THE HAPPIEST RECAP

50 Years of the New York Mets As Told in 500 Amazin' Wins

Volume 1—First Base: 1962-1973

Greg Prince

by Greg W. Prince

D0861644

Micah,

As a wise man once said,
"Mookie! Mookie!"

Greg

© Copyright 2012 Greg W. Prince.

All Rights Reserved.
No part of this book may be reproduced, stored in a retrieval system
or transmitted by any means without the express written consent of the author,
except in the case of brief excerpts in critical reviews or articles.

First published by
Banner Day Press in November 2012.

Inquiries may be addressed to
thehappiestrecap@gmail.com

http://www.thehappiestrecap.com

Printed in the United States of America.

First edition

Manufacturing by CreateSpace

Interior and cover designed and illustrated
by Jim Haines.
jim.haines@verizon.net

ISBN-13: 978-0615665284
ISBN-10: 0615655289
BISAC: Sports & Recreation/Baseball/History

To
BOB MURPHY

When he'd praise
Mets fans for being "knowledgeable,"
I became determined
to never let him down.

CONTENTS

WELCOME TO OUR PREGAME SHOW

T he record topping the WABC Silver Dollar Sound Survey unveiled on Tuesday, April 10, 1962, was "Mashed Potato Time," a dance ditty served up on the peppiest of platters by 16-year-old Dee Dee Sharp of Philadelphia. Yet with apologies to young Miss Sharp (real name Dione LaRue), the latest and the greatest sound on "Radio 77" that week...the pick hit ready to rock and roll the New York Metropolitan Area airwaves like nothing else before it...was this:

> *"Well, hi there, everybody, this is Bob Murphy, welcoming you to the first regular-season game in the history of the New York Mets — brought to you by Rheingold Extra Dry. Tonight, the New York Mets meet the Saint Louis Cardinals, right here in Saint Louis. Lindsey Nelson, Ralph Kiner and I are on hand to bring you every bit of the action.*
> *"Yes sir, the New York Mets are on the air in their first great season."*

The skies were mostly cloudy. The temperature was in the high forties. Yet except for the announcer's explicit meteorological reportage, who could tell on Wednesday evening, April 11, 1962, that the stars of WABC's newest nighttime programming, the brand new New York Mets, weren't already bathed in warmth and wrapped in sunshine? That's how Bob Murphy made them sound from that very first pregame introduction in that very "first great season," through every game he delivered over every frequency on which he broadcast across the subsequent 42 years.

WABC-AM, in the early stages of its Top 40 glory when it signed on as the first flagship station of the New York Mets radio network, referred to its disc jockeys in 1962 as the Good Guys. No offense to the likes of "the Morning Mayor of New York" Herb Oscar Anderson, Big Dan Ingram or Bruce Morrow — a.k.a. Cousin Brucie — but you couldn't have asked for three *better* guys to inaugurate New York Mets baseball than the trio on hand right there in St. Louis to bring us every bit of the action.

They were a team, just as much as the team taking the field for the first time at the first of the three ballparks to be known as Busch Stadium, yet like the players whose hits, runs and errors they were about to transmit to a waiting audience, each brought a distinct asset to the Mets' radio and television booths. Kiner was the big-time slugger who knew the National League game from the inside — Ralph would prove popular and beloved among Mets fans. Nelson was the smooth network pro whose fluid style added a dab of aural sheen to a start-up enterprise — Lindsey would prove popular and beloved to Mets fans, too. Ultimately, though, it was Robert Allan Murphy, the Oklahoman, U.S. Marine and veteran of the Boston Red Sox and Baltimore Orioles microphones whose endurance, familiarity and unstinting sincerity earned him the sobriquet "Voice of the New York Mets" for generations to come. He was popular, beloved and certifiably ours.

On the tube, for the seventeen seasons they worked together, you knew Murph, Ralph and Lindsey would always be right where you left them, on WOR-TV, Channel 9. Radio was a different story, though. 77 WABC would give way to 1050 WHN in 1964. WHN would give way to WJRZ at 970 AM in 1967. WJRZ would send the radio rights back to WHN in 1972. WHN would hand them off in 1975 to WNEW 1130, which would ship them to AM 57 WMCA in 1978, which would, as if by force of habit, shift them once more, come 1983, to WHN, which became WFAN in 1987 and moved its revolutionary all-sports format to 660 AM during the 1988 playoffs. Plus, there'd sometimes be alternate carriers for weekday afternoon games; there'd be affiliates throughout the Northeast and south to Florida; there'd someday be the Internet. Yet no matter who claimed flagship radio station status from 1962 to 2003, and no matter how a listener managed to tune in, town to town, up and down the dial, Bob Murphy was almost always on the air in New York, as much a part of the Mets to the Mets fan ear as any athlete who ever wore the uniform.

The first New York Met player chronologically was center fielder Richie Ashburn, leading off against Cardinal starter Larry Jackson in what would soon reveal itself as an 11-4 loss for the visitors on 4/11/62. Bob Murphy called Ashburn's initial plate appearance: *"Jackson is into his windup, and the Mets are in business!"* The last New York Met alphabetically was (and remains) third baseman Don Zimmer. Bob Murphy called his maiden at-bat, too: *"A ground smash, over the mound, over second, a base hit to center field."* Firsts, lasts and everything in between fell to the Voice of the New York Mets to communicate, sometimes on radio, sometimes on television, always with the sense that there was no better place to be, Metwise, than in the company of Bob Murphy.

Murphy wouldn't have put it that way. He was in the business of telling you about Mets, not Murph. Ashburn and Zimmer were his cause. Later, Seaver, Koosman and Gentry; Matlack, Millan and Milner; Mazzilli, Youngblood and Henderson; Hernandez, Carter and Strawberry; Bonilla, Brogna and Kent; Piazza, Alfonzo and Leiter...ringing every Bell from Gus to Derek to Jay and keeping up with seven different Joneses. From the age of Hobie Landrith to the rise of Jose Reyes, the Voice of the New York Mets was solely about the New York Mets.

About coming out to the Polo Grounds or Shea Stadium, where plenty of good seats were still available if you happened to be in the area.

About Rheingold Extra Dry and Viceroy Cigarettes and Kahn's Hot Dogs.

About twinight doubleheaders and Helmet Day and pitchers going so well that they were wearing the hitters on their watch chains.

About games in which putting a couple of runners on base would bring the tying run into the on-deck circle.

About scores that demanded you fasten your seatbelt.

About flies popped so high that they could've been hit in a silo.

About pencils and how they came with erasers because everybody makes mistakes.

About baseball as a game of redeeming features.

And if a Mets fan was lucky — which could be as few as 40 times and as many as 108 times in any given season — about a happy recap: the topline details and totals of the New York Mets victory just accomplished, which Murph would be back with after this word from our sponsor on the New York Mets radio network.

The Mets needed to win if Bob Murphy was to proffer a happy recap. Not that he didn't already sound pretty darn happy to be announcing a baseball game, whatever the result. Murph was scrupulously evenhanded in his praise of the players and teams it was his pleasure to describe. He was just as fair about spreading criticism around: he hardly said a bad word about any Met or any Met opponent. And he never made a big deal about himself, let alone what became the signature phrase and legacy of his four-plus decades as a New York institution. There was drama, tension and emotion informing his calls if the Mets had the winning run on base in the bottom of the ninth, but none of it was ever prefaced with an explicit nod to himself, no *"we really want a happy recap here!"* or anything so unbecomingly bush.

But for Mets fans, the happy recap was the best part. It meant the Mets won. Bob Murphy, his classy neutrality notwithstanding, would agree. He didn't openly root for the Mets, but he was clearly in favor of their prevailing. Of course he was. He was with them, home and road, almost every day of every season for the longest time. The man, weary from travel, once checked into his accommodations under the unintentional *nom de plume* Robert Mets.

So if he didn't wear his heart on his sleeve, he had no problem displaying it on a hotel register.

It is in the spirit of the sunny and warm Voice of the New York Mets, the one that saw little worse on his team's horizon than a few harmless, puffy, cumulus clouds, that the pages that follow offer the only thing that could be better than a happy recap.

That would be a Happiest Recap — 500 of them, to be precise.

WINNING STREAK WITHOUT END

Winning isn't everything. It's also not the only thing. There can be much to be gleaned from a Mets loss for even the most devoted of Mets fans. I consider myself in that category and continue to swear more than a dozen years after I toweled off the sweat, tears and fleeting euphoria attendant to it that my favorite game ever was Game Six of the 1999 National League Championship Series, a see-saw affair that featured the highest of Met highs and the lowest of Met lows spanning eleven innings forever seared in my consciousness.

That the final score was Braves 10 Mets 9 and the Mets' dream of a pennant died when Kenny Rogers walked Andruw Jones with the bases loaded doesn't detract from the immensity of the night of October 19 and earliest morning of October 20, 1999, for me. It barely detracts from the trip to the gates of Met heaven that the final thirty exhilarating days of that extended Met campaign represents in my life as a Mets fan. No matter who won or who lost, I'll put it up against any baseball game ever played as one of the greatest.

But you won't read about it in *The Happiest Recap*.

Actually, you probably will, but, as with other Met setbacks that can't help but come up throughout this four-volume history of a franchise that has lost quite a bit more than it's won, only as necessary punctuation to the winning stories that surround it. Losses serve as our ellipses, our em-dashes and occasionally as our periods, but make no mistake regarding the expedition on which we are about to commence.

The Mets are going to win.

The Mets, in fact, are about to go undefeated, piling up a record of 500-0. Every single game we're about to revisit, from 1962 to 2011, is going to be — per Casey Stengel's early and accurate assessment of the team he all but invented — utterly Amazin'. Each entry in *The Happiest Recap* has been chosen to tell a segment of the story of the New York Mets' first 50 years of existence. I have no objective formula to assure you these are the "greatest" games the Mets have ever won, but I am confident in their Amazin' properties.

These games are...

• the games that launched legends;

• the games where standards were established;

- the games that introduced us to characters we would come to know as if they were related to us by blood;

- the games that left behind images that defy erasure;

- the games that set and reset the course of Metropolitan events;

- the games in whose results we reveled before relegating them to the deepest recesses of our collective subconscious;

- the games hindsight presents to us as milestones hidden in plain sight;

- the games that are leavened with irresistible curiosities, only some of which may show up in the box score;

- the games that were mammoth in their day and require just a spoonful of context to stir back to life;

- the games marked by epic team efforts;

- the games defined by superb individual feats;

- the games featuring the extraordinary exploits of protagonists hardly heard of before and barely heard from since;

- the games that nudge us toward tales too tantalizing to let sit boxed, warehoused and obscured by time's inevitable march;

- the games that illustrate how we've lived and how we've evolved as Mets fans these past 50 years;

- the games that were Marvelous early, Terrific before you knew it, and Wright as could be by their conclusion;

- the games that weren't over until they were over;

- and the games that made miracles possible.

Some of these are games you saw and whose most intricate details you can recite at the drop of a cap. Some you're going to recognize even if you don't remember them first-hand. Some will seem at least vaguely familiar. Some you've never heard of — which is all right, since some I'd never heard of until I dove headfirst into the Met annals in search of...

In search of what, exactly? Why exactly do I have 500 Amazin' wins to bring you?

The Happiest Recap has its roots in the summer of 2009, when little regarding the Mets was happy, and recapping their nightly foibles was more a matter of chore than cheer. As co-author of the blog Faith and Fear in Flushing — the blog for Mets fans who like to read, as my partner and fellow Met traveler Jason Fry and I like to call it — I required an upbeat diversion from the day-to-day drudgery of documenting my 70-92 team. In a season peppered by worsts, I started thinking in terms of bests.

With the franchise's 50th anniversary on the horizon, my idea was to craft an ideal Mets season comprised of only Mets wins. The twist was the slots in my season had to correspond to the junctures at which the Mets played games in previous seasons. Thus, Game 1 in my blog series, which ran on Faith and Fear while the 2011 campaign unfolded, had to be the "best" Opening Day win the Mets ever played. Game 2 had to be the "best" second game of a Mets season. And it went like that until I highlighted the "best" 162nd and (as circumstances insisted) 163rd games in Mets history. I place "best" in quote marks because there is no quantitative analysis that will determine that a three-hit 1-0 shutout is better than a contest decided on an extra-inning three-run homer...or one in which a black cat wandered by or a pitcher stole second base. As I plumbed further on my archival expedition, I found myself progressively less concerned with what would win an objective argument for "best" Game Number Whatever. Mostly, I found myself wanting to tell as many Met stories as I could, whether the games in question were familiar to all of Faith and Fear's readers or came as news to most of them.

Though my blog series completed its mission of constructing the mythical ideal season, my head was left crammed with so many statistics and anecdotes dug up during my two years of research that I found myself wanting to tell *more* Met stories. So that's what I'm doing here, opting for a somewhat more conventional chronological framework in which to tell them. Since 50 years of Mets baseball had been officially put in the books, 500 wins seemed a nice, round number through which to explore virtually every aspect of the Mets experience.

After several more months of research — more statistics, more anecdotes, one more round of immersion in literally every single box score that recounted a Mets triumph — I had well over 500 wins that I (as an uncommonly attentive and retentive Mets fan born the same year as the franchise itself) judged to be of surpassing significance. From there, I chopped, I pared, I debated...and eventually I had the 457 regular-season and 43 postseason wins that constitute the raw material for these four volumes. Emerging from the individual stories the 500 games spawned is an organic narrative that I sincerely believe amounts to a modern-day sports saga.

One in which the Mets always win, of course.

If you are a Mets fan, this is your family history...which I guess makes me the obsessive but well-meaning uncle who thought to jot it all down so as to make sure everybody who shares these bloodlines would know how we got here.

GETTING TO FIRST BASE

" **A**ll right, let me show you where the bases are."

The New York Mets were busy being born. Who better to slap them on the rear, turn their heads around and lead them to their destiny than Casey Stengel? In February of 1962, amid the brisk late-winter winds whipping off the Florida Gulf Coast, their destiny was simply to put one foot in front of the other until both feet found themselves on the field of play, the Mets no longer a wish or a concept, but an actual ballclub...or something very much like one. Casey, who had in 1958 testified to Congress that he'd had "many years that I was not so successful as a ballplayer, as it is a game of skill," was determined to give his newest charges the benefit of his experiences as a not altogether unsuccessful practitioner of the game, especially in New York. He had once led the National League in on-base percentage as a Dodger, topped the circuit in hit-by-pitches as a Giant and won the first World Series game ever played at Yankee Stadium via inside-the-park home run. "What do you think," he was reported to have asked an incredulous Mickey Mantle as he attempted to give the young man a hands-on fielding lesson decades later, "I was born old?"

Stengel, 71 during 1962's Spring Training, wasn't born yesterday, that much was for sure. Having parlayed a decent and vividly colorful major league career into a string of managerial gigs that impressed no one until he captivated everybody by helming the Yankee dynasty through an unprecedented string of October appointments (twelve seasons, ten pennants, seven world championships before his services were no longer required), the Ol' Perfesser still relished his role as baseball's most tenured tutor. "In the baseball business" since 1910, as he put it when Congress sought his myriad thoughts on the sport's antitrust exemption, he knew a few things. For one, you can't even commence to thinking about winning until you're certain of which direction your feet should be taking you once they find that field they're supposed to be on. Guiding a unit filled primarily with the overripe and underdeveloped fruit of the 1961 expansion draft, Casey couldn't take any chances.

So in St. Petersburg, where the former Dodgers and Giants and Cubs and Reds and Pirates and Phillies and Cardinals and Braves had gathered to train to take on the teams that had tossed them onto the National League discard pile, the first Mets manager was going to show the first Mets players where the bases were.

"Like a pied piper," Maury Allen would recall a veritable Met lifetime later, in 1969, Stengel "marched his forty players from base to base on the practice field." The first stop on their trek? First base, naturally.

"Now if you get to first base, you can make a living in New York," Stengel explained, by Allen's account in *The Incredible Mets*, "because everybody wants to support a new team and the public expects their best and the Polo Grounds is an old field but a new one is being built."

There was more to it than that — there was always more to a Casey Stengel monologue than a man driving in verbal circles, because the Ol' Perfesser's mind came factory-equipped with the sharpest GPS available — but the key to the manager's lesson in geography, economics, public relations and urban planning was getting to first base was paramount if the Mets were going to get anywhere.

Far be it from me to contradict Casey Stengel. He commenced the birth of the New York Mets with first base, so this four-volume series on the 500 most Amazin' wins in Mets history also begins with First Base. That's "volume one" for you literal thinkers, roughly the first quarter of the Mets' first 50 years, encompassing 127 Amazin' games the Mets won from 1962 through 1973.

This period, which takes us from the franchise's infancy to the threshold of its adolescence, is pure Mets — Mets classic, you might say. The Mets at their core, even in the present day, are the product of their earliest upbringing. Their inherent identifiability presented itself almost immediately. Their quest for basic competence and their general inability to secure it didn't turn potential Mets fans off. It attracted them.

- When a well-connected lawyer named William Alfred Shea began shaking the oaks of power in hopes of rustling the baseball establishment's leaves (those antitrust hearings were but one step on the road to expansion), *this* wouldn't seem to be what he was working toward.

- When a heartbroken New York Giants fan of considerable means named Joan Whitney Payson was moved to bankroll the operation that was conceived to replace both her old team and their sorely missed local rivals, the Brooklyn Dodgers, in a National League market left barren by a westward gold rush, *this* wouldn't seem to be what she was buying into.

- When the architect of Stengel's Bronx dynasty, George Martin Weiss, was lured from reluctant retirement to build from scratch an entirely new and prosperous baseball business...he was all business as far as anyone could tell...*this* wouldn't seem to be what he was planning on.

But Charles Dillon "Casey" Stengel got it and latched onto it. He understood that when not showing his players the way to first base, he would have to serve as the face of the franchise. That it was a remarkably etched face connected to a voice that could go on all day and all night about what an Amazin', Amazin', Amazin', Amazin' ballclub he was bringing to New York clicked instantly and brilliantly with the media ("my writers") assigned to cover him. Stengel understood no more World Series rings were in his immediate future, so he constructed a Met image that was every bit as important as and, it turned out, longer-lasting than that new field he mentioned as succeeding the Polo Grounds:

The Mets were lovable.
The Mets were adorable.
The Mets were human.

Until there was a stadium named for the immensely helpful Bill Shea (and even after it opened its gates) and until a steady stream of George Weiss's promising prospects could get the hang of its field (and for a while longer besides), Mrs. Payson and everyone else in Ol' Case's orbit was going to have to have to — in the 21st century patois — go with it.

The lovable, adorable, human Mets inspired shouts of "Let's Go Mets!" no matter how tough the going got. The lovable, adorable, human Mets elicited homemade placards of support that first struck management as dangerous until it dawned on one and all that free customer-generated advertising was an asset and not a liability. The lovable, adorable, human Mets frustrated the instinctive rooting impulse for positive results again and again, yet instead of dampening enthusiasm, they energized it.

And when the lovable, adorable, human Mets went against accepted form and snatched victory from the jaws of routine defeat, it was a cause for celebration. Those festive occasions form the basis of the first passages of First Base, spanning 1962 through 1964, the last days of the Polo Grounds to the dawning of Shea Stadium.

Before the Mets could show grudging signs of necessary maturity, Casey Stengel exited the stage. That's all right, though. He did what he had to do. He got the Mets to the point where their followers could attempt to imagine them growing up big and strong. It didn't happen overnight...not until it did, which is 1969's verified fable, of course, but the interregnum between the Original Mets and the Miracle Mets deserves its own examination, which is what the second chapter — 1965 to 1968 — is all about. The Mets are still lovable, adorable and human, and their wins are still set rather far apart, but enough is happening to indicate a Mets fan could love them and respect them at the same time.

Respect, embodied in every sense of the word by the manager who takes over in 1968, Gil Hodges, changes immediate perceptions of the ballclub. They're human, but now human means expecting the team to, as impatient New Yorkers might put it, act like a person already. Under Hodges, the Mets come to respect themselves and the league is forced to respect them.

Then 1969, when what it means to be the Mets becomes multidimensional. Now you can't help but love them because you can't help but respect them for what they're doing, which is not just not losing, but winning. The Mets shatter every pane of conventional wisdom en route to the most unlikely story any baseball team has ever written in one season's time. Because the lovable Mets became champion Mets so suddenly if not exactly quickly (it had taken a very long seven seasons to prepare them for their quantum leap), the Mets now stood as an avatar for impossible dreamers everywhere. After the 1969 Mets, whose miraculous doings take up a chapter of their own, being a Mets fan means thinking anything can happen — anything good, that is.

Such a spirit can't help but inform the next phase of the First Base era, 1970 to 1972.

The Mets are indeed capable of generating anything here — anything good, yes, but only so much of it. The good can be plenty good, but once you've partaken of great, it's tough to swallow anything of a lesser nature that comes along in its wake.

Which brings us to our final First Base chapter, 1973, wherein the Mets teeter on the brink of inescapable mundanity, maybe worse, yet revive in the last act to craft one more set of trademark Metsian characteristics. This is the time when Mets fans don't just believe in the impossible; they believe in believing. That the belief pays off at almost every stage of this multilayered absurdist action-drama only hardens the Mets fan's determination to believe, no matter what, no matter when.

When you can't help but love the Mets, when you can't help but wait on the Mets, when you can't help but dream for the Mets, when you can't help but put up with the Mets and when you can't help but keep faith in the Mets, that's the legacy of 1962 through 1973 come to life. The Mets are what they are in large part because of who they were at their start.

The Mets got to first base.

It was some kind of trip.

1962-1964

BABY,
IT'S YOU

It had to happen sooner or later, right? No franchise goes through its life never winning. Even the Cleveland Spiders of 1899 infamy went 20-134. The Spiders' web was all but spun out by the beginning of the 20th century, yet even they got off the schneid faster than the 1962 Mets. The Spiders lost their first four contests prior to defeating the Louisville Colonels in their fifth game.

The Colonels, like the Spiders, were rewarded with imminent contraction — the National League didn't screw around in 1899.

Anyway, nobody, no matter how abysmal, loses 'em all, and the 1962 Mets were rapidly indicating they'd be taking abysmal to new depths. First game ever, at St. Louis: a loss. Six-game homestand at the Polo Grounds followed, as did a half-dozen defeats. Hitting the road again, the road hit Casey Stengel's inaugural squad right back, with the Pittsburgh Pirates taking the first two games of a three-game series. That second loss dropped the Mets' record — 1962 and all-time — to 0-9. Meanwhile, the Bucs had blazed their way to a 10-0 start, meaning the Mets were already 9 1/2 games out of first place...or a margin greater than the total amount of games they had ever played.

No, it couldn't go on forever, and twelve days after the Mets were born, they learned to crawl.

At Forbes Field, on a Monday night literally like no other that had come before it, the Mets won. Sparked by three sacrifice flies in the first two innings, the Mets lunged to a 6-0 lead and handed their fate to starter Jay Hook. Hook's legend, courtesy of Stengel, was that as the holder of an engineering degree, the righty could tell you why a curveball curved, but he couldn't make one curve in practice the way he did in theory.

The hook worked fine for Hook, however. His entire arsenal did. Jay went the distance, stopping the Pirates' winning streak at ten and, of more cosmic significance, introducing the Mets to the sensation of not losing. They won, 9-1. Their record was 1-9. For the 1962 Mets, it was the spiritual equivalent of going .500...and, mathematically speaking, it was one of the last times their all-time record was a single-digit number under .500.

Sure the bad start buried the franchise in a statistical hole from which they will likely never fully dig out (they ended the 2011 season 338 regular-season games shy of the break-even point), but look at it this way — the New York Mets have won a whole lot more than the Cleveland Spiders have since 1962.

Ten-thousand, four-hundred ninety-two souls won the lottery. Those lucky stiffs weren't stiffed. They became the first Mets crowd to experience the satisfaction and perhaps bliss of going to a Mets home game and leaving it having seen a Mets home win.

This new baseball team had previously tried its hand at homestanding, and they could barely maintain their balance. Six games at the Polo Grounds led to six losses between April 13 and April 19. One of those went extra innings, which could be interpreted as Casey Stengel's crew hanging in there as long as they could, but also meant it just took longer for them to lose. Perhaps the spirit of those first home games was best captured by Leonard Shecter in *Once Upon The Polo Grounds*, when he found a fan in right field begging for the Mets, trailing the Cardinals, 15-5, with two out in the bottom of the ninth, for "one more run, just one more run."

When asked why one more run was so important given that the Mets trailed by ten, the fan explained that instead of five runs, the Mets would have six, and "then you could say if they got any pitching, they woulda won."

The same, one supposes, could have been said as the Mets set out on their second-ever homestand. Fortified by their first win of any kind, at Forbes Field, the 1-11 Mets scored four runs off the Phillies' Cal McLish — given name Calvin Coolidge Julius Caesar Tuskahoma McLish, as Bob Murphy was fond of reminding listeners — and another five against Frank Sullivan. Problem was, they didn't get any pitching, and they didn't win. The firm of Craig, Anderson, Moford & Moorhead was roughed up for 11 hits and 15 runs (Ken MacKenzie did, however, pitch a 1-2-3 ninth) and the result was an already familiar 11-9 defeat.

Seven home contests, seven home setbacks. Hard to attract fans with that kind of advertising, but just as the Mets were bound to win one somewhere eventually, so too were they on a collision course with probability at the Polo Grounds. Their day to cash in was a Saturday that started out more or less like every day in the Mets' infancy. The Phillies hung an immediate four-spot on starter Jay Hook by way of Tony Gonzalez's three-run home run and Don Demeter's solo shot. Stengel saw enough and gave Jay the hook. In came Bob Miller (Bob *L*. Miller; the need to differentiate was on the horizon) and he calmed down Phillie bats, holding them to only one more run through the fifth.

It would take until the bottom of the sixth, with the Mets trailing, 6-1 — Charlie Neal had homered to lead off the home second but Demeter returned the favor against Dave Hillman to start the top of the sixth — to say they got enough hitting to match their relief pitching. When it came, it came in a barrage. After Phillie starter Jim Owens walked Gus Bell, Frank Thomas homered, his fifth of the young year (he'd wind up with a longstanding team record 34). Then Neal homered again. Jack Hamilton immediately replaced Owens, but he couldn't put a plug in the Mets' power surge; Gil Hodges greeted him with a homer of his own.

Three blows to the Philadelphia body placed the Mets back in the game, 6-5. Once back, they decided not to leave. After recording an out and allowing a walk to Chris Cannizzaro, Hamilton exited in favor of Sullivan. But the Mets were beginning to like being on base. Sammy Taylor hit for Hillman and walked. Rod Kanehl ran for Taylor while John DeMerit pinch-ran for catcher Cannizzaro. Richie Asbhurn's grounder to the right side pushed both runners up a base. Gene Mauch replaced Sullivan with Chris Short — it was taking four Phillie hurlers to quell one Met uprising — and Short rewarded his skipper's confidence by unleashing a corker of a wild pitch, wild enough to score DeMerit from third and Hot Rod from second.

The Mets had a lead! At home! And it grew bigger when Jim Hickman homered off Ed Keegan in the eighth! The Mets were on top, 8-6. Roger Craig — the starter from the night before and the closest thing Stengel had to an ace — had come on in the seventh to attempt to nail this sucker down. The Phillies didn't score on him in the seventh or the eighth. In the ninth, Johnny Callison fouled out to Hodges at first, Gonzalez grounded to Neal at second and the Phillies' final hope, Frank Torre, grounded out to Hodges. The Mets won, 8-6, for the first time delighting their home fans not just by existing but by excelling. Or their version of it.

Ten-thousand, four-hundred ninety-two souls bought tickets to see the Mets at the Polo Grounds, the eighth time a person could do that, but only the first time a person could do that and feel completely rewarded for having done so. Every darn one of those 10,492 hit the jackpot.

MAY 6, 1962
METS 7 PHILLIES 5 (12)
CONNIE MACK STADIUM

The recently born Mets never say die this Sunday, scoring two to knot the Phillies at five in the eighth inning in Philly, and then take the lead in the twelfth when Gil Hodges singles home Rod Kanehl and Gus Bell. Casey Stengel calls on his ostensible ace Roger Craig (knocked out of the box in the first inning two nights earlier) to preserve the 7-5 win for Craig Anderson. Despite allowing a leadoff double to catcher Clay Dalrymple and wild-pitching him to third, Roger strikes out Roy Sievers to give the 4-16 Mets their first-ever extra-inning win. It wouldn't be an official statistic for seven years, but the scoreless twelfth also earns Craig the first save in Mets history.

Were the Original Mets stunning? Twice they were, with the Milwaukee Braves the most stunned of all. After coming from behind in the first game of a Saturday doubleheader at the Polo Grounds — when Hobie Landrith touched Warren Spahn for a two-out, two-run

MAY 12, 1962 (2ND)
METS 8 BRAVES 7
THE POLO GROUNDS

homer in the bottom of the ninth for a 3-2 Mets win — the expansioneers set out for their first-ever twinbill sweep in the nightcap. It wouldn't be easy, as a back-and-forth affair ensued, tilting in the Braves' favor by the top of the eighth when Milwaukee grabbed a 7-6 lead (with four of their runs driven in by Hammerin' Hank Aaron).

But these Mets weren't about to let their big day be split in half. In the bottom of the eighth, Elio Chacon singled home Rod Kanehl from second base for the tying run, and in the bottom of the ninth, with one out, none other than old Dodger hero Gil Hodges hit the day's second walkoff home run. The Mets won, 8-7, nailing their first doubleheader sweep and making a winning pitcher out of reliever Craig Anderson twice in the same day. Anderson's distinction would be earned by only two other "daily double" Met pitchers over the next half-century (Willard Hunter in 1964 and Jesse Orosco in 1983).

With the Mets trailing the Cubs, 5-4, in the bottom of the eighth, Gil Hodges took advantage of the Polo Grounds' unique dimensions and launched a fly ball to center field which, amid the rolling pastures under Coogan's Bluff, became the first inside-the-park home run in Mets history. Gil's interior blast helped send the game into extra innings where, in the eleventh, Felix Mantilla's infield single with the bases loaded brought home John DeMerit to give Casey Stengel's squad a 6-5 Wednesday win. The victory catapulted the 9-18 Metsies into an eighth-place tie with the Colt .45s. It was also their second consecutive extra-inning win, both coming at the expense of last-place Chicago...the victims of the Mets' first-ever series sweep.

In one very literal sense, things would never get better for the Mets than they did after completing a Sunday doubleheader sweep of Milwaukee in Milwaukee, 9-6. Overall, New York took the final three of this four-game set, meaning the eighth-place Mets now had their

longest winning streak ever. They held leads over ninth-place Houston and tenth-place Chicago and were only a game behind the Braves, against whom the Mets now held a lifetime 5-3 series edge.

And speaking of lifetime, by having taken 12 of their previous 22 contests, the Mets' composite record was now up to 12-19. As a franchise, they were seven games from .500 for the first time...and for the last time...ever. The high of sticking it to the Braves wore off as the Mets winged their way to Houston to take on their fraternal twins, the brand new Colt .45s. A long and arduous night of travel bled into the harsh Texas morning and even the indefatigable Casey Stengel could barely stand as the Mets checked into their hotel. If anybody wanted him, he let it be known, "Tell 'em I'm being embalmed."

The same could be said for the Mets' recent winning ways. The next time they won a ballgame, their record would rise to 13-36. In between victories, the Mets lost a club-record (then and now) 17 in a row.

A tradition begins that would seem just fine on its own if not for one fundamental flaw. Certainly Al Jackson was fine. He was never better — no Mets pitcher ever was and, in a sense, no Mets pitcher ever would be (as far as could be told after fifty years). Jackson gave up a one-out single to Joey Amalfitano of the Colt .45s, the second batter he saw in the opener of this Friday twinighter at the Polo Grounds. And then he gave up no further hits to Houston, going all the way for a 2-0 win...a one-hitter, the first in Mets history. Over the next half-century, Mets pitchers would pitch 34 more. Some were combined,

a couple were rain-shortened, one went into extra innings, but none outdid Jackson's. They were all one-hitters. Put another way, none was a no-hitter. But one-hitters are pretty good, too.

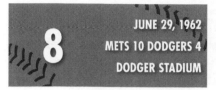

The Mets may not have been very experienced, but on this Friday night in Chavez Ravine, they demonstrated that they knew enough to take what was given them... and walk like hell with it. Against Joe Moeller of the Dodgers, the Mets started their evening accepting one gift after another. Richie Ashburn led off with a walk. After Rod Kanehl mysteriously swung and flied to right, Gene Woodling picked up on Ashburn's cue and walked. Then Frank Thomas walked. Then Charlie Neal walked. The Mets went up, 1-0, by not taking their bats off their shoulders.

Ron Perranoski replaced Moeller in body if not in spirit. He walked Sammy Taylor with the bases loaded. He walked Felix Mantilla in the exact same situation. Those successive bases on balls made it 3-0, Mets. Elio Chacon tried to follow his teammates' example but struck out looking for the inning's second out. But pitcher Jay Hook — the Mets' ninth "hitter" of the inning — was more successful just standing there. Jay walked, and it resulted in the fourth Met run, every one of them scored the same way. Finally, Ashburn decided to mix it up by swinging; Whitey singled in two of the previous walkers (or walkees) to put the Mets ahead, 6-0. That was it for Ron Perranoski, to say nothing of Dodger dignity. Phil Ortega came on to get Kanehl for the third out of the inning, the second Hot Rod had to endure. Totals for the top of the first: six runs on one hit, seven walks and no errors. The score: Mets 6 Dodgers coming to bat.

By the time the night was over, the Mets would walk SIXTEEN TIMES, eight of them courtesy of L.A. reliever Stan Williams, en route to a 10-4 victory. It's still the record for most walks by any Mets team in any one game. Hook himself would walk three times, or one fewer than the number he himself permitted in going the distance. It was the first win the Mets earned against (or were handed by) one of the former National League ballclubs they replaced back home. The Dodgers and Giants had been a combined 13-0 against the expansion Mets to that point in 1962. It was about time one of them sent a baby gift.

Two of the veterans with whom George Weiss was so intent on stocking the first Met roster showed they could still play a little bit. Thirty-nine year-old Gene Woodling, a contributor to Casey Stengel's first five championships in the Bronx, stroked a two-

run pinch-homer in the fifth inning at Busch Stadium (the facility formerly known as Sportsman's Park) to complete a four-run rally that brought the Mets from a 5-3 deficit to a 7-5 lead over the Cardinals. That Saturday's eventual 9-8 win would be secured via the contributions of another graybeard, 35-year-old Richie Ashburn, who went 4-for-5 on the day and, doing his best Maury Wills impression, swiped two bases.

Though Ashburn, like Woodling, was on his figurative last legs, playing his final big league season, he was going out with as much of a bang as any 1962 Met could detonate. Two days after playing a big role in a rare Mets win, Whitey would return to one of his old stomping grounds, Wrigley Field, to participate in that summer's second All-Star Game as the Mets' lone representative. The former Cub and Phillie (mostly Phillie) singled and scored…and, as was the case so often in 1962, Ashburn's team lost.

When league action resumed, Richie didn't slow down, finishing the Mets' inaugural season as their leading hitter, sporting a nifty .306 average. Before Ashburn exited New York, he was honored by Met beat writers as the team's first MVP. That is to say he was considered the most valuable member of the worst team ever.

And the boat the landlocked Nebraskan received as a prize sank while docked in New Jersey.

The team that was regaled for, among many other oddities, having traded an ineffectual backup catcher for himself — Harry Chiti for Harry Chiti — doubled down and attempted to clone one of its least successful players.

10 AUGUST 4, 1962 (2ND)
METS 3 REDS 2 (14)
THE POLO GROUNDS

Well, not exactly, but it makes for a better story that way, and sometimes it seems the whole point of the 1962 Mets was to produce anecdotes that could be told repeatedly for the next half-century (usually by first-hand witness Ralph Kiner).

In most of the telling, the Mets lose, which makes mathematical sense given the club's final record of 40-120, but now and then — say, 40 times — the strangeness worked out just fine.

Need proof? Never mind Harry Chiti (technically purchased from the Indians and sent back to Cleveland after batting .195 in fifteen games). Just ask the two Bob Millers.

One was the righty with the middle initial "L" who'd been with the team all season and had yet to rack up a "W". That Bob Miller, 23 years old, was 0-7 after 23 appearances. And then there was the lefty with the same first and last names whose middle initial was "G," spent most of the previous four seasons at Double-A and Triple-A and just wanted to go home once the Mets dealt Don Zimmer to Cincinnati to nab him, his 21.94 ERA and Cliff Cook in May. This second Bob Miller, pushing 27 and suddenly exiled from the defending National League champs, was convinced to hang in there, refresh his left arm at Syracuse and accept a callup to the bigs in due time.

Miller II, if you will (a.k.a. Lefty Miller; also a.k.a. the Bob Miller to whom Casey Stengel didn't mysteriously refer as "Nelson," which is what he sometimes called Bob L. Miller), became a Met for real in late July — and really became a Met by absorbing a loss in his first appearance as a Met and pitching in nothing but losses in his first four games as a Met.

That was Bob G. Miller's tough luck. Bob L. Miller's tougher luck was the 0-7 record and what was befalling him in the nightcap of this Saturday doubleheader at the Polo Grounds. Righty Miller was pitching well — allowing only two runs to lefty Miller's old team, the Reds, in seven innings — and righty Miller was, naturally, losing. His teammates felt so bad about his fate that they waited until the bottom of the eighth to tie the score on a Charlie Neal triple and a Frank Thomas sac fly. By then, Willard Hunter was the pitcher of record for the Mets. No way Miller could win.

But at least he couldn't lose, which for a 1962 Met pitcher was a victory unto itself.

The game went on a good, long while after it was knotted. Hunter would depart in favor of Yale man Ken MacKenzie, on the verge of turning himself into another element of the 1962 Mets' legend. MacKenzie gave Stengel 4 2/3 scoreless innings, but when it came to the game's bottom line, he made like Bob L. Miller and got nothing tangible for his yeoman work, save perhaps for an encouraging "Boola Boola" from his manager.

Probably not, actually, as Ol' Case had to figure out who would pitch after MacKenzie departed for a pinch-hitter in the thirteenth. If he was looking for "Nelson," he was going to be disappointed, as "Nelson" — Bob L. Miller, that is — was out of the game. The next best thing, of course, would be the next Miller in line.

So Casey went that way, with the other Bob Miller. And the other Bob Miller went after his former teammates in grand style, setting down the Reds 1-2-3 in the top of the fourteenth. That made him the pitcher of record entering the bottom of the inning, which was a good thing to be, because Thomas chose that instant to clobber a Moe Drabowsky pitch for a leadoff home run, making the Mets 3-2 winners...making the Mets doubleheader sweepers, for that matter, as Roger Craig had won the opener.

For the first time all season, the winning pitcher was Bob Miller. OK, so it was a Bob Miller, specifically the relatively new Bob G. Miller rather than the long-beleaguered Bob L. Miller. Seeing as how Bob G. Miller was at least keeping it in the proverbial family, it's doubtful Bob L. Miller minded all that much that he couldn't be the first Miller on the 1962 Mets to notch that elusive W.

This was the first time both Bob Millers pitched in the same game. It would happen four more times in 1962, but it would never again result in a win for the Mets.

Which may be why they never got around to rechristening the Polo Grounds Miller Park.

T he most Marvelous way to break yet another mammoth losing streak was with more Marv Throneberry, not less.

The legend of Throneberry as avatar of laughable failure on every conceivable side of the ball in the franchise's inaugural season is littered

AUGUST 21, 1962 (2ND)
METS 5 PIRATES 4
THE POLO GROUNDS

with everything that went wrong for his disaster of a team. Some of it was even true. Just as true, though, is that these fellows were human, and no human being likes to be laughed at...or provide anybody watching them a reason to snicker.

The Mets, however, were their own worst enemies in that regard. Their record wasn't fabricating that they'd just lost their 13th consecutive game (their third losing streak of ten or more games) to start a doubleheader versus the Pirates at the Polo Grounds. They really were bad enough to have entered this Tuesday twinighter 51 games out of first place. Maybe the stress of it all got to be too much for third base coach Solly Hemus, for Solly argued a call with umpire Frank Walsh and got tossed from the nightcap for his troubles. In those days, there weren't bench coaches and batting coaches routinely filling the dugout, so Casey Stengel needed someone from the ranks of his players to fill in near first after he shifted first base coach Cookie Lavagetto to the third base box. His original choice was veteran Gene Woodling, but then he used Woodling to pinch-hit, so he needed somebody else to pat fannies and handle helmets.

Who else for such a delicate assignment but Marv Throneberry?

Well, why not? The Mets were a mere 65 games under .500 at the moment Stengel required a volunteer and Richie Ashburn volunteered Marv. The 4,184 who trekked to Coogan's Bluff in search of a full evening's entertainment were tickled to death. They cottoned quickly to the concept of Marv Throneberry, first base coach.

But not as much as they would adore the notion of Marv Throneberry, pinch-hitting hero.

The Mets were three outs from their 14th consecutive loss when Ashburn led off the Mets' ninth with a single to right. After Buc starter Harvey Haddix walked Joe Christopher, Pittsburgh skipper Danny Murtaugh opted to bring in relief ace Roy Face. Face fanned Charlie Neal for the first out of the bottom of the ninth, but then allowed a run-scoring single to Felix Mantilla. After Frank Thomas flied to center and the Mets were down to their last out, Casey wanted a lefty batter to face the righty Face. Thus, to pinch-hit for the righthanded Jim Hickman, he chose the people's choice of 1962.

"We want Marv! We want Marv!" the fans cried. So Ol' Case gave 'em what they wanted.

So did he who was Marvelous. Throneberry blasted a three-run homer to right. The Mets won, 5-4 — the same score by which Bobby Thomson's three-run homer won the pennant for the Giants in the very same inning in the very same ballpark eleven years earlier.

Hard to decide which was the bigger miracle under Coogan's Bluff.

AUGUST 22, 1962
METS 5 GIANTS 4
THE POLO GROUNDS

The presence of Ken MacKenzie, Yale '56, in the class photo of Mets '62 brings to mind Gerald Ford's alleged campaign slogan for 1976 (as alleged on *Saturday Night Live*, at any rate): "If he's so dumb, how come he's president?" MacKenzie may have pitched his way from the Ivy League to the National League...but if he was so smart, what was he doing stuck in the Senior Circuit cellar?

Such a query could have been directed at any number of highly educated early Mets. As William Ryczek noted in *The Amazin' Mets, 1962-1969*, the club's first pitching staff certainly made good grades if not great pitches. Jay Hook, for example went to Northwestern and earned a master's degree in mechanical engineering. Craig Anderson matriculated at Lehigh and would go on to hold a master's in education. Al Jackson, Galen Cisco, Bob G. Miller — all college men when that designation was still rather unique in the baseball profession.

Yet at the head of the class, at least when it came to the tales the 1962 Mets generated, was MacKenzie, known for two things that long outlasted his modestly successful pitching career.

The first was Yale. That was unusual for the highest rung of pro baseball. MacKenzie was only the twelfth Bulldog to bark his way into the bigs in the twentieth century. None would follow him until Ron Darling joined Ken's N.L. alma mater in 1983. MacKenzie's collegiate background made for a couple of good lines. Like Ken, by the Eli's amused reckoning, being the "lowest-paid" member of the Yale class of '56... and like his manager telling him the secret to retiring enemy batters was to "make like they're the Harvards."

Must've worked, for the second and most relevant thing repeated on behalf of Ken MacKenzie after 1962 was he was the only Mets pitcher from that staff to compile a winning record — 5-4 in 42 appearances. In a season when losses accosted his colleagues by the bushel (Anderson, 17; Hook, 19; Jackson, 20; Roger Craig, 24), the lefty reliever gained his eternal statistical advantage in Amazin'ly Metsian fashion.

He blew a lead. Not only that, but he blew a lead for Bob L. Miller, the Bob Miller who staggered into his late August home start against the second-place Giants at 0-10. Miller, however, appeared on the verge of getting off the cruelest of schneids this Wednesday by holding San Francisco to a single run over seven innings. It was Mets 4 Giants 1 when righty Bob encountered a bit of trouble in the eighth. With one run in and two men on base, Stengel pulled Miller for MacKenzie. Two batters later, it was 4-4, which is how the visitors' eighth ended.

Miller was, per usual, out of luck, but MacKenzie wasn't out of the game. Stengel let him hit for himself against Don Larsen and it all worked perfectly for Ken. The pitcher reached on an error and departed for a pinch-runner, Joe Christopher, who eventually came around to score to make it 5-4, Mets. Roger Craig preserved that score in the ninth, which resulted in MacKenzie's fifth triumph in nine decisions. That's where his record stayed for the rest of the year, and that's the mark that gets referenced to this day, sometimes even by Ron Darling on SNY.

Lowest-paid Yalie from 1956? Maybe. Highest-profile thanks to a 1962 win that even Yale's Department of Ornithology would have to judge vultured? Definitely.

With the last of their dates in Upper Manhattan completed, the Mets said goodbye to the only home they had ever known... or so they thought. They were playing their final scheduled game ever at the Polo Grounds. Come 1963, the Mets were destined to move to their new home in Flushing Meadows, Shea Stadium. Hence, the big horseshoe-

13

SEPTEMBER 23, 1962
METS 2 CUBS 1
THE POLO GROUNDS

shaped yard on the edge of Harlem, site of baseball history since the Giants rebuilt it after a devastating fire in 1911, was about to host its last baseball game.

The Mets may not have made much history there in their one year at the Polo Grounds — certainly not the triumphant kind — but they treated the occasion with requisite significance. Public address announcer Jack E. Lee provided an appropriate soundtrack of popular standards throughout this sentimental Sunday afternoon, starting with "This Ole House" and heart-tuggingly proceeding to "Auld Lang Syne". In between, the Mets placed their own punctuation at the end of a 48-season period of Manhattan baseball when, in the bottom of the ninth, Frank Thomas singled home Choo Choo Coleman with the winning run to create one final great New York victory under Coogan's Bluff, as the Mets beat the Cubs, 2-1.

That it was only the Mets' 39th win of 1962, and only their 22nd in the ole house, didn't make it any less marvelous. That Thomas, the man who got the final hit, was the same man who (as a Pirate) caught the final putout in the first "final" game played there five years earlier as the Giants vacated certainly made it more intriguing. That it included the first hit in the big league career of 17-year-old rookie Ed Kranepool couldn't help but make it hopeful. That it came against Chicago on the 54th anniversary of Fred Merkle's Boner (which was committed by the young Giant first baseman against the enemy Cubs at the version of the Polo Grounds that predated this one) made it all the more historically poignant. Not that poignancy was in short supply, per Robert Lipsyte of the *Times*, who reported "Till We Meet Again" echoed from the speakers before giving way to "Auld Lang Syne," which accompanied the sight of Casey Stengel making the final march "alone on an empty field, 475 feet to the clubhouse with his right hand in his back pocket."

Sentimentally, the tableau made for the ideal bridge: the 1962 Mets leaving behind the past they were conceived and convened to continue as heirs to the Giant and Dodger legacy while heading to a new borough for a new ballpark, intent on constructing new Queens dreams. But the 1962 Mets had been redefining what was ideal from the day they played their very first home game (at which point they were already 0-1). Leave it to these Mets to step on their graceful adieu. They had to — Shea Stadium wasn't going to be ready for Opening Day 1963. It wasn't going to be ready at any time in 1963.

This meant the final baseball game ever at the Polo Grounds that 10,304 thought they'd attended was actually the 82nd-to-last. There'd be plenty more Lang Syne heard by the banks of the Harlem River come April.

SEPTEMBER 29, 1962

METS 2 CUBS 1

WRIGLEY FIELD

One last loose end was taken care of on the inaugural season's penultimate day. Bob L. Miller got his. Oh and twelve and perpetually confused for his same-named roommate, the righty became a winner when he went the distance on a seven-hitter that assured he wouldn't be remembered as the first pitcher ever to go 0-13 in an entire season. Bob Miller went 1-12, which was the literal expression of better than nothing. By securing the Mets' 40th victory of the campaign, Miller figured he'd have plenty to talk about when the team's beat reporters approached him in the clubhouse.

Except there was no approach. There were no beat reporters around on the final Saturday of the season. The men who covered the Mets had abandoned the sunken Met ship to cover the sizzling Dodger-Giant pennant race in California. So much for a happy ending.

And if that wasn't proof enough that the 1962 Mets couldn't go out on their own terms, they still had one game left to play the next day at Wrigley. It was another loss, the 120th of the *annus horribilis*, this one accented by the eighth-inning triple play hit into by catcher Joe Pignatano. Piggy would never again play in the majors after the game that left the maiden Mets forever imprinted with a 40-120 mark. Neither would Richie Ashburn, who was caught off second base on Pignatano's ball...nor would Sammy Drake, who had been on first when the TP unfurled.

That last loss left the tenth-place Mets with their instantly recognizable won-lost-lost-lost winning percentage of .250, but 1962 wasn't quite done tormenting them. Because the Giants and Dodgers wound up in a first-place tie, league rules mandated they play a three-game playoff, which in those pre-divisional days counted as part of the regular season. The Giants took the series in three, which was bad news for the Dodgers, yet somehow managed to kick the downtrodden Mets with one more spiteful footnote. When the Mets finished playing, they were 60 games out of first. As they scattered into history, they lost yet another half-game in the standings. Therefore, the team that was 9 1/2 behind after only nine games of existence completed its appointed rounds 60 1/2 behind three days after there technically stopped being 1962 Mets.

Is it any wonder so many of their so few wins so stand out?

 **1963**

S hea Stadium wasn't yet ready, and maybe the Mets still weren't, either, but a couple of flickers of Polo Grounds progress couldn't be denied. For one, there was the Mets getting to the business of their first win of their second season 10% sooner than they had in their first

15
APRIL 19, 1963
METS 5 BRAVES 4
THE POLO GROUNDS

year. True, it's a nice way of saying that instead of getting off to an 0-9 start, they commenced to winning after losing eight straight to begin 1963. The ninth game's first blow toward a brighter future came in the bottom of the second when 18-year-old Ed Kranepool — the Mets' glamour signing the summer before — struck his first major league home run to stake Roger Craig to a 1-0 lead. The next bright, young faces to succeed emerged in the fourth, when sophomore Jim Hickman (25) and rookie Ron

Hunt (22) tripled consecutively to extend the Mets' margin to 3-0.

Growing pains, however, were still part of the Met story this Friday afternoon, and by the top of ninth, Eddie Mathews's bases-loaded walk off Ken MacKenzie would put the Braves up, 4-3. The last response the Mets had for Milwaukee was their best: second baseman Hunt racking up his third hit of the day, a two-run double off Frank Funk to give the Mets a last at-bat, 5-4 win that touched off the Mets' first-ever four game winning streak. Four years in the Brave farm system weren't enough to get Hunt's original parent club to give him a chance in the bigs. The kid made his old would-be teammates pay. By the end of '63, Hunt wound up polling second in National League Rookie of the Year voting and everybody in the N.L. knew New York's gain was Milwaukee's loss.

In the same stadium where Floyd Patterson regained his heavyweight championship belt from Ingemar Johansson three years earlier, the Mets showed they could take a punch and prevail in a slugfest, doing whatever it took to earn a split decision in this hard-fought twinbill.

MAY 12, 1963 (2ND)
METS 13 REDS 12
THE POLO GROUNDS

One Met in particular knew no limits when it came to effort. Casey Stengel had once let it be known that if any Met found himself at bat with the bases loaded, fifty American dollars could be his if he "accidentally" allowed himself to be hit by a pitch. Fifty bucks was not insubstantial to the early 1960s ballplayer, yet only one Met was determined to cash in on the offer. With three on and one out, hustling Hot Rod Kanehl stepped up and stepped into a delivery from the Reds' John Tsitouris. That was using his head and his body, for Rod's welt lengthened the Mets' third-inning lead over Cincinnati at the Polo Grounds to 5-0.

Kanehl's HBP RBI was truly money because the Mets would eventually require every last run they could scrounge up in the second game of this Sunday doubleheader. Unaccustomed to pitching with a lead, Jay Hook gave it all away, and by the middle of the fifth, the Mets and Reds were tied at six. The Mets, however, came roaring back with five in their half of the fifth, capped by a three-run homer from Duke Snider. Suddenly it was 11-6, Mets.

Then, just as suddenly, it wasn't. Relievers Ken MacKenzie and Larry Bearnarth — abetted by a Tim Harkness error — allowed the Reds right back into the game, then into the lead by allowing six sixth-inning runs. The Mets trailed, 12-11, and stayed behind until the eighth when a pair of walks and a Harkness single set up Jim Hickman's tying sacrifice fly and Choo Choo Coleman's go-ahead single. The Mets led, 13-12, heading to the ninth and, shockingly, won, 13-12, as starter Tracy Stallard came in to stop the madness with a scoreless inning of relief, striking out rookie second baseman Pete Rose (who had been on base four times) to end the game.

If this nightcap didn't contain enough mythic elements already, consider that in their history, the Mets have given up exactly a dozen runs in 59 different games. This is the only one of those they've ever won.

The old guy from Brooklyn transformed himself into a new hero in Manhattan. Such a role for prematurely gray, seventeen-season veteran outfielder Duke Snider would have been unimaginable as recently as six years earlier, but so would have been the Mets in 1957.

JUNE 7, 1963
METS 3 CARDINALS 2
THE POLO GROUNDS

The longtime Dodger star glimmered at the even longer-time home of the Giants, socking a one-out, bottom-of-the-ninth, three-run homer off Diomedes Olivo of the Cardinals to pull out a 3-2 Mets win at the raucous Polo Grounds.

Prior to the ninth this Friday night, the tenth-place Mets had collected only two hits against St. Louis starter Ron Taylor and appeared on their way to wasting a complete game effort from Al Jackson. But after retiring Jim Hickman to start the ninth, Taylor gave up a single to Frank Thomas (pinch-run for by Rod Kanehl) and walked Ron Hunt. Johnny Keane opted to replace Taylor with Olivo, whose work for the evening consisted of a passed ball that moved the baserunners up to second and third and the 399th home run of Snider's illustrious, multiborough career.

A week later, the Duke attained a nice, round number when he blasted a first-inning, two-out pitch from Cincinnati's Bob Purkey out of Crosley Field. When Snider drove himself and Ron Hunt home, it gave the all-time Dodger great the 400th home run of his career, making him the eighth player in big league history to hit that many. The Mets would go on to beat the Reds, 10-3, and seventeen summers later, a plaque would hang in Cooperstown featuring Snider's likeness and a notation that somewhere between 1947 and 1964, the Duke of Flatbush logged time with NEW YORK N.L.

JUNE 23, 1963 (1ST)
METS 5 PHILLIES 0
THE POLO GROUNDS

As milestone home runs went, Duke Snider's 400th dinger was four times as impressive as that a teammate of his would produce the same month, yet only a fraction as famous. For while Snider had shown uncommon power, he had nothing on the production values of Jimmy Piersall.

Jimmy Piersall was one of a kind: longtime American League outfielder who suffered and overcame a nervous breakdown; had his story made into a book — *Fear Strikes Out* — that became a major motion picture; was judged contemporarily, per Leonard Koppett, as either "a little crazy" or as "a master put-on". Fear may have struck out in the '50s, but Piersall was still active come 1963, a 33-year-old Washington Senator whose game was falling off as he aged. Naturally, he became a Met — unofficial compensation for Gil Hodges (the straightest baseball person imaginable) being let out of his Met player contract so he could manage in D.C. If Piersall's reputation as a character preceded him to New York, whatever he was known for as a player had pretty much abandoned him.

Piersall was batting .210 in the month since the Mets acquired him, knocking in only eight runs, stealing no bases — one of his specialties in the A.L. — and remaining stuck on 99 career home runs. Not hitting homers gave him plenty of time to think about what he might do once he launched his first as a Met, his prospective hundredth as a big leaguer. Piersall's goal became to "do something different".

Boy, did he ever.

In the fifth inning of this Sunday doubleheader opener at the Polo Grounds, the Mets were leading Philadelphia, 1-0, primarily on the strength of Carl Willey's sublime pitching. The Maine native had a perfect game going into the fourth and kept his shutout through the top of the fifth. He would keep his shutout all the way to a most pleasing 5-0 complete game, a two-hitter as it turned out (one of four shutouts Carl crafted for a 51-win team). Yet it also turned out that nobody would remember this game as the day Carl Willey blanked the Phillies.

This was Piersall's show, at least once he got ahold of a Dallas Green delivery and took it over the Polo Grounds fence. Jimmy did it — he got his 100th home run. Not the stuff of the Duke, exactly, but a pretty admirable total.

What he did next was a matter of taste. Piersall turned around and ran to first... backwards. He continued his trot facing the wrong way, until he arrived at home plate, the number 34 on his back greeting the next hitter, Tim Harkness.

"I hit my 400th homer and all I got was the ball," Snider was reported to have told Piersall. "You hit your 100th and go coast-to-coast."

It was different, all right. It was different from Piersall's original plan, which was to run first to third, then to second and so on, but the umpires told him to forget that idea. It was also the beginning of the end of Jimmy Piersall's Mets career. Casey Stengel (who, as a player, once doffed his cap to reveal a sparrow) did not particularly care for Piersall's act even before he stuck his baserunning in reverse. And Piersall was on record as not much caring for Stengel: "He isn't a manager anymore. He's just on display."

The outfielder was entitled to his opinion, but Stengel was plenty capable of displaying his managerial prerogative of wanting nothing more to do with someone he decided was a showboat, a malcontent and, most significantly, a player who wasn't producing anything else besides a single home run and accompanying spectacle in forty games as a Met. With his Met average down to .194 in late July, Piersall was released...along with a parting shot from the perpetually self-aware Stengel:

"There's only room for one clown on this team."

Snider's analysis would prove prescient. Piersall literally went coast-to-coast, being picked up by the Los Angeles Angels and sticking with them until 1967. He hit four home runs in parts of five seasons in Southern California, the last of his dingers being dung before they moved to Anaheim, next door to Disneyland.

Thus, there went Jimmy Piersall's chance to do something really Goofy for a home run trot.

The Mets giving a game away was nothing unusual given their brief, inglorious history. But the Mets taking one back — the very same one? Was that allowed? It would take fourteen innings to confirm that it was.

JUNE 26, 1963
METS 8 CUBS 6 (14)
THE POLO GROUNDS

To be fair, the Mets did a nice job of burrowing their way into this Wednesday matinee versus the Cubs at the Polo Grounds. Down, 4-0, by the middle of the fifth, Duke Snider drove in Ron Hunt with a sixth-inning double and Frank Thomas followed behind him with a two-run homer. Frank was Thomas on the spot in the eighth, knocking in Choo Choo Coleman to knot the score at four. The Mets' pitching staff was doing a heckuva job in the meantime: starting with Al Jackson getting the last out of the fifth and going through his next inning of work, then two from Larry Bearnarth, one from Tracy Stallard, two from Carl Willey and two and two-thirds from Galen Cisco, the Mets actually threw the equivalent of a no-hitter for nine innings' worth of Cubs outs. That streak was snapped, however, when, with two out in top of the fourteenth and Don Landrum on first via walk, Billy Williams lined a ball to left that Thomas — known as the Big Donkey — got a poor jump on. It took off to distant precincts of the PG outfield and Williams's hit became a two-run inside-the-park home run, giving the Cubs a 6-4 lead.

If the game had climaxed there, it would have been...not unusual. But the Mets had hung around this long, so they might as well hang in there a little longer. Jim Hickman singled to open the home fourteenth and the Mets seemed to have a rally going when Ron Hunt singled, too, but Hickman, in his haste to make something happen, overran second base for the first out of the inning. After Jimmy Piersall walked, Cubs "head coach" Bob Kennedy (Chicago did not believe in managers in the early '60s, opting to employ a "college of coaches" instead) chose to change pitchers, replacing Jack Warner — who'd produced boffo results since entering the game in the ninth — with Paul Toth. Toth was assigned the heavy task of getting out Thomas, who had four hits on the day. The strategy worked, as Frank flied to left for the second out. Toth was then removed by non-manager Kennedy in favor of Jim Brewer. Brewer experienced a prohibition on control, walking Sammy Taylor to load the bases for first baseman Tim Harkness.

Harkness had three hits already, including two in his previous at-bats in the eleventh and the thirteenth. Extra innings were apparently Tim Harkness's kind of innings, the fourteenth in particular. Sure enough, Harkness ended the game right then and there, on a three-two pitch, with his first career grand slam. It was a mighty wallop over the right field wall that gave the Mets an 8-6 win that, in turn, unleashed delirium among however many hundreds of fans who remained to the joyous end. Although the numbers were fewer and the stakes absolutely lesser, Harkness was called out by Mets fans who gathered at the foot of the steps to the Mets' center field clubhouse (as fans were permitted to do in days of yore) and cheered "WE WANT HARKNESS!" until the man of the moment emerged on the balcony to acknowledge their rapture much as Bobby Thomson did a dozen years earlier when the home team at the Polo Grounds was the Giants and the shot that set off shock waves was heard 'round the world.

"We just about had to end it there," Casey Stengel offered with impeccable logic after deploying 20 players across four hours and eight minutes of baseball, "because I'd run out of men."

"I couldn't believe it was me who hit that," Harkness, a .208 hitter when the day began, confessed. "It doesn't seem like good things happen to me." That might have been a blanket statement for the Polo Grounds Mets, but their New Breed of loyalists recognized the good thing that had befallen them and they never forgot it. Witness the response this game has generated post-2000 at Ultimate Mets Database from those who attended and those who followed the action from afar:

"That afternoon in 1963 at the Polo Grounds is still my most memorable and favorite baseball recollection."

"When it really did happen, you can imagine how great it felt."

"It sounded like 50,000 people were there."

"What I remember was the pandemonium after the game, in the corridors leading out of the Polo Grounds and down into the subway. Everyone was just chanting 'Let's Go Mets' and the sound was bouncing off the walls. It was so much fun."

AUGUST 9, 1963
METS 7 CUBS 3
THE POLO GROUNDS

20

Forget that line about how you have to be a pretty good pitcher to lose twenty games. You have to be a plenty strong human being to endure being a twenty-game loser by the first week of August. And to arrive at such a humbling mark in a fashion in which you'd have to believe Somebody Upstairs (besides George Weiss) was telling you to find another profession?

Let's just say Roger Craig dug deep to persevere as long as he did in 1963. The veteran of two world champion Dodger clubs already knew what he was in the midst of after emerging as the ace of the 1962 Mets. That team was loaded with "pretty good pitchers," which is to say four of its hurlers lost at least 17 games. Nobody lost more than Craig, who took 24 defeats in the Mets' inaugural season. On the flip side, he led those Mets in wins with 10 — or exactly a quarter of their 40 victories. By comparison, that year's Cy Young winner, Craig's old Los Angeles teammate Don Drysdale, won 25 games, but his total represented a lesser percentage of his team's 102 wins.

Hard to believe the Cy Young voters overlooked Roger completely.

Come 1963, Craig commenced to setting a much more encouraging pace for himself. When he beat L.A. on April 29, he evened his record at 2-2. Maybe his second year as a Met would be different from his first.

It would. Oh, it would.

Only one of the "2's" in Roger Craig's record would hold steady and it wasn't the one on the right. The win column remained stubbornly unchanging for Craig, but the other column, where they keep track of the losses? The updates would be frequent. Beginning on May 4, with a 17-4 shellacking at the Polo Grounds at the hands of the Giants, and winding through the spring and into summer, Craig did nothing but lose.

There would be a few blowouts, to be sure, but most of Craig's losing was of the excruciating variety: 4-2...4-3...1-0...like that. As the defeats mounted, the luck grew harder. When Roger lost his 18th consecutive decision on August 4 — the one that made him a 20-game loser with 52 games to go in the season — it was in a 2-1 game at Milwaukee's County Stadium. Twelve of those 18 straight losses charged to Craig were contests he lost by one, two or three runs. His luck was typified by the way he lost the eighteenth: the Brave run that beat him scored when a pickoff attempt went awry.

And Craig was known to have a great pickoff move.

"If he bought a graveyard," Tracy Stallard said of his teammate, "Nobody would die."

Craig somehow kept his perspective alive as long as his unwanted streak insisted on living, too. "I try not to think about how many games I've lost, or think about how many I might lose," he said after the 17th consecutive defeat. "Sure, maybe I joke about it after a game, but I'll tell you this: If I ever find myself thinking about losing during a game, I'll know it's time to quit."

Roger's fellow Mets certainly thought of ways to make him a winner. Long before a black cat would take on more positive connotations in Mets lore, catcher Norm Sherry sought to track one down for Craig to bring to the mound with him when he warmed up. That didn't exactly work out, but anything would go as far as a potential upturn in fortune was concerned. When the streak was at 13, of all numbers, Stallard loaned Craig his uniform digits, 36. Craig pitched beautifully in them, carrying a 1-0 lead into the bottom of the ninth at Philadelphia. Alas, with one out, he surrendered a triple to Tony Gonzalez and a game-losing home run to Roy Sievers. With 36 having yielded him nothing more than a 14th straight loss, Craig returned to wearing No. 38.

Still, nothing was beyond trying, including yet another numerical stab in the dark. At the behest of a dream Polo Grounds clubhouse guard Ted Decker shared with him — as chronicled in Jerry Mitchell's *The Amazing Mets* — Craig switched from 38 to 13 before his August 9 home outing against the Cubs. Decker told Roger he dreamt he saw him winning a game with No. 13 on his shirt. That's all a pitcher with a 2-20 mark needs to hear to be spurred to sartorial action (though Craig would, many years later, credit his kids for the idea).

No Met had yet worn 13, according to *Mets By The Numbers* by Jon Springer and Matthew Silverman. Baseball was as superstitious as any endeavor in 1963. You didn't see 13th floors in skyscrapers or Row 13 on any airplane, either. But few of those entities had suffered luck as rotten as Roger Craig's, so why not tempt fate? And why not up the stakes, as Craig did at the end of the pregame meeting Roger ran as part of his duties as Mets player representative? He completed the business at hand and then added an addendum:

"I'd really like to win this one tonight, boys."

Maybe that's what was holding Roger back all those months — maybe he simply forgot to tell his teammates what he wanted. Or maybe it was the sight of No. 13 taking the hill under Coogan's Bluff that appeased the baseball gods. Or perhaps it was just the streak's time to take a powder.

Whatever it was, it wasn't going to be easy, not even with Craig holding Chicago in check for seven innings and the Mets clinging to a 3-2 lead. As had happened so often before, one bad pitch bit the pitcher, in this case, one that resulted in a leadoff eighth-inning triple for Billy Williams, which was followed by a Ron Santo fly to center that tied the score at three and put Craig's streakbusting in jeopardy. Roger hung in there and didn't give up anything else in the eighth or ninth. It stayed 3-3 heading to the bottom of the final inning of regulation.

With one out, the Mets tried to rescue Roger from an 0-19 span — which would have matched Philadelphia Athletic Jack Nabors's all-time worst single-season losing streak from 1916 — and a 2-21 overall mark for the year. Joe Hicks singled off Cubs starter Paul Toth. Choo Choo Coleman struck out, but Al Moran doubled, sending Hicks to third. Lindy McDaniel relieved Toth. Casey Stengel had no choice but to pinch-hit for Craig. He chose Tim Harkness, a hero earlier in the season when he beat these very same Cubs on a fourteenth-inning grand slam. Cubs head coach Bob Kennedy wouldn't give Tim that kind of chance again, intentionally walking him. That loaded the bases with two outs and brought up Jim Hickman.

Jim Hickman — two days removed from completing the first cycle in Mets history — happily played the role of Harkness this time around, working the count to three-and-two before lifting a fly to left field that took advantage of the Polo Grounds' singularly weird dimensions. "It just ticked the overhang of the upper stands," Mitchell wrote, "before falling to the field."

All that mattered is it left the field of play fair for a grand slam home run — the grand slam home run that gave the Mets the 7-3 victory to make a winner at long last out of Roger Craig. Of course no one was quicker out of the dugout to greet Hickman than the winning pitcher.

"The first thing I had in mind," Craig said, "was to make sure he touched home plate. I'd have tackled him to make him do it if I had to."

As of Friday the Ninth, No. 13 was 3-20 and keeping a death grip on that uniform for the rest of the season. It proved sort of lucky, as Roger went on a three-game winning streak before backsliding to a final record of 5-22, 15-46 in two seasons as a Met. Finally, the fates smiled on him by getting him traded to St. Louis after the season for outfielder George Altman and reliever Bill Wakefield. By October of 1964, he'd be pitching in the Fall Classic and earning his third world championship, as a Cardinal. As Mitchell put it, "No prisoner ever received a pardon with more sincere expressions of gratitude."

Indeed, Craig evinced no bitterness over his experience in New York, just as he never pointed fingers at an offense that didn't score for him or fielders who might have made a few more plays on his behalf. "My two seasons with the Mets were a blessing," he said. "It taught me how to cope with adversity."

A star was born, even if it was destined to flame out almost immediately. The southpaw supernova that briefly brightened the Mets' sky — clad in No. 41, no less — was Grover Powell, 22 and arguably the Mets' first breakthrough pitcher. He broke through in

21 AUGUST 20, 1963 (1ST)
METS 3 PHILLIES 0
CONNIE MACK STADIUM

style, certainly. In his first start (following nine relief appearances), Pennsylvanian Powell held his home state Phillies scoreless for nine sublime innings at Connie Mack

Stadium. Backed by two runs in the eighth and a Frank Thomas two-run dinger in the ninth, Powell came away the 4-0 winner of this Tuesday twinight opener.

After nearly two seasons of flailing and failing, maybe the Mets were finally onto something: they had a young pitcher who dazzled the opposition. Powell was an instant sensation. Between games of the doubleheader, he had each of his teammates autograph the game ball to commemorate his four-hitter. "I'm going to stick it in my front window," he promised. Later that night, he was the apple of the Mets' beat writers' collective eye, as they at last had something positive to chronicle (never mind the Mets losing the nightcap). Grover even drew the attention of a most unusual reporter.

Manager Casey Stengel, perhaps giddy from the Mets having matched their entire 1962 victory total when Powell raised the team's record to a sassy 40-85, picked up a pencil and notebook and joined the journalistic scrum. While other gentlemen of the press inquired after Grover's nerves (he had plenty) and sought predictions regarding his next start (he'd probably get bombed, he allowed lightheartedly), Ol' Case injected the perfect non sequitur for the interrogatory occasion:

"Wuz you born in Poland?"

It wasn't (or wuzn't) where Powell had come from, it was where he was going. Stengel thought the kid looked 14 ("just imagine what he'll be like when he's 16") but he had just pitched one of the young Mets' most mature games. He'd definitely grown up quicker than anybody else in orange and blue. His future could only grow brighter.

Except there was no future to Grover Powell as a Met pitcher. His next start, against Pittsburgh, was derailed when a Donn Clendenon liner caught him in the face, and he didn't win another game in 1963. Grover had adjusted his pitching motion after the injury and it not only made him less successful, it led to tendonitis in his left elbow. He injured his moneymaker in winter ball and, despite pitching professionally through 1970, never returned to the majors. Leukemia would cut him down at the age of 44.

But oh, what a night, late August, back in '63.

22

SEPTEMBER 11, 1963
METS 4 GIANTS 2
THE POLO GROUNDS

The Mets' *second* final game ever at the Polo Grounds came to pass on September 18, 1963, an unceremonious 5-1 defeat at the hands of the Phillies in front of 1,752. Counting the Giants' departure in 1957, this was the third time in a six-year span New York was compelled to bid "Auld Lang Syne" to the PG, so it wasn't really a very big deal at that point. No pomp and little circumstance attached itself to Goodbye III — "I don't remember any fanfare," Craig Anderson told Nick Diunte of examiner. com in 2011— but a legend was born even as a ballpark was being given its third set of last rites.

The *Times* reported, "Movies were taken as part of a Met promotional film. Casey Stengel waxed eloquent Stengelese all over the place for a couple of hours prior to and following the game." That alleged rambling was, in fact, the classic "Metsie, Metsie, Metsie" rant that has lived on in the Mets fan consciousness for most of a half-century (and remains in heavy rotation, thanks to SNY's continual reairings of *Mets Yearbook: 1963*).

The final Mets *win* in the Polo Grounds came a week earlier, on September 11, as the home team defeated its predecessor in this space, the now San Francisco Giants, 4-2. Tim Harkness went 3-for-5 that Wednesday with a pair of RBIs and Al Jackson threw a seven-hitter. Of course there was no way of telling that was the final Mets win in Manhattan, even though that would have been a reasonable guess, considering this was a 49-97 club. They had seven more home games remaining and they lost all seven. Their subsequent nine-game road swing to end the season brought them another seven losses, consigning the Mets to a 51-111 sophomore season.

Not that too many minded too much to watch. As Gordon White noted in the *Times*, "What seems most amazing is that this club, though still a sad bunch of major leaguers, drew 157,754 more fans than in 1962, when the newness of the Mets was the main factor in their good showing." Indeed, these cellar-dwelling Mets of 1963 cracked the one-million mark in attendance back when that sort of thing simply wasn't done by last-place teams. Obviously, Mets fans would be back for more in '64, which led White to extend a helpful bit of commuting advice after the *final* final Polo Grounds game was over:

> *"For those New Breeders who want to see the next Met game, remember, don't take the D train to 155th Street; take the IRT to Willets Point."*

 **1964**

Two years of waiting didn't dim the enthusiasm one iota. Once it opened, there was no holding back the thrill Mets fans felt at having a ballpark of their very own. "You've gotta see this stadium," announcer Bob Murphy urged his radio listeners in advance of the inaugural game there. "Every seat is a beautifully painted individual seat." It was probably no accident Murph mentioned that little fact, as the scramble to ready Shea Stadium for its previously postponed closeup was so frenzied that the paint was still drying as customers were finding their way up its 21 gleaming banks of escalators.

23

APRIL 19, 1964
METS 6 PIRATES 0
SHEA STADIUM

Something else wasn't quite 100% ready that sunny Friday afternoon: the Mets. As was the case in 1962 and 1963, the 1964 Mets were masters at not getting off to a good start. They lost their first pair of games in Philadelphia, then came home to big, bright, beautiful Shea Stadium only to blow a 3-1 lead to the Pirates. As the stadium settled in Saturday, so did the Mets...into their usual rut, absorbing yet another defeat, this one 9-5 to Pittsburgh.

Can't anybody here christen this thing?

It fell to "Little Al Jackson," as Murph was fond of calling him, to make the Mets winners in their new home for the very first time. Jackson figured as the prime candidate for the assignment, as it was he who tossed the first Met shutout ever two years earlier. Now Little Al would put the team on his formidable back and do at Shea what he did as admirably as any early Met could possibly hope to at the Polo Grounds — lead the worst team in baseball to one of its infrequent triumphs. Jackson threw nine scoreless innings versus the Bucs on Shea's first Sunday, scattering six hits and striking out six batters. A four-run fourth, built on two-run singles from Rod Kanehl and Ron Hunt, provided Jackson ample support.

Bigger wins awaited in Shea's future. That was hard to imagine in 1964. The way the Mets played back then, it was hard to imagine any wins awaited in Shea's future, especially its immediate future. Good thing Little Al Jackson came up so big.

MAY 26, 1964
METS 19 CUBS 1
WRIGLEY FIELD

For what very good teams could do in one year, the toddler Mets required two-and-a-quarter seasons: namely win their 103rd game (ever). But how much the Mets scored to win their 103rd game was more than some teams managed in a week — like the 1964 Mets, for example.

In the seven days before they touched off an offensive outburst for the ages, the Mets played seven games, lost six of them and scored twelve times. Pretty typical stuff for the Mets in their formative years, which is what made the events of this particular Tuesday in Chicago so Amazin'ly atypical.

Come to think of it, maybe those weren't really the Mets out there at Wrigley Field. Their lineup featured two guys named Smith: Dick, batting leadoff and playing first, and Charley, playing third and hitting sixth. Smith is one of those names a fellow uses when he's pretending to be somebody he's not. Dick and Charley masqueraded as superstars, going a combined 8-for-12 with seven RBIs between them. Then again, guys who tended to register at motels under every possible Met name — from Christopher and Cannizzaro to Hunt and Hickman to Thomas and McMillan — were registering base hits and runs batted in and just about everything positive a box score would allow.

Each member of the Mets' starting lineup hit. Dick Smith alone tripled, doubled and singled thrice. Charley Smith contributed a three-run homer and five ribbies. Hickman drove in three, scored three and notched three singles. Overall, in 49 official at-bats, the Mets collected 23 hits, a total that remains unsurpassed as the most the Mets have ever accumulated in a nine-inning game.

The beneficiary of all this largesse was Jack Fisher, a 1-for-6 batter himself, but mostly a four-hit complete game pitcher. When all the dust the Mets kicked on the Cubs settled, he was the winner of a shocking 19-1 decision.

"This," announced Bob Murphy, in a masterstroke of understatement as the final out approached, "is some kind of a day, I want to tell you."

Clearly, the best line to come out of this unforeseen explosion was the one that stretched out across the Wrigley scoreboard:

But there were a few other lines that, like the Mets' club-record 18-run margin of victory, still stand the test of time.

Like Tracy Stallard's, after the Mets tacked on a six-run ninth: "That's when I knew we had 'em."

Like Casey Stengel's, after finally not being on the receiving end of a blowout: "I suppose most of the club owners will be trying to contact me now to get my players."

And, most enduringly, like that uttered by the eternally quoted caller to the sports department of the *Waterbury Republican,* a Connecticut gentleman who sincerely wanted to know if what he thought he'd heard was true...that the cellar-dwelling Mets had actually scored 19 runs that afternoon. When he was told yes, they most definitely did, the fellow offered the follow-up question that, given the state of the Mets since there had been Mets, absolutely needed to be asked:

"But did they win?"

W hen you say "long man," you be sure to pronounce it "Larry Bearnarth." That's how Casey Stengel did it in the opener of a twinighter at Shea this Tuesday night. He said Bearnarth, and he kept saying it.

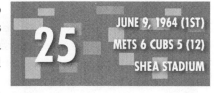

25
JUNE 9, 1964 (1ST)
METS 6 CUBS 5 (12)
SHEA STADIUM

First, however, the Ol' Perfesser said, "Al Jackson," but Jackson's pitching said he didn't have it. Little Al faced seven batters in the opening inning at Shea; five of them reached base; three of them scored; three of them were on base when Stengel decided he'd seen enough. Jackson was pulled in favor of Bill Wakefield, who got the Mets out of the first trailing, 3-0.

The Mets had their first big opportunity to get even and, perhaps, then some in the second, so once the Mets got two on with two out and Wakefield was due up, Stengel pinch-hit for him with Hot Rod Kanehl. Kanehl didn't let him down, singling home two runs and taking second on the throw in from right field. Jim Hickman followed with another two-run single and now the Mets led, 4-3.

In to pitch came Tom Sturdivant, who promptly lost Stengel's confidence by surrendering a leadoff triple to Ron Santo, a run-scoring single to Ernie Banks and another single to Billy Cowan. That was enough Tom Sturdivant. Enter Bearnarth, making his first appearance since the infamous 23-inning loss to the Giants on Memorial Day. In that wacky May 31 affair, the St. John's alum gave Casey seven solid innings of shutout relief. His encore, against the Cubs, began in promising fashion, as a flyball, a grounder and a strikeout untangled Sturdivant's mess.

At this point, the Mets had played three defensive innings and used four pitchers. A second game remained after this one, so if Stengel needed anything, it was length. And length became Larry's middle name (though, for the record, Lawrence Bearnarth's middle name was Donald). There'd be a hit batsman and a few walks, but Bearnarth gave up no hits from his entrance in the top of the third clear through to one out in tenth. That added up to seven-and-one-third hitless frames from the righty reliever, though it bears noting his streak was saved by Kanehl, who stayed in the game to play center and conjured an outfield catch-and-throw that served as an unknowing precursor to one Endy Chavez would make 42 years later.

Santo led off the seventh with a walk. Banks belted a Bearnarth pitch an alarming distance. What happened next is best described by Bob Murphy:

> *"Here's the pitch on the way…a drive in the air to deep center, Kanehl a long way to go, way back, WAY back, against the wall — OH WHAT A CATCH! WHAT A CATCH, THE PLAY OF THE YEAR! HE MAY GET A DOUBLE PLAY! Ron Hunt has a relay throw to make… here it comes…DOUBLE PLAY!"*

At that moment, Kanehl was the long man of long men on the Mets, but soon enough it was Bearnarth out there extending himself even more. Banks and Dick Bertell singled for the Cubs in the tenth, but nobody scored. Lou Brock singled in the eleventh, but he, too, was stranded. Finally, in the twelfth, in Bearnarth's tenth inning of relief, the Cubs got to him, when Bertell singled home Santo. The Cubs led, 5-4.

But not for long. In the bottom of the twelfth, Joe Christopher singled with one out and Charley Smith reached on shortstop Jimmy Stewart's ground ball error. Bearnarth finally left the game for a pinch-hitter, Amado "Sammy" Samuel. Samuel — facing Lindy McDaniel, who had just replaced Chicago starter Dick Ellsworth (who had gone 11 1/3 innings), singled, sending Christopher home to tie the game at five. One intentional walk later, catcher Jesse Gonder made a winner of Bearnarth by singling to center. Charley Smith scored and the Mets prevailed, 6-5, in twelve.

Larry Bearnarth's ten innings of relief in one game established a Mets record that has never been matched. No Mets reliever, in fact, has come within two innings of Bearnarth's length since June 9, 1964. That span includes the second game of that doubleheader, one which was lost 5-2 in regulation. The starter and loser for the Mets? Galen Cisco, who had set the record Bearnarth had broken when Cisco pitched nine relief innings in…yup, that 23-inning loss to San Francisco on Memorial Day. Galen pitched the 15th through the 23rd immediately after Larry pitched the 8th through the 14th.

The Mets might not have been very good in 1964, but they didn't let opponents know that for sure any sooner than they had to.

26 JUNE 20, 1964
METS 7 PHILLIES 3
SHEA STADIUM

It was time to bash an eight-game losing streak into submission, and the Mets had just the pair of sluggers to tackle the task this Saturday at Shea.

In the third inning of a scoreless duel, left fielder Joe Christopher strode to the plate with one out and put the Mets on the board with a solo home run off Phillie starter Dennis

Bennett. After Charley Smith doubled and Rod Kanehl struck out, catcher Hawk Taylor put the same kind of hurt on Bennett that Christopher had. Another home run, this one making it 3-0, Mets.

Four innings later, the Mets clung to a 4-3 lead. Christopher replicated his earlier feat with a leadoff homer versus reliever Jack Baldschun. And three batters after that, with Dick Smith on second, Taylor did as Christopher had and encored: another two-run homer. The Mets were up, 7-3, snapping that eight-game losing streak and marking the first Mets win in which two Mets homered twice.

Were the paired power-hitting exploits of Joe and Hawk contagious? Let's just say there's no inoculation for an outburst of slugging momentum quite like the next day's starting pitcher. The Mets came back to work Sunday, Father's Day, and — with Christopher and Taylor each in the lineup and rarin' to go — went a combined 0-for-27. Philadelphia's Jim Bunning threw a perfect game.

JULY 31, 1964 (1ST)
METS 3 COLT .45s 0
SHEA STADIUM

In a sense, it had already been a dream month for Ron Hunt. He began it by representing the Mets as the starting second baseman for the National League in the All-Star Game at Shea Stadium. Hunt, the Mets' first All-Star starter, did the host club proud by singling on the first pitch he saw from the Los Angeles Angels' Dean Chance when he led off the bottom of the third for the N.L. Six innings later, he joined Willie Mays, Hank Aaron and the rest of his temporary teammates in congratulating the Phillies' Johnny Callison on his game-ending three-run homer off the Red Sox' Dick Radatz. At 23 years old and carrying a .311 batting average into the Midsummer Classic, there was every chance Hunt would become known as the Senior Circuit's premier second baseman for years to come.

As it happened, he was swiftly becoming known for something else — something productive if painful. As a rookie in 1963, Hunt gained a reputation for taking one for the team. As a matter of fact, he took 13 for the team. Ron's 13 Hit By Pitches were second in the league to Frank Robinson of the Reds. Proving his courage was no fluke, Hunt wasn't shying away from inside pitches in 1964. By the end of July, he'd already been nicked, battered and/or bruised seven times entering a Friday twinighter at Shea.

Did somebody say eight? Hunt did. In a scoreless duel between the Mets' Frank Lary and the Colt .45s' Don Larsen, Ron took matters into his own hands...his own body, at any rate. With the bases loaded on three consecutive singles in the bottom of the fifth, the versatile infielder, playing third in this game, leaned into one and took his eighth HBP of the year. In trotted shortstop Roy McMillan from third to give Lary and the Mets a 1-0 lead. Frank did the rest, spinning a two-hitter and beating Houston, 3-0. Ron had to feel fine that he put the Mets ahead for good, but ironically he had to leave the second game of the twinbill after fouling a pitch off his left big toe.

Hunt would again finish second in the N.L. in HBP, with 11 (behind the Phillies' Tony Taylor). The kid's legacy was being written in black and blue. Before his 1966 trade to the Dodgers, Hunt would be hit by 41 pitches, still a Met career record (though nine short of the 50 body blows Hunt, by then an Expo, absorbed in 1971 for the modern single-season record). Larsen's wayward pitch at the end of Hunt's idyllic July 1964 was the only time, however, that one of those 41 resulted in an RBI.

28

AUGUST 17, 1964
METS 5 PIRATES 0
SHEA STADIUM

Dennis Ribant brought to mind one of the great utterances in baseball history, one certainly in tune with Casey Stengel's "Youth of America" movement. Ribant, 22, made his second big league start at Shea and dazzled the Pittsburgh Pirates. He retired the first eleven batters to face him this Monday night and let only one baserunner get as far as third. Aided by a pair of Charley Smith home runs, the wiry righty won going away, 5-0. Dennis dominated as no Met hurler before him dominated. His was the first complete game shutout to be delivered with double-digit strikeouts (10) in team history — and he didn't walk a single Buc.

His performance came some 53 years after a 25-year-old second baseman playing for the New York National League team of yore exulted to none other than Damon Runyon that "It's great to be young and a New York Giant." The infielder who was so overjoyed to be playing under John McGraw at the Polo Grounds in 1911 — when Ol' Case was still a busher for the Aurora Blues of the Class C Wisconsin-Illinois League — was Larry Doyle, a triples-hitting whiz in his day and still very much alive in 1964. Lee Allen of *The Sporting News* had caught up with Doyle the previous summer in upstate Saranac Lake, a town that liked Larry so much they had recently honored their "most noted citizen" by crowning him King of the Winter Carnival.

Doyle, no fool at the age of 76, told the Chamber of Commerce that if they wanted him to serve as king, they'd have to get him a queen. They took his royal demand seriously and imported that distaff avatar of aristocracy, Miss Rheingold of 1963, Loretta Ann Rissell. Miss Rheingold was pretty famous in those days, just as Rheingold was already known far and wide as the Extra Dry Beer of New York's new National League team. Thus, Allen invoked Doyle's "regal association" with Miss Rheingold and suggested it "would seem to give him kinship with the Mets, providing a strain of old blood for the New Breed." Naturally, Lee was compelled to wonder of Larry, "What did he think of the Mets anyway?"

He asked him directly, and you have to love the literary license the *Sporting News* scribe took. Allen wrote, "You forget what he replied, you remember that he smiled and, surely, like all old Giants, he wished them well. It's great to be old and a Met fan."

As for Ribant, he'd be 24 and compiling his best Mets season in 1966, putting together a crisp 11-9 record with a 3.20 ERA, arguably the best Met starting pitching season to date. Dennis's ultimate Met value, though, came not on the mound, but in the subsequent offseason trade that brought veteran Don Cardwell to New York. Cardwell's impact on the Mets wouldn't be felt until the franchise was a little older and a lot greater.

S top the presses — the Mets were in a pennant race! True, they were only visiting, but the third-year expansion club, buried in last place under another three-digit avalanche of losses, was about to have a say in how 1964's World Series tickets were going to be printed.

29

OCTOBER 2, 1964
METS 1 CARDINALS 0
BUSCH STADIUM I

Would they indicate Games 1, 2, 6 and 7 (if necessary) were to be played in Cincinnati? Philadelphia? St. Louis? Barely two weeks before the Mets' final series of the year, there was no question that the answer was Philly: the Phils led the Reds and Cards by 6 1/2 with twelve to play. Only a series of unimaginable events would prevent the National League pennant from flying over Connie Mack Stadium.

Imagination got quite a workout as the 1964 Phillies became synonymous with the word "collapse". As the Mets headed to St. Loo to finish out their season, everything had changed. The Cardinals were now in first, a half-game up on the Reds, who in turn were two in front of the devastated Phils. The Redbirds hadn't clinched anything, but with the 51-108 Mets as their guests, it would surely be a formality to roll over their inept visitors en route to their first flag since 1946. After all, it wasn't just political jibing that produced the sentiment behind a campaign button spotted in this presidential election year:

"Mets Rooters! Edsel Owners! Back A REAL Loser! Goldwater!"

In accordance with the polling of the day, Barry Goldwater would be snowed under by Lyndon Johnson's electoral landslide come early November, but baseball wasn't necessarily so predictable one month ahead of LBJ going all the way. The National League in 1964 had already inverted every assumption a baseball fan held about pennant races, so why shouldn't the Mets?

Al Jackson certainly wasn't ready to wave a white flag in front of the Cardinals, not even with Bob Gibson as his mound opponent. Gibby entered the action 18-11, Jackson at 10-16. Yet there was no evidence each hurler wasn't trying to pitch his team to the postseason this Friday night in Missouri. Boosted by a third-inning RBI single from Ed Kranepool, Jackson bested Gibson, 1-0, going the distance on a five-hitter. With the Phillies beating the Reds, the National League was as tight as the season was late.

Forty-four years later, Jackson recalled for *Newsday* his role as a roadblock on the Cardinals' path to glory. When his opponents spotted him after the game, he chuckled, "Oh, did they call me a bunch of names."

Presumably the list included "winner" as well as "spoiler." Jackson's teammates gladly lined up for such epithets the following afternoon as they spanked Ray Sadecki and a parade of relievers to prevail again, 15-5. The Phillies and Reds were idle and the Cardinals were in trouble, tied with Cincy and only a game up on Philly. If the Phils could pull themselves out of their tailspin for good — and if the Mets could maintain their newfound flair for October baseball — a three-way tie for the pennant would result, with the Metsies' fingerprints all over an unprecedented round-robin playoff.

The Mets' first flirtation with pennant race drama came to an end on Sunday, as Gibson emerged from the bullpen to extinguish the upstarts from New York, 11-5. Cincinnati lost, allowing the Cardinals to finish first by a single game over its two closest rivals. They went on to win a seven-game World Series against New York's other ballclub, a set that couldn't have been a whole lot more stressful than the trio of contests they barely survived against Casey Stengel's suddenly never-say-die dead-enders.

1965-1-5-1968

REACH
OUT OF
THE
DARKNESS

Allowing baserunners was never a problem for the Mets during their first three seasons. It was hardly the objective of their games, but they permitted them by the multitude, as evidenced by the 120, 111 and 109 games they lost across those initial campaigns.

But that was then. This was 1965...which would, soon enough, prove the Mets were still stuck in "then" mode. But for one half-inning on one Thursday afternoon, they at least figured out what to do about those pesky enemy baserunners.

The newly rechristened Houston Astros orbited Shea in the usual visiting manner. In the top of the second, trailing 1-0, Walt Bond led off by reaching Jack Fisher for a single. Bob Aspromonte followed with a single that chased Bond to third. Two on, nobody out, the kind of situation that had been flummoxing Met pitchers since 1962.

Today, though, it was the other expansion team that got flummoxed. Toy Cannon Jimmy Wynn shot a flyball to rookie right fielder Johnny Lewis. It appeared to the 'Stros good enough for a sacrifice. They'd gladly trade an out for a run. But the Mets weren't in such a swapping mood. Lewis threw home after catching Wynn's ball and nailed Bond at the plate for a double play. All that activity inspired Aspromonte to tag up and take second...but Chris Cannizzaro, who had tagged out Bond, had other ideas. He fired to shortstop Roy McMillan and another out was chalked up.

That was three outs. That was the Mets' third triple play ever. The previous two — including one from the legendary 23-inning game against the Giants in 1964 — were turned in losses. Losses are an occupational hazard of allowing baserunners. Even if you erase three at once, there's a pretty decent chance there are more where those came from in other innings.

Sure enough, the Astros would regroup, particularly Aspromonte, who walked with two outs and nobody on in the ninth, and Wynn, who followed that base on balls with a two-run homer off Fisher to tie this, the third game of the Mets' season, at four. Already having lost their first two, the Mets seemed to be limping to their usual futile overall start.

Things would not necessarily be what they seemed when the tenth inning rolled around. In the top of the frame, 18-year-old righthander Jim Bethke wriggled out of a jam by throwing an unconventional 5-4-6 double play ball (though what's unconventional when you've already seen a 9-2-6 triple play)? And in the bottom of the tenth, Bobby Klaus led off with a game-ending home run. The Mets were 5-4 winners and owned a 1-2 record, their best ever after three games.

Baby steps, perhaps. But every team learns to walk in its own time.

If the rest of America would come to see San Francisco in the 1960s as practically otherworldly (not that the natives would mind — columnist Herb Caen had long before lovingly dubbed his city Baghdad By The Bay), the Mets were suddenly finding it an exotically intoxicating place to win ballgames in all kinds of exotic fashion.

Like plural, even.

It didn't seem the Mets on Saturday at Candlestick could top what they had pulled off on Friday night. On Friday, it was downright lunatic by 1965 Met standards. The visitors from the east trailed 6-1 after two and 8-2 after seven, yet they not only didn't lose, they won; it's the kind of distinction one feels compelled to make when it comes to the Mets of this era. A four-run ninth keyed by pinch-homers from rookie sensation Ron Swoboda and Jesse Gonder propelled the Mets to extra innings. In the eleventh, Joe Christopher walked, stole second, took third on the throw and scored on Charley Smith's fly to center. Dennis Ribant's second inning of solid relief preserved the 9-8 win.

So how about an almost immediate encore? Saturday afternoon's affair was more competitive from the get-go, yet the Mets found themselves trailing through eight once again. But the ninth belonged to New York, thanks to a crowded rally that included a leadoff bunt single from Smith, a pitcher's error on the Giants' Bob Shaw that let Chris Cannizzaro reach, a pinch-running appearance by Al Jackson, a pinch-*hitting* appearance by 44-year-old Warren Spahn — the pitching master just passing through Mets Land — and, penultimately, a two-out intentional walk to Johnny Lewis. The Mets, down 6-4, found their fate in the hands of Danny Napoleon, the 23-year-old rookie who had batted twice thus far in the big leagues and whose career would be over before he turned 25.

Casey Stengel's hunch that youth should be served and Napoleon should pinch-hit for Roy McMillan (who'd been playing since 1951 but was batting only .079) paid off. Danny blasted a fly to right that eluded the grasp of Jesus Alou. It went for a three-run triple that put the Mets up, 7-6, and gave Napoleon 43% of his lifetime seven RBIs. The bottom of the inning made for a nervous ninth, as Stengel had to play several men out of position and call on Ribant to pitch in relief once again — Willie Mays got as far as third base — but it all worked out for a giddy 7-6 final.

How giddy? Giddy enough so that Casey, who didn't really go back so far as to have personally known Napoleon's ostensible namesake, roared, "Vive La France!" in the victorious clubhouse. Never mind that Danny Napoleon went to high school in New Jersey; back-to-back wins generated after trailing in the eighth inning each time will cause a feller to express joie de vivre in historic terms. And make no mistake, there was history made at Candlestick that weekend, at least when you consider how long the circumstances surrounding those wins went into exile. Consecutive comebacks from eighth-inning deficits wouldn't be manufactured again by the Mets for another 46 years, when the 2011 club overcame similarly late Padre leads across two August nights at Citi Field.

Though without "Vive La France!" being bellowed, the Napoleonic comeback code tends to get a little lost in translation.

There was rarely a penalty for any pitcher deciding to pitch the game of his life versus the New York Mets in their first four years. Ask Jim Bunning, whose 1964 perfect game at Shea Stadium raised his profile so high that it probably edged him into the Hall of Fame and maybe Congress. Ask Sandy Koufax, who would pitch plenty of "games of his life" before he was done, but chose the 1962 Mets for his first no-hitter. Ask most every ace moundsman nine National League staffs sent to face the basement babies throughout '62, '63, '64 and well into '65.

But don't ask Jim Maloney. He didn't get to take full advantage of excelling against the Mets, not on this Monday night at Crosley Field. But, oh, did he excel, and oh, was he taking advantage of the generally easily duped Mets.

From striking out Billy Cowan to lead off the game to striking out the side in the third and striking them out again in the eighth, Maloney was untouchable. His only imperfection was walking Ed Kranepool to open the second...and choosing the wrong night to go so long without being touched.

His opposite number on the mound was Frank Lary, known in his American League days as the Yankee Killer, but he was doing an admirable job of snuffing out Reds. He wasn't as close to flawless as Maloney, but for eight innings, he did what he had to do, holding Cincinnati to five hits, three walks, a hit batsman and — this is key — no runs. In the top of the ninth, Casey Stengel pinch-hit for Lary with Joe Christopher, but Maloney struck him out. He did the same to Cowan for the third time in the evening.

By the middle of the ninth, Jim Maloney had faced 28 Mets batters. One of them walked. Twenty-seven of them made outs. Fifteen of them struck out. But Maloney wasn't winning. He was only tying because of Lary, also known as the Mule. Frank was at his most mulish in the eighth when after hitting Tommy Harper, Harper stole second and raced to third on Chris Cannizzaro's bad throw. With the go-ahead run ninety feet away, Lary grounded Pete Rose back to the mound to erase the Red menace.

Met defense had been surprisingly obstinate, too...after a fashion. In the fourth, Vada Pinson made it to second on a stolen base attempt in which Cannizzaro's pitchout worked beautifully until shortstop Roy McMillan dropped the throw. Gordy Coleman (who would later make a dazzling stop on the Mets' only bid for a hit in regulation) continued his at-bat and struck out, but strike three got by Chris, who chased the passed ball. While he did so, Pinson kept running from second. Cannizzaro found the ball and fired it to Lary, who tagged him at home.

In the bottom of the ninth, it fell to Mets reliever Larry Bearnarth to display a little stubbornness, and he proved plenty recalcitrant. Pinson flied to Johnny Lewis in right before Frank Robinson drew a walk. But Bearnarth bore down, getting Coleman to foul to Gonder (who had replaced Cannizzaro behind the plate) and Deron Johnson to ground to McMillan, forcing Pinson at second.

For Maloney to cash in on his incredible night's work, he'd have to keep going. So he did. Chuck Hiller lined out to start the tenth. Charley Smith struck out swinging. Kranepool stuck out looking. Maloney had now pitched ten hitless innings and collected seventeen strikeouts. "A catcher's dream," Cincy backstop Johnny Edwards would call him.

Yet he still wasn't winning.

An Edwards single to lead off the bottom of the tenth and a sacrifice of pinch-runner Chico Ruiz by Leo Cardenas got a Red into scoring position for the fourth time all night, but Ruiz never got past third. It was 0-0 heading to the eleventh.

Lewis led off for the Mets. On a 2-1 pitch, he homered to center. There — just like that, Maloney was not only not winning, he was losing, 1-0. He'd recover to strike out Ron Swoboda for his 18th K of the game and two batters later, after allowing a single to McMillan, get a double play ball out of Gonder. But the spell was broken. Bearnarth made sure it stayed that way by pitching a scoreless eleventh, and the Mets came away with a 1-0 win.

Despite being no-hit for ten innings. Despite being struck out eighteen times. Despite being the 1965 Mets.

"I can't help but feel good," Lewis, who had struck out thrice, said afterwards. "But it was a heartbreaker for Maloney to lose. He threw good, real good. In fact, I never saw a pitcher throw as hard to me as Maloney did."

What was hard on Maloney was losing the game of his or most pitchers' lives. "I'd just as soon win ballgames as pitch a no-hitter," the flamethrowing righty insisted before taking his postgame shower, though he acknowledged he knew the no-no was in progress and that he really wanted it. He may not have felt terribly enriched by the experience of losing a game he judged "by far the best I've ever pitched," but Reds owner Bill DeWitt immediately announced a $1,000 raise for Maloney, big money in those days for the son of a California car dealer.

Not bad for losing to the last-place Mets.

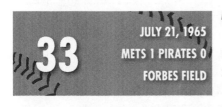

JULY 21, 1965

METS 1 PIRATES 0

FORBES FIELD

The long and intermittent tease begins. Al Jackson, author of the first one-hitter in Mets history, seems destined to take the franchise's next step when he sets down the Pirates for seven innings on nothing more than an error and a walk. He's nursing a 1-0 lead, but more potentially monumentally, he's six outs from fashioning the first no-hitter in Mets history. If he gets six outs this Wednesday night in Pittsburgh, he truly alters how every Mets fan views this very situation for the rest of the first half-century of Mets baseball. There is no sense of being cursed or haunted or luckless. There is a no-hitter on the books. The Mets, by that theoretical logic, are just another team when it comes to this brand of pitching gem.

But the Mets are not just another team by most reckonings, especially this one. Jackson retires Bill Mazeroski to begin the eighth and reduces the countdown to five outs. The countdown, however, expires when Willie Stargell singles to left. The closest the Mets come to a no-hitter to date is 7 1/3 innings without a hit allowed. Jackson has to "settle" for a two-hit victory in which he outduels Don Cardwell, 1-0. That's nothing to sneeze at in any season, especially one in which actual destiny involves the Mets, last place and 112 losses (twenty of them ultimately on Jackson's ledger).

Great game...just not great enough. Rinse and repeat that phrase periodically for decades to come.

Something that occurred 1,904 previous times occurs for the final time, though it can't be confirmed for a little while longer that it will never happen again.

JULY 23, 1965
METS 3 PHILLIES 2 (10)
SHEA STADIUM

On a Friday night, the Mets are where they've been since they were born, in last place. Progress is slow for New York's expansion beloveds, but goodness knows they're trying. They get to the tenth inning at Shea, tied at two with the Phillies. With one out, the Mets' first great hope, Ed Kranepool, singles. Chuck Hiller follows with a single of his own. Then it's up to Johnny Stephenson, he who struck out to end Jim Bunning's perfect game against these same Phillies a year earlier. Facing Jack Baldschun, Stephenson singles to right. Kranepool barrels home with the winning run. Mets win, 3-2. And congratulating his players is the man who's been there for every all-too-rare Mets win, manager Casey Stengel. That night, Stengel will go home after leading his club to its 175th win ever and look forward to managing another game the next day.

He'll never be able to anticipate that again, for the next game is played on the heels of Old Timers Day. After the festivities (and the Mets' 404th-ever loss — to Bunning, no less), Stengel, the embodiment of old-time baseball, goes out on the town with his comrades from days gone by for the Old Timers' party at Toots Shor's. Casey's no wallflower when it comes to having a few. He's been in baseball for more than fifty years. He knows his way around. But on this Saturday night/Sunday morning, he can't do it anymore. He loses his footing on a slippery men's room floor and breaks his hip. Stengel winds up in the hospital in no condition to manage the Sunday doubleheader at Shea nor partake of the 75th birthday cake he was to be presented. Wes Westrum moves in on an interim basis.

Soon enough, it will become apparent that Casey Stengel, after 3,766 games played to their conclusion and nearly as many legends, is finished as a major league manager. Thus, that Friday night walkoff win — with two Original Mets (Jim Hickman and Chris Cannizzaro) and two who'd someday be known as Miracle Mets (Kranepool and Ron Swoboda) in the lineup — will go down as his 1,905th and last victory...not counting those he accumulated in the postseason, let alone his most enduring triumph: inventing, nurturing and making irresistible the team he tabbed the *Amazin', Amazin', Amazin', Amazin'* New York Mets.

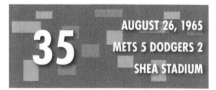

AUGUST 26, 1965
METS 5 DODGERS 2
SHEA STADIUM

David had Goliath. The Mets had Sandy Koufax. Just about everybody did, but the Mets more than most.

The first time the Mets faced Koufax, they pounded him for 13 hits...and lost. Sandy Koufax scattered those 13 hits for a complete game 13-6 victory at the Polo Grounds. Is it only that the 1962 Mets could pile up those kinds of offensive numbers against the premier pitcher of his generation and still be blown out, or is it that only Sandy Koufax in his prime could sustain a 13-hit attack and brush it off like lint?

A compelling philosophical question, but hardly an issue worth contemplating the second time the Mets faced Koufax. On that occasion, exactly a month later at Dodger Stadium, the Mets did nothing with Koufax. Nothing at all. Well, five walks, but no hits. That's what you call a no-hitter, the first dropped upon the young Mets' heads.

And it took them only 73 games.

That was life with Koufax whenever he and the Mets crossed paths. Three encounters in 1962 left the Mets 0-3 versus Sandy. They took him on four times in 1963 and provided him with a 4-0 component of what would become a Cy Young/MVP campaign. Koufax gave up two runs to the Mets in 31 innings that year, but only one of them was earned.

In 1964, Koufax started against the Mets three times, and the Dodgers won all three games. The Amazins did lead him in the last one, 3-2 in the eighth, and Walt Alston was forced to pinch-hit for him, but Wally Moon smacked a double off Tracy Stallard to tie the game and get Sandy off the hook. Tommy Davis put the Dodgers ahead to stay thereafter. But Koufax, who was 9-0 in nine previous starts versus the Mets, was finally saddled with a no-decision.

All hail moral victory.

1965: More of the same. He won, 2-1, in April; 5-0 and 2-1 in June; and 4-3 on August 10 at Dodger Stadium, giving Sandy his 20th win of the year and a 13-0 lifetime mark at the expense of the Mets.

Would it ever end? Would the Mets ever stop being Sandy Koufax's patsy? He didn't lose to many teams, and the Mets didn't beat many pitchers, so when you combined these two entities, it was hard to imagine the prevailing winds were likely to soon shift.

Enter, from stage left, a fresh-faced southpaw who would alter that little slice of Met futility.

Frank Edwin McGraw was an excitable 20-year-old rookie who spent four months not particularly distinguishing himself as a lefty reliever for Casey Stengel or Wes Westrum in 1965. Finally, as another Met season rushed rapidly down the tubes, Westrum gave the young man known as "Tug" his second major league start (three weeks after his first one lasted all of seven batters). Tug threw a nine-inning gem on August 22, beating the Cardinals in the second game of a doubleheader, 2-1. With nothing to lose, Westrum gave the kid another start four days later, a Thursday night at Shea, against the Dodgers.

Against Koufax.

1965: *Still* more of the same, at least in the first, before Koufax had even touched the ball. McGraw surrendered a leadoff single to Maury Wills (who'd go 4-for-4). Wes Parker bunted Wills to second, and Maury scored when Lou Johnson doubled. It put the Mets in a 1-0 hole as they prepared to face a pitcher who entered the evening's action with a 21-5 record and a 2.18 ERA, never mind his total mastery of the Mets since 1962.

But you gotta play each of these games to find out what happens next. The Mets did, and on the strength of a leadoff walk by Ron Hunt, a Roy McMillan double and a Jim Hickman single, the Mets fused a pair of runs to give McGraw a 2-1 lead over Koufax after an inning.

Tug and Sandy each settled down from there. For Sandy, it was business as usual: 16 Mets batters faced from the second to the sixth, only one single (to McMillan in the third) allowed. For Tug, there was no usual business. It was his first year in the majors, his third start overall, and he was still settling into the role of big league baseball player. Nevertheless, he was as composed as his more celebrated (*much* more celebrated) rival, giving up only four hits from the second through the seventh, never more than one per inning. It remained 2-1, Mets, as they batted in the home seventh.

With one out, Ed Kranepool doubled off Koufax. After intentionally walking Chris Cannizzaro, Sandy pitched to pinch-hitter Bobby Klaus, who grounded to short, forcing Cannizzaro at second. That put runners on first and third with two outs and Tug coming up. It was a recipe for extrication: the greatest pitcher on earth against a pitcher batting .111. And, sure enough, McGraw grounded to Don LeJohn at third.

It was all a perfect setup for a Dodger escape, except LeJohn made a bad throw. Tug was safe at first as Kranepool scored to increase the Mets' lead to 3-1. It was a much better margin than 2-1 for McGraw to nurse in the eighth, for after he grounded out Jeff Torborg to start the inning, Koufax's spot in the order was due up.

But not Koufax. Alston sent in a pinch-hitter, meaning Sandy was out of the game, with no chance to beat the Mets. Dick Tracewski walked in his place. Tug surrendered a single to Wills, which sent Tracewski to third; Wills, however, was thrown out by center fielder Hickman as he failed to stretch his hit into a double. That proved huge, as the next batter, Parker, tripled home Tracewski to cut the Mets' lead to 3-2. Westrum finally removed McGraw in favor of Jack Fisher, the Mets' ace starter. Jack walked Jim Gilliam but grounded out Johnson to end the top of the eighth with the Mets still up by one run.

The new Dodger pitcher, Johnny Podres (like Koufax, a holdover from the team's Brooklyn days), was struck for back-to-back homers by Joe Christopher and Ron Swoboda in the bottom of the eighth. And Fisher held that 5-2 lead in the ninth.

The Mets won. Tug McGraw was the victor. And for the first time in the history of the world, Sandy Koufax was the losing pitcher in a game he pitched against the New York Mets.

The New York Mets beat Sandy Koufax.

McGraw remembered it fondly nearly a decade later in his autobiography, *Screwball*, when he referred to the sensation as "unreal" and the event a perfectly valid reason for "jumping up and down". Young Tug (older Tug, too) could have been the template for Warren Zevon's "Excitable Boy," but given the significance of what he had just accomplished, McGraw was gratified that "nobody went around the locker room saying McGraw's some strange cat."

Technically, though, he was. Tug McGraw was the oddest duck in Mets history because he was the Met who bested Sandy Koufax. Nobody else would be able to say that until just over a year later, on McGraw's 22nd birthday, as it happened. Tug started against Koufax again on August 30, 1966. During that season, Sandy had started another four games against the Mets and won them all. In this rematch, though, each starter was bombed and out of the game by the third. By then, the Mets led the Dodgers, 6-2, and went on to a 10-4 victory. Bob Friend earned the win in relief, while Koufax took the loss, diminishing his lifetime ledger against the Mets to a paltry 17-2.

That was the last the Mets would see of Sandy Koufax from a major league mound. His left arm was in too much pain to carry on, and 1966 wound up being his final year in baseball. He went out on a high, posting a 27-9 won-lost mark, a 1.73 ERA and 317 strikeouts in 323 innings.

But also on a one-game losing streak versus his latent nemeses, the New York Mets.

The exclusive clubs of Mets who have hit for the cycle and Mets who have hit three home runs in one game could claim an overlapping membership of two after fifty years. Jose Reyes cycled in June 2006 and homered thrice one night in August of the same year. Somehow in a  divisional championship season, the Mets lost both of those games. Thus, it falls to Jim Hickman to claim the franchise's most successful degree of isolated offensive Met splendor.

Hickman took care of the cycle on August 7, 1963, a 7-3 win over the Cardinals at the Polo Grounds. In fact, he rolled a natural, as it were, singling, doubling, tripling and homering in successive at-bats. Amazingly, generating the Mets' first-ever cycle wasn't even the standout highlight of Hickman's week. That came two days later against the Cubs, when he took the game's final swing, belting the grand slam that ended Roger Craig's eighteen-game losing streak.

Jim's sense of occasion reasserted itself on a Friday night in St. Louis two years later — also his sense of efficiency. There was a solo homer in his first plate appearance; then another solo shot in his second; then a two-run job in his third. By the sixth inning, Hickman had been to bat three times and had produced three home runs (all against Cardinal starter Ray Sadecki), the first Met to do so. That meant he was sure to get a chance to swing again and maybe join the likes of Lou Gehrig, Gil Hodges and Willie Mays in hitting four home runs in one game.

Didn't happen. Hickman's final at-bat amounted to a single. Still, 4-for-4 in a 6-3 win, with three homers and four runs batted in, was a pretty good night's work. Though Jim never really broke out more than for a spectacular game here or there as a Met, the record shows he was the team's stalwart run-producer in its first half-decade. From 1962 until his trade to Los Angeles — with Ron Hunt for Tommy Davis — in 1966, no Met hit more homers (60) or drove in more runs (210).

He came out of Fresno High School in Central California. He was a promising righthander, capable of mowing down batter after batter. He was young. He represented a genuine sign of progress for a team that was still groping for some sign of maturity after spending its developmental years going nowhere in the standings.

Sound familiar? The legend of Tom Seaver should...but this isn't the legend of Tom Seaver. This is about Dick Selma, a Seaver contemporary (one year older) from the same neck of the woods, answering to the same general description and — very early on — putting up the kind of eye-popping performance that would imbue any fan base with faith that a better future was rapidly approaching.

It took only two starts for Selma to start boggling the mind. The 21-year-old's first appearance at Shea left the Sunday crowd of 13,500 salivating for more. Several of Milwaukee's best succumbed to his stuff right away, as Selma struck out Rico Carty, Eddie Mathews and Joe Torre in his first inning.

The tone was set. Selma was dominant frame after frame. His opposite number, Bob Sadowski, wasn't so bad himself, which is why the game stayed scoreless for a very long time, but this afternoon was all about Selma and how he tamed the Braves. The man worked ten innings, scattered four hits, walked one batter and struck out a Mets record thirteen. No way Wes Westrum was taking his starter out and no way the kid couldn't be rewarded. So it came to pass that in the bottom of the tenth, Charley Smith drove home Joe Christopher with the only run of the day. Dick Selma was a 1-0 winner.

References to overpowering righthanded starters from Fresno would come to indicate something and somebody else altogether before too long. But for now, in September of '65, Dick Selma's was the arm on which Mets fans could eagerly hang their hopes.

 **1966**

Better late than never? Try better earlier than ever. Better, in fact, than the Mets had ever been describes the team three games into its fifth season.

The Mets waited only until their second game to visit the win column in 1966, besting

the newly situated Atlanta Braves at Shea, 3-1, on Jack Hamilton's five-hitter. That put the Mets in a position to claim something that had never before been in their grasp beyond Opening Day: a winning record. Sure, it would be only 2-1, but as was so often the modest rallying cry surrounding the incremental advances the Mets had earned since 1962, ya gotta start somewhere.

On a Sunday at Shea, the Mets started quickly, staked to a 1-0 lead in the first when 1964 N.L. MVP Ken Boyer (acquired in the offseason for Al Jackson and Charley Smith) doubled home Johnny Lewis. Ed Kranepool's third-inning single upped the Mets' margin to 2-0, but starter Dick Selma couldn't stand prosperity and by the eighth, the Mets were down, 4-2.

That's when Boyer showed why he was not long before considered more valuable than any player in the National League, driving home Ron Hunt and Lewis with his third double on the day. The moment of truth arrived an inning later when, with the bases loaded, Ron Swoboda graciously accepted ball four from Billy O'Dell. Billy Murphy, who had started the bottom-of-the-ninth rally with a walk of his own, trotted home from third with the winning run. The Mets' 5-4 victory was their second of the season, against one loss...and for the first time, the Mets peeked their heads above .500.

Like the groundhog who draws everybody's attention briefly every February 2, the moment was akin to Punxsutawney Phil spotting his shadow. The Mets burrowed back below .500 by their fifth game of 1966, and a few more years of winter ensued where their winning percentage was concerned. But on this chilly April day in Queens, 26,965 Mets fans could feel confident forecasting that somewhere along the distant horizon, here came the sun.

MAY 6, 1966
METS 2 CUBS 1
SHEA STADIUM

After two auditions, one of the Mets' brighter prospects was getting his first extended trial by National League pitching. And seven months after posting the most unfairly unrewarded mound performance in Met history, one of their young arms received his due.

Cleon Jones appeared in his first starting lineup on September 14, 1963, just in time to say he was part of the good old days. But the last Met to make his major league debut at the Polo Grounds was all about the future, and on this Friday night at Shea, the 23-year-old centerfielder from Mobile, Ala., showed he was going places by belting a game-ending home run in the bottom of the ninth off Cub rookie lefty Ken Holtzman. In winning the contest for the Mets, 2-1, Jones ensured a W on the ledger of Rob Gardner.

Gardner held the Cubs to four hits while striking out eight to earn his first big league win after four unsuccessful attempts in 1965 and two more in '66. Yet it had to seem like Gardner had been out there pitching with a paucity of run support for a far longer time than that because his signature game as a Met was about as epic as epic could get.

To fully appreciate the beauty of Gardner getting the decision against Chicago — and his driving in a run himself in the fifth — consider what he experienced as a 20-year-old callup on October 2, 1965. Rob gave the Mets fifteen scoreless innings. And the Mets gave Rob *bupkes*. They failed to tally a single run on his behalf as he threw what added up to one-and-two-third complete games. In the second game of a Saturday doubleheader at Shea on the preceding season's final weekend, Gardner allowed the Phillies five hits and two walks...and no runs. His opponent, Chris Short, was just as effective and a bit more spectacular: nine hits and two walks (with eighteen strikeouts to Rob's seven) in fifteen innings. Short also surrendered no runs. The relievers who followed them for another three frames also put up zeroes.

At last, New York's Saturday night curfew law kicked in and the nightcap — a doubleheader unto itself — was declared an eighteen-inning 0-0 tie (one of eight in

Mets history). For the Mets' and Phillies' trouble, they had to make it up the next afternoon as part of yet another doubleheader (dropped by New York), and Gardner had to head home for the winter with nothing to show for his extraordinary effort. Jones's home run to make him a winner the following May provided him something tangible for his record at last.

I n the heart of the Swingin' Sixties, the Mets got into the spirit of the times in a big way this Saturday at Shea. Call the fashionable young men who beat the Giants the Swingin' Singles...or at least recognize how successfully they swung for singles.

MAY 14, 1966
METS 11 GIANTS 4
SHEA STADIUM

There was no Met power, but the Metropolitan Area had proved it could thrive in a blackout the previous November, so why not the Metropolitans a half-year later? The Mets' acoustic set consisted of seventeen singles unleashed on Bobby Bolin and three San Francisco relievers. Cleon Jones, Ron Hunt and Johnny Stephenson produced three apiece. Nine different players, including starting pitcher Jack Fisher, recorded at least one single. But nobody doubled, tripled or homered.

Singles, however, were all the Mets needed to construct their 11-4 romp. Two San Francisco errors, four walks and a wild pitch by Giant hurlers — plus a couple of Eddie Bressoud sacrifice bunts — didn't hurt, either. Seventeen hits of exclusively the single-base variety added up to a team record for, shall we say, the most successful power outage in Met history. It's a singular mark that's been equaled only once, in a 1982 6-3 Mets win over the Dodgers.

JUNE 10, 1966
METS 5 REDS 0
SHEA STADIUM

Y ou want out-of-the-box success? Then you want Dick Rusteck. No Mets starting pitcher was ever better sooner than the 24-year-old lefty from Chicago. And, judging by the relatively few households in which his name became enduringly recognizable, no Mets starting pitcher of surpassing promise ever disappeared quite so quickly.

But nobody envisioned that while Rusteck was doing his thing...his one and only thing, just about.

The Notre Dame graduate was having a fine year in Triple-A Jacksonville (pitching alongside first-year pro Tom Seaver) but "didn't expect to get called up," he told reporters. "My record was 4-0, then 5-0, then 6-0 and I wasn't called. Then I lost one and I got hit by a batted ball [in BP, by Suns teammate Bud Harrelson] — and I couldn't throw. I was sure they wouldn't call me up."

Perhaps it was the Metsian way of doing things to wait until a prospect was incapacitated to give him his big break, but Rusteck was ready for the big time, as personified by the Cincinnati Reds of Tommy Harper, Pete Rose, Vada Pinson, Deron Johnson, Tony Perez and Leo Cardenas. The raw rookie wasn't nervous, concentrating on trying to "force myself to pitch the way I did at Jacksonville."

A Friday night at Shea, in front of nearly 34,000, and Rusteck treated the whole scene as if it were just another outing in the International League. He no-hit the Reds for four innings and maintained his poise after Perez broke up his bid for immortality with a leadoff single in the fifth. That would be one of only four hits the Reds would collect on the night, all of them singles. Backed by two Eddie Bressoud homers, Rusteck cruised to a complete game 5-0 shutout in his major league debut, the only Met starter to achieve that kind of instant success (Grover Powell threw a shutout for the Mets in his first big league start in 1963, but he had pitched several times in relief before that). Dick struck out four and walked only one in defeating Cincinnati ace Jim Maloney.

The reviews were raves. Ralph Kiner, watching from the Mets' broadcast booth, said, "His fastball moves. A couple of times the ball jumped more than half a foot as it came up to the plate." Home plate ump Ed Sudol testified that Rusteck's fastball "has a tendency to rise at the last instant. It had the batters off balance and was probably the main reason they popped up so much."

Because baseball is baseball, and baseball is rarely predictable and only occasionally fair, Dick Rusteck's debut shutout was his last win in the majors and 1966 was his only season in the bigs. "Four days later," he would recall for author William Ryczek, "I tried to pick up a ball and I could hardly lift my arm. I had a real sharp pain in my shoulder. They pleaded with me to start, because after pitching a shutout, how could you possibly not come out for your next turn?"

Rusteck was bombed by St. Louis in one-plus innings of ill-advised work in that second try. One more start, in early July versus the Pirates, didn't go much better. There'd be a trip to the disabled list, a few games out of the bullpen and a return to Jacksonville in 1967...and 1968. Rusteck would bounce around the minors clear to 1977 when he wound down his career on the unaffiliated Salem Senators of the Northwest League. His left shoulder healed, but his left elbow went bad, as did his luck. One day in Rochester, for example, a piece of glass fell from a building and cut his non-pitching shoulder badly enough to require seventeen stitches.

But for one night, at 24, Dick Rusteck had the art of pitching successfully in the major leagues all sewn up.

You didn't get to be a perennial cellar dweller because you enjoyed a surplus of outstanding players at every position. The early Mets did not have that so-called pleasant problem. A half-decade into their existence, they were still groping for a full-time center

fielder who would be comfortable on both sides of the ball. They had yet to settle on a third baseman for more than one season at a time. And catching had yet to be mistaken for a strong suit.

Despite using their first expansion pick on a catcher (Hobie Landrith, because, as Ol' Case explained, you need a catcher lest you wind up with a plethora of passed balls), it would be difficult to say manning the position had been a Met priority. Everybody from the notoriously taciturn Choo Choo Coleman to the legendarily quotable (and temporarily unretired) Yogi Berra tried on the chest protector for Casey Stengel and Wes Westrum — the latter himself a catcher in his playing days — but nobody took control behind the plate until a relatively minor deal began to pay major dividends.

In the fall of 1965, the Mets sent Tom Parsons, a righthanded pitcher who had just gone 1-10, to Houston for a 23-year-old backstop who had hit .181 in 100 games in 1964 and spent all of the subsequent season in the minors. The Mets wanted him anyway. If Jerry Grote could learn to hit, fine. But if he could catch, that would be enough to fill one gaping Met hole.

Grote put his many tools on display this Wednesday night in St. Louis's new round ballpark, as good a place as any to unleash a cannon arm. The Cardinals were breaking in the second Busch Stadium, one big enough to suit the emerging Runnin' Redbird style of play. Their leadoff hitter, swift Lou Brock, was about to kick his career into high gear — in 1966, he would lead the National League in stolen bases for the first of eight times. But against Jerry Grote, Brock would learn discretion was sometimes the better part of thievery. In the sixth inning of a 0-0 duel between Jack Fisher and ex-Met Al Jackson, Brock singled with two out. He soon took off for second, the kind of play on which he'd be successful 74 times in '66.

He wasn't so lucky this time. Grote nailed him. As Brock's fame would grow, he'd be asked regularly which catcher was toughest for him to steal against. His answer? Jerry Grote of the Mets.

Grote's defensive reputation went beyond a dynamite arm. Nobody was considered a better bet to track down a foul pop, and against the Cards, Jerry hauled in three of them. And though he was known as a temperamental Texan, Grote knew how to nurse a pitcher through a tough game. Westrum entrusted a pair of Jacks — Fisher and Hamilton — to his care and neither pitcher gave up anything to the Cards. Appropriately enough in what hindsight would reveal as a breakout game, it was Jerry Grote who doubled with one out in the top of the tenth and it was Jerry Grote who came around to score the go-ahead run in what became a 2-0 Mets victory.

After making due with fourteen underwhelming catching candidates in their first four years, the Mets had finally caught on to a real, live catcher.

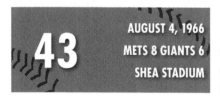

43

AUGUST 4, 1966

METS 8 GIANTS 6

SHEA STADIUM

If you can't beat your nemesis, at least deprive him of another win at your expense...and then beat his successor. No better advice was dispensed in 1966 and there was no better font of wisdom on the subject than the bat of Ron Swoboda.

The larger point, one supposes, is that the Mets couldn't beat their San Francisco nemesis, Juan Marichal. And "couldn't" is not an exaggeration when you consider from the time they were born to this, the first year they began to do anything but curl up in the fetal position of tenth place in the National League, they were incapable of doing a thing with the man his legion of admirers called the Dominican Dandy.

And for the Dandy, pitching against the Mets was like taking candy from a toddler of a franchise.

Marichal versus the Mets, from June 3, 1962, through August 2, 1966: 16-0 in 20 appearances. All of the righty's decisions against the runt of the expansion litter were, by definition, dandy, at least for him. Really they were closer to TKOs than decisions. During a period when the Mets were a punching bag for many talented arms throughout the N.L., they were barely sparring partners for the Giant ace. Or if we can avail ourselves of one more boxing metaphor, no responsible governing body would have sanctioned a fight between Juan Marichal and the New York Mets.

But baseball bouts don't necessarily boil down to what one heavyweight can do. Sometimes he's got to have help from his corner. This rule held true even in the era of the complete game's primacy. Marichal was a great practitioner of going the distance, completing 25 of his 36 starts in 1966, second best in the league. There was little reason for Giants manager Herman Franks to think he'd need more than one pitcher this Thursday afternoon at Shea. Marichal carried a perfect game to two outs in the sixth when Dennis Ribant, of all people, broke it up with a single. The Mets' starter, however, barely had a chance to acclimate himself to first base, as Chuck Hiller flied to left to end the Mets' mini-threat.

By then, San Francisco led, 3-0. And by the seventh-inning stretch, their lead was 5-0, as Ribant was knocked out after giving up a double, a single and a walk, and reliever Darrell Sutherland surrendered an RBI base hit to Willie Mays. Cleon Jones's run-scoring single in the bottom of the seventh was quickly countered when Tom Haller went deep off the next Met pitcher, Dallas Green, to lead off the eighth (Willie McCovey and Jim Ray Hart had earlier led off innings with homers).

A 6-1 deficit with six outs to go and Juan Marichal on the mound. There couldn't have been much doubt this game was over for the Mets. Johnny Stephenson's two-run pinch-homer and Larry Elliot's RBI single made it close in the eighth, but once Marichal retired Jones with two on and two out, it could be reasonably assumed the Mets had had their fun for the day and Juan would be up to 17-0 in a matter of minutes.

After Jack Hamilton pitched a scoreless top of the ninth, Marichal — who posted a rare relief win in the series opener two days earlier — returned to finish what he started. Ken Boyer, however, finished him with a leadoff home run. Now it was 6-5 and Franks had no choice but to remove the Dandy and ask his bullpen to record those last three outs. His first call was to righty Lindy McDaniel, who gave up a single to Eddie Bressoud before grounding pinch-hitter Ron Hunt to short, forcing Bressoud at second. Stephenson, who had remained in the game to catch, singled, putting two on with one out.

Franks could brook no more of McDaniel and replaced him with lefty Bill Henry. Wes Westrum responded by removing Hiller and sending up 22-year-old righty slugger Ron Swoboda to pinch-hit. Swoboda had blasted 19 home runs as a rookie in 1965 but had slowed down as the season ended and had failed to resume his powerful pace once 1966 began. His three homers in the first half of his sophomore season were hardly emblematic of a player nicknamed Rocky, but things had been turning for Swoboda of late. Most notably, he broke a 2-2 tie in the tenth inning at Candlestick Park on July 20, a game the Mets went on to win, 3-2, after spending most of it losing to Marichal.

Rocky didn't hit that home run off the Dominican Dandy, however. He hit it off Bill Henry.

Now they met again, fifteen days later. Not only was the game on the line, but so was the Giants' position near the top of the National League. If they could beat the Mets, they'd be tied for first with the Pirates and open up a four-game lead on their archrivals, the Dodgers. But first they'd have to beat the Mets, something that might have seemed a foregone conclusion while Juan Marichal was pitching. Marichal was gone now, and the fate of the game was in Bill Henry's hands.

That is before it jumped off Ron Swoboda's bat.

Lindsey Nelson set the stage:

> "So, here we are in the bottom half of the ninth inning, the Mets trailing by one run, have runners at first and second, one man out. Ron Swoboda's batting for Chuck Hiller. Bill Henry has relieved Lindy McDaniel on the mound.
> "Juan Marichal is still the pitcher of record on the winning side for the Giants — to this point. Ron Hunt the runner at second, Johnny Stephenson the runner at first. One man out."

Henry threw the first pitch high. Swoboda swung anyway for strike one. Rocky took the second delivery for a ball.

The third, by the reckoning of the Times's Robert Lipsyte, "was thrown with the stuff that dreams are made on." Swoboda hit it high to left, where it soared to the left of the 371 marker...and over it.

Lindsey at the Met mic:

> "Deep to left, it's going, going, gone for a home run, the Mets win the ballgame! The Mets win the ballgame as Ron Swoboda hits a three-run homer! Ron Hunt is coming on to score! Johnny Stephenson is coming on to score! Ron Swoboda is coming on!
> "For him, his eighth home run, and the Mets win the ballgame!"

Ron Swoboda came on, all right, and didn't the visitors from the West know it? Lindy McDaniel took the loss. Bill Henry was saddled with the infamy. Juan Marichal's dual excellent records — 17-4 on the season, 16-0 against the Mets — remained unsullied, but although their ace was off the hook, the Giants were clearly knocked for a loop. They did not reach first place that Thursday, and when the year was over, they finished second, 1 1/2 games behind L.A. Give them back those two swings Swoboda took against Henry, and the 1966 pennant quite possibly flies in San Francisco.

Not Rocky's problem. He had no problems after clinching the 8-6 win for the Mets.

The 22-year-old Maryland strongboy — "stronger than dirt" according to one Shea banner — decided this game was "just like a fairy tale. It was a storybook game. Holy cow!"

As far as taking care of the Dominican Dandy was concerned, the Mets finally hung a loss on Marichal on July 4, 1967, beating him and San Francisco, 8-7, raising their record to date versus the eventual Hall of Famer to a spiffy 1-19.

SEPTEMBER 16, 1966
METS 5 GIANTS 4
CANDLESTICK PARK

Down in the second division, the stakes aren't high to the naked eye, but the games the schedule dictates must be played can provide a proving ground to a young player who's getting a good look from his organization. Those circumstances were perfect for a prospect like skinny Bud Harrelson to slip into the Mets' long-term plans.

Shortstop hadn't necessarily been one of those positions that had previously baffled the Mets, at least not to the extent third base and its parade of practitioners (28) had since 1962. Veteran Roy McMillan lent the middle of the infield an air of stability in 1964 and '65, but he was on his last legs by the time he was done at Shea. Eddie Bressoud imbued short with a burst of power in 1966, whacking ten homers (no shortstop would hit more for the Mets until Jose Reyes popped nineteen some four decades later), but the old New York Giant wasn't an answer beyond the present.

Harrelson was going to be given every chance to make himself the logical response to *"who's going to be our shortstop?"* as 1966 closed out. He would craft most of his declaration of intent with a reliable glove, but punctuate his bid for the job with a most memorable Friday night along the Candlestick Park basepaths.

Buddy — whose listed weight of 160 pounds was understood to include the qualifier "soaking wet" — led off the game by tripling against San Francisco starter Ray Sadecki. His opening statement proved that much more effective when he dashed home on Ken Boyer's fly to center, giving Jack Fisher a 1-0 lead.

The 22-year-old shortstop helped keep the Mets in the game from there with heady defense, turning two double plays (3-6-3 in the second, 6-4-3 in the eighth), before turning back to his less obvious skill in the top of the ninth, the Mets trailing, 3-2. Hawk Taylor tied things up with an RBI single and his pinch-runner, Johnny Lewis, represented the go-ahead run with two out when Harrelson came up again. And again, Harrelson tripled. His newfound extra-base power gave the Mets a 4-3 advantage... but what's a lead without a little insurance?

Harrelson decided he was the best policy the Mets had and took off from third for home with Bressoud at the plate and Lindy McDaniel on the mound. The former didn't get in his way and the latter couldn't get him out. Harrelson was safe on a steal of home. The Mets went up, 5-3.

Good thing, too, as the Giants staged a last-ditch rally that netted them a run in the bottom of the ninth. Buddy's insurance turned out to be the difference-maker, as the Mets emerged 5-4 winners and Harrelson edged a little closer to taking over short on a permanent basis.

45

Bud Harrelson collected three hits and scored three runs. Cleon Jones drove in three. Ron Swoboda knocked in two more. These youngsters had begun to form the foundation of a unit across 1966 and now, on a Sunday afternoon in Cincinnati, they and their teammates combined to...not finish last.

It was true. The Mets were no longer the worst team in the league. By beating the Reds, 8-4, they clinched ninth place. Maybe only the Mets as they were popularly perceived after five seasons could have been said to have clinched something as inauspicious as next-to-last, but you can't turn a corner without at first approaching it.

The Mets were undeniably on the right side of the street. By winning their 64th game of the year, they knew they'd finish ahead of the Cubs. It didn't really matter who they topped. They needed to top somebody. Now they knew they weren't going to be at the bottom of the National League standings. And neither would they lose 100 games. That, in addition to not being last, was another delectable first.

Anything else the Mets achieve as Wes Westrum's first full season as skipper concluded relatively successfully? Well, they had nothing to do with it, but any Mets fan who took a moment to scan how things stacked up in the other league after this Sunday couldn't help but notice that as the New York Mets gripped ninth place in the N.L., there was an unfamiliar bunch stuck in the cellar of the A.L.

The junior circuit's tenth-place tenant? None other than the recently dynastic New York Yankees. Sure enough, one week later, the Yankees — world champions for the 20th time in 1962 as the Mets were wallowing in heretofore unexplored ineptitude — went into the books as the last-place team in the American League for the first time since 1912. They'd only two years before won the pennant. Now they were finishing at a lower latitude than the suddenly ascendant Mets, who themselves ramped up their record from 50-112 in 1965 to 66-95 in '66.

It was too soon to ask if wonders would ever cease. It was enough to know they were ever so slightly commencing to exist.

 **1967**

Someday he'd be an attraction, among many other things. But on an inconspicuous Thursday afternoon, he was just a rookie making his second major league start and seeking his first major league win. No wonder no more than a typical-for-the era crowd of 5,379 gathered to

46

watch. Whatever those Shea Stadium attendees' motivation was, they picked a good day to go to a Mets game, for they bore witness to the birth of the Franchise.

Tom Seaver was 0-0. His first start was a no-decision — a win for the team, but nothing to show from a bottom-line pitching perspective, even if he did impress: two runs over five-and-a-third versus the powerful Pirates, striking out eight. For his second start, against the Cubs, that little bit of big league experience the former Jacksonville Sun, Alaska Goldpanner, USC Trojan, United States Marine and, most critically, disallowed Atlanta Brave prospect had accumulated against the Bucs served him well. After two scoreless frames, Billy Williams reached 22-year-old Seaver for an RBI triple in the third, putting Chicago up, 1-0. But Tommy Davis evened matters in the fourth with a solo home run off veteran Curt Simmons.

From there, it was mostly Seaver, bestowed upon to the Mets barely a year earlier when Commissioner William Eckert plucked the club's name out of a hat in what amounted to the luckiest lottery drawing of all time. Tom retired the Cubs in order in the fifth and again in the sixth. With a two-run lead by the seventh, he got fly balls to center out of Ernie Banks and Randy Hundley, both nabbed by Don Bosch. Two singles followed, but pinch-hitter Clarence Jones popped to Buddy Harrelson at short. Through seven, Seaver had given up just the one run on seven hits, with five strikeouts to his credit.

The eighth would be Seaver's last inning. Don Kessinger singled to lead off. Glenn Beckert then lined a pitch deep to left, which headed toward the wall. It took a leaping, spearing catch by Davis to turn it into an out. Then the rookie pitcher did something that impressed one of his most experienced teammates. Third baseman Ken Boyer visited the mound and asked Tom how he was feeling.

Seaver admitted to being "pooped". Young pitchers rarely came clean so readily, but Seaver wasn't just about a promising fastball. As Boyer recognized, he brought maturity to his job, and this may have been the first tangible sign of it. With Williams about to come up, and Tom's hard stuff losing a little something late in the game, he didn't hesitate tell the truth. Wes Westrum arrived at the mound, ascertained the situation and pulled the kid.

It worked out fine. Don Shaw came on and teased a double play grounder from Williams. The Mets padded their lead to 6-1 in the bottom of the eighth and Shaw set down the Cubs in the ninth.

Winning pitcher? Tom Seaver (1-0). It was the first of 198 Terrific Mets wins and the first of 311 in what would soon enough reveal itself as a career for the ages.

MAY 9, 1967
METS 3 REDS 2 (11)
SHEA STADIUM

The distance that got everybody's attention when it was over was the distance from home plate to somewhere past the 371-foot mark on the left field fence at Shea Stadium. That's how far Tommy Davis's eleventh-inning, game-winning homer off Cincinnati reliever Mel Queen traveled, thereby allowing the Mets to beat the Reds, 3-2, on a Tuesday night in 1967. Also of interest was how far Davis had come in the previous four years.

Tommy Davis was one of baseball's best players as a Dodger in 1962 and 1963. He was darn near the MVP of the National League in '62 when he drove in 153 runs, and won batting titles in both seasons. Then things took a downward turn as Davis endured a broken ankle, a dislocated leg and a reduced role in Los Angeles. In the 1966-67 offseason, the Dodgers sent the Brooklyn native back home, or one borough over. A fresh start awaited Tommy in Queens, and he was happy with what he was experiencing in the early going.

"This," he said after his walkoff clout, "is the first time I've had anything to cheer about since 1963."

If the heartwarming ending — and the transcontinental journey — belonged to Davis, something else about distance needed to be said for that night's winning pitcher. The Mets' Jack Fisher kept his team in the game the entire game...all eleven innings of it. Jack gave up two runs (one earned), six hits, three walks and struck out five. But the most impressive thing about his line was his IP. He pitched a complete game victory.

Fisher didn't come out in the eighth even after pinch-runner Dick Simpson, inserted for Reds pinch-hitter Art Shamsky, scored the tying run on a John Sullivan passed ball. Wes Westrum left Jack in to pitch a 1-2-3 ninth as well as a tenth that saw him give up a leadoff single to Leo Cardenas but then erase it on a ground ball double play. When the Mets got runners on first and second with nobody out in the bottom of the tenth, Westrum sent Fisher to the plate to bunt them over. The strategy didn't work to perfection (lead runner Tommie Reynolds was gunned down at third) and the Mets didn't score, but Jack went back to the mound to pitch the eleventh. He gave up a leadoff single to Vada Pinson, but then induced three consecutive fly balls from Pete Rose, Tony Perez and Lee May. Center fielder Cleon Jones snagged them all.

One starting pitcher; eleven innings. Unimaginable in the 21st century, isn't it?

Yet it wasn't unprecedented in Mets history to that point. Six times a Met starter had gone at least — *at least!* — that long in a game. The most recent incidence of extreme endurance took place exactly a week earlier, and it was committed by the very same Jack Fisher, who went 11 2/3 against the Giants. Unfortunately, Fisher (known maybe not entirely endearingly as Fat Jack) threw his last pitch to Willie Mays, which Mays belted for an RBI single, causing Westrum to remove Fisher in favor of reliever Don Shaw (who retired Willie McCovey and vultured the win when the Mets scored twice in the bottom of the twelfth).

But against the Reds — with a mighty assist from Davis — Fisher accomplished something no Met pitcher had done before: win an eleven-inning start. Jack's 3-2 victory over the Reds set a record for the longest complete game win in Mets history, and it's never been exceeded. Bob Shaw managed to match the feat a month later, and though there would be nine starts of that length or longer between 1968 and 1983 (including four by Tom Seaver and three by Jerry Koosman), no Met starter has won a complete game of such impressive distance since 1967.

The day had a Hollywood beginning. And a Hollywood middle, for that matter. Each amounted to scenes orchestrated by two successful directors — Gene Saks, working for Paramount, and Wes Westrum, calling the shots for the New York Mets.

On the Tuesday afternoon Shea Stadium was borrowed to help make a major motion picture out of the Broadway hit *The Odd Couple*, it was Westrum taking a rare star turn when

he scripted a moment of comic one-upmanship worthy of Neil Simon. He realized Pirate skipper Harry Walker was employing a batting order that did not match the one on the lineup card he submitted to home plate umpire Al Barlick. There had been a communication snafu that resulted in one version of the Pittsburgh lineup on the scoreboard and a different one in Barlick's possession. Westrum picked up on the confusion early but kept that realization in his pocket for when it mattered, namely the top of the third.

A Pirate rally was in progress against Met starter Dennis Bennett, one that included Gene Alley reaching base ahead of Jose Pagan, and Pagan doubling Alley and Donn Clendenon home with two outs...except Westrum knew Pagan was, by the official lineup card's dictum (which takes precedence over whatever it says on the scoreboard), supposed to be batting before Alley, not after. Barlick couldn't argue and negated Pagan's plate appearance and, with it, his two RBIs. The "next" batter, Jim Pagliaroni, was called out for not having batted directly after Alley as the lineup card said he was supposed to. The Mets, who led 5-2 before Pagan's double seemed to have made it 5-4, got out of the inning leading 5-2, which became the day's final score.

Pagan's pair of runs batted in never made it into the box score, and neither did the triple play Bill Mazeroski banged into to end the game. That omission was less confusing since the around-the-horn rally-killer was part of the filming of *The Odd Couple*, which preceded the matinee performance that counted in the standings. It's the scene in which sportswriter Oscar Madison (Walter Matthau) covers the Mets and Pirates from the Shea Stadium press box. Oscar is hard at work in the ninth inning — the Mets are up by one but the Bucs have the bases loaded against Jack Fisher — when he gets an urgent phone call from his old friend/new roommate, Felix Unger (Jack Lemmon), transmitting the urgent message not to eat any hot dogs at the game because he's making franks and beans for dinner. The distraction pulls Oscar's attention from the field, forcing him to miss the unlikeliest of finales. It's left to real-life journalist Heywood Hale Broun to inform Oscar what had just transpired:

"A triple play! The Mets did it! The greatest fielding play I ever saw, and you missed it, Oscar! You missed it!"

Maybe, but it wasn't as embarrassing as Harry Walker missing the discrepancy between the lineup he wrote down and the lineup that got posted...and unlike Oscar, Harry the Hat couldn't blame any of it on fussy Felix.

M ets fans had grown used to losing for five years, but in the sixth, they got a sense of what consistent winning looked like. They got to spend a season with Tom Seaver. Before it was over, they had statistical confirmation that they'd never had a

bigger winner in their midst.

Observationally, proof built throughout the campaign. The rookie from Fresno, winning more than he was losing (not a common condition among Met moundsmen), established himself as an inspirational figure to his up-and-coming teammates. Seaver on the mound meant "these guys plain work a little harder," his catcher, Jerry Grote, marveled. Shortstop Buddy Harrelson noticed the instant ace's "concentration," and if Seaver was that into the game, then "playing behind him, you try to match it."

Walter Alston thought Seaver's 1967 matched up well with those of Juan Marichal, Don Drysdale and Bob Gibson and named him to the National League All-Star team, making him the first Met pitcher to ever earn that honor. And it was earned: at the break, Tom owned an 8-5 record and an ERA of 2.65. Those were not Metlike numbers, at least before Seaver.

The defining experience of Seaver's first All-Star Game, on July 11 in Anaheim, seemed destined to take place before anybody threw a pitch. The rookie was so fresh-faced that starting left fielder Lou Brock mistook him for one of the clubhouse kids. Brock asked Seaver to go get him a soda. He did as asked. Even Tom Terrific was a neophyte once.

Many hours later, Tom was an All-Star among All-Stars. Alston's request was more up Seaver's alley than Brock's — he handed Tom the assignment of preserving a 2-1 lead in the bottom of the fifteenth inning. As if it was no more challenging than slaking a teammate's thirst, Seaver poured it on against A.L. batters. Tony Conigliaro flied out. Carl Yastrzemski (en route to a triple crown) walked. Bill Freehan flied out. Ken Berry struck out.

Marichal got the start. Drysdale got the win. Seaver got the save. Suddenly it wasn't strange to think of a Mets pitcher in that kind of company.

As the regular season resumed, Tom showed himself to be peerless in Met history. When he faced Pat Jarvis and the Braves on a Wednesday night in mid-September, he made it official, prevailing in a 2-1 duel for his fourteenth win of the season (earned against an Atlanta team that signed him as a collegiate, only to be stripped of his rights on a technicality in 1966). Fourteen was the most victories compiled by any Met pitcher yet. The previous record-holder was Al Jackson, whose thirteen wins in 1963 were, as if by law, coupled with seventeen losses. That had been the Met way, for the most part: lose more than you win.

It wasn't Seaver's way. Seaver's way was to overcome the one run he gave up in the second, on a Rico Carty double, and carry the Mets to a 1-1 tie through eight. He was helped along when Ron Swoboda robbed Tito Francona of a potential homer in the sixth and helped himself by striking out Hank Aaron — his boyhood idol — to escape a jam in the seventh. In the top of the ninth, Grote singled with two out to give the Mets a lead...by the same 2-1 score he protected for Drysdale two months earlier. Tom protected his own this time, setting down Carty, Felix Millan and Mike Lum to raise his won-lost total to 14-12.

Seaver's final mark would be 16-13, with the Mets' best-yet ERA of 2.76 and a franchise-record 170 strikeouts. It was easily the top Mets pitching season to date and just as easily the premier 1967 put forth by any freshman at any position in the senior circuit. No wonder the Mets' wonder would soon be voted National League Rookie of the Year. The young man accepted the honor graciously, but admitted his real goal: "I want to pitch on a Mets pennant winner and I want to pitch in the first game in the World Series. I want to change things...I don't want the Mets to be laughed at anymore."

For the 1967 Mets, Tom Seaver loomed as the happiest harbinger of what might come next for a heretofore object of mass derision, but unfortunately he couldn't completely blot out all the personnel chaos that went on around him. Though his team played adjacent to a stop

SEPTEMBER 19, 1967
METS 6 DODGERS 3
SHEA STADIUM

on the IRT in Queens, its roster too often resembled rush hour at Grand Central Terminal...and reflected the team's unfortunate 61-101 express ride back to tenth place.

The Mets used a National League record 54 players in 1967, including 35 making their inaugural appearance for the club. There were youngsters, there were oldsters, there was everyone in between. Seventeen of those who played their first game as a Met in 1967 also played their final game as a Met in 1967. Ten other 1967 Mets who came to the team earlier wouldn't be there later — of the 54 players who took the field for the team in its sixth season, fully half would be forever done with the team by the time its seventh season started.

Sic transit Metropolitan, indeed.

Yet for every Al Luplow who had come and was now gone, or every Al Schmelz who was over and out in a blink, there were holdovers and newcomers with a future. The Kranepools, Joneses, Swobodas, McGraws, Grotes and Harrelsons each continued to mature, albeit at varying rates. Several veterans — pitchers Don Cardwell, Cal Koonce and Ron Taylor and third baseman Ed Charles — arrived in time to prove themselves able-bodied and levelheaded enough to be called on for 1968 and beyond. Rookies Jerry Koosman (pitcher) and Ken Boswell (second baseman) each drew first looks, if not quite as long as the one Seaver earned, and they, too, would be back.

And then, chronologically, there was the 35th new Met of the season, the 12th to make his big league debut and the 54th of 54 Mets to take part in at least one game in 1967. In his case, however, the last was also a first, for Les Rohr already held a distinction in New York Mets history no one else could claim.

Rohr had been the first player picked by the Mets in professional baseball's inaugural amateur draft in 1965. The hard-throwing lefty went second overall as the National League's top choice (a pick the Mets earned by finishing last in 1964). In a sense, the Montana high school star was the Mets' answer — or parallel, at least — to their Shea Stadium co-tenant's first pick from the same year, the New York Jets' Joe Namath. But while Namath began lighting up American Football League scoreboards relatively quickly, earning AFL Rookie of the Year honors in 1965, the Mets had to wait on Rohr, who was only 19 when drafted.

He spent 1966 in the minors and split 1967 between the Carolina League and the United States military. The Mets were finally able to call up their first-ever pick and station him on the Shea Stadium mound on the third Tuesday night in September. His first major league opponents were the Los Angeles Dodgers, finishing up an off year following two consecutive National League pennants.

Young Les, by now 21, acquitted himself well enough to justify the organization's faith in him: six innings and two earned runs (three overall), with six strikeouts, including two — Wes Parker and Jeff Torborg — in his very first inning of work. Wes Westrum removed Rohr with a 4-3 lead after six and Dick Selma pitched the final three innings to secure a 6-3 win for the rookie's first decision.

Les Rohr was 1-0. Two starts would follow to close out the season: a 4-2 loss at home to the Astros and eight innings of a combined shutout (with Ron Taylor) in L.A. on the season's final weekend. The brief taste Les got of the majors — like that the Mets had of Les — was tantalizing. He went 2-1 with the kind of ERA (2.12) that figured to have the team calling him up to New York again in the near future. But as it happened, Les Rohr wound up 1967 pitching half the big league games he ever would. An arm injury sustained in the Mets' 24-inning, 1-0 loss to Houston the subsequent April limited him to two appearances in 1968, both losses. There'd be one more late-season shot in 1969, exactly two years after his debut. It didn't go well. The first amateur the Mets ever selected through the baseball draft would be through as a pro by 1970, all of 24 years old.

So much for Broadway Les.

Because of less-than-stellar finishes through most of the 1960s, the Mets were regularly granted one of the top four choices in the June draft in the seasons succeeding their tenth- or ninth-place standing. These golden opportunities yielded them Rohr in 1965, catcher Steve Chilcott in 1966 (with the No. 1 pick overall, just ahead of the Kansas City A's selection of Reggie Jackson), lefty pitcher Jon Matlack in 1967, infielder Tim Foli in 1968 (with another overall No. 1 pick) and righty pitcher Randy Sterling in 1969. History would reveal that Rohr's results, while disappointing in the long term, were hardly the worst the Mets' early first-selection drafting would yield.

51

SEPTEMBER 22, 1967 (2ND)

METS 8 ASTROS 5 (10)

SHEA STADIUM

The first manager to lead the Mets out of the basement couldn't stand being the first manager to take them right back where they started. A stressed-out Wes Westrum resigned with less than two weeks to go in the 1967 season. His replacement — the first solely interim manager in Mets history — was coach Francis James "Salty" Parker. True to the temporary pilot's nickname, his first night on the job turned a little spicy.

The first game of a Friday twinighter against the Astros wasn't exactly an advertisement for keeping Parker around as 1968 approached. The Mets lost, 8-0, which is to say they gave up twice as many runs as they used Jerrys.

Which, in turn, is to say Parker started rookie Jerry Koosman on the mound (he lasted an inning); finished the game with eternally hard-luck Jerry Hinsley (whose injury-riddled career consisted of eleven Met appearances, every one of them in a Met loss); had Jerry Grote behind the plate for the first six innings (his average sunk to .194 on an 0-for-2); and pinch-hit infielder Jerry Buchek for Bud Harrelson and left him in to complete the game at short.

Four Jerrys, no winning. But the nightcap was a different story, and it took only one Jerry to make things very merry.

The Mets trailed the Astros, 4-2, in the eighth when Bob Johnson — who was one of several infielders to have bumped Buchek from his regular second base slot as 1967 wound down — singled. Tommy Davis did the same. After Parker pinch-ran Cleon Jones for Davis, Buchek, at shortstop again, came up and put the Mets in the lead with a three-run homer off Carroll Sembera. Score one for the Jerrys!

Then take one away, as a two-out single clanged off Buchek's glove in the top of the ninth and the Astros tied the game at five.

But Jerry's bat would have the last word. Buchek came up with two on and two out in the bottom of the tenth and launched his second three-run homer of the second game, this one off Tom Dukes. The Mets were 8-5 winners, Salty Parker was a victorious major league manager for the first time and Jerry Buchek, with the twelfth and thirteenth homers of his unusually powerful season, had just set the all-time single-game record for most runs batted in by a Met in a Met win with six. (Frank Thomas drove in six in a loss in 1962.)

That mark has since been surpassed, but no manager since Salty has thought to pepper a box score — let alone a roster — with such a generous serving of Jerrys jubilee.

1968

APRIL 11, 1968
METS 4 DODGERS 0
DODGER STADIUM

L ose on Opening Day, there's always tomorrow. Tomorrow is what the Mets depended on after every Opening Day that kicked off their earliest campaigns, back when the only luck they had on Opening Day was typified by getting stuck in an elevator (as happened to a passel of them before their first Opening Day in 1962).

Ergo, you had to seek solace in the second game of the season, and the Mets really needed it in 1968. They came so close to breaking their first-game jinx in their seventh year. They had their first certified ace, Tom Seaver, starting his first Opening Day, in San Francisco, and he carried a 4-2 lead into the ninth. Alas, even Tom Seaver, sophomore deluxe, wasn't impervious to whatever it is that kept the Mets from getting off on the good foot. Seaver came out with a lead. The Mets lost, 5-4.

Which made Jerry Koosman's emergence as the ultimate No. 2 starter in the second game of the 1968 season that much more crucial. Kooz had sipped his share of coffee during brief stints in 1967, but he had yet to make an impression in the win column. He, like the '68 Mets, had something more in mind when they headed down the coast to Los Angeles to try and even their record.

Koosman, who avoided release in the low minors only because he owed the Mets some money for car repairs, was a revelation as he revved up his career. The 25-year-old lefty from Morris, Minn., went the distance, shutting out the Dodgers, 4-0. New manager Gil Hodges considered taking the rookie out when he seemed to be tiring but explained afterwards, "When you see a kid still have that kind of stuff so late in the game, you know he's got the ability to win up here."

Hodges proved a prophet. In what would become known as the Year of the Pitcher, Jerry Koosman stepping up and joining Tom Seaver atop the Mets' rotation assured Mets fans would be able to proudly use the plural — "pitchers" — for many years to come.

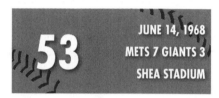

53

JUNE 14, 1968

METS 7 GIANTS 3

SHEA STADIUM

On this Flag Day, you could forgive the Shea faithful if they had visions of something besides the stars and stripes flying high on the center field pole.

The Mets under Gil Hodges suddenly had the air of winners about them. They weren't winners yet where the National League standings were concerned, but they had never gotten this close this late in their young lives before. Certainly they had never been so far removed from losing for this long.

Consider that the team that would intermittently go a week without winning the way some people might occasionally work through lunch had, as 1968 approached the one-third mark, not lost more than four in a row at any point of the season. The Mets had never delved that far into their schedule without encountering a more sizable skid...usually much more sizable. But for these Mets, losing four in a row was as bad as it had gotten in the first couple of months of '68.

And then things began to get good. Very good. Not just good for the Mets, but good for any team.

The progress commenced in earnest on a June road trip of 7-2 that saw the Mets sweep both the Cubs and the Dodgers and come home to face the only team that had just bested them away from Shea, the Giants. Mets fans were ready not for anything — they were ready for payback. A packed house of 54,259 showed up to see just how real the ascendant objects of their affection were.

They were plenty real this Friday night, gaining a quick lead on Ed Charles's first-inning RBI single and breaking it open on two homers in the third, a leadoff shot from 1967 center field washout Don Bosch and a three-run blast courtesy of Jerry Buchek. The rest of the heavy lifting in the 7-3 victory was performed by Jerry Koosman, whose seven-hit complete game outing improved his record to a most unMetlike 10-2.

Then again, Kooz cost himself a double in the seventh inning when, in the tradition of Marv Throneberry, he failed to touch first. So who was to say what was Metlike anymore?

Hodges was instilling in his charges the idea that winning was the name of the game.

This game brought the Mets their eighth triumph in ten contests and inched them to within one game of the heretofore unattainable .500 mark at 26-27. Though mired in eighth place, it was as strong an eighth as the jumbled National League had to offer. The Mets sat only six games from first place, a mere two lengths from second place.

The air of a winner proved a little too rarefied for the 1968 Mets, who would not crack .500 this year nor move up in the N.L. The progress slowed after a fashion, but it didn't stop. It, too, was plenty real.

I magine if the Franchise opened an outlet store. Imagine if the best starting pitcher the Mets ever had decided to fill his days between starts with relief assignments. Imagine Tom Seaver as not just your ace but your closer.

54

JULY 8, 1968 (2ND)

METS 4 PHILLIES 2

CONNIE MACK STADIUM

Once a year, with something approximating regularity, Gil Hodges availed himself of this fantasy. He handed Seaver the ball not in the first inning, but in a late inning. The first time he did it, it made for a successful if unusual finishing flourish.

The Mets and Phillies were winding down the first half of the 1968 season with a Sunday doubleheader at Connie Mack Stadium. The opener was lost in most heartbreaking fashion. Dick Selma had pitched seven shutout innings, but was removed in favor of Ron Taylor after Johnny Callison reached him for a leadoff homer in the eighth to cut the Mets' advantage to 3-1. Hodges's confidence in Taylor, the reliever who would finish more games for the Mets than any other that year, was justified when he allowed no further damage in the inning. So confident was Gil that he let Ron bat for himself in the top of the ninth, even though the Mets had the bases loaded. Dick Hall struck Taylor out to keep the game at 3-1.

After Ron retired Cookie Rojas to start the bottom of the ninth, the walls fell in: two singles and then Richie Allen belting his 15th homer of the season — the third of a record-tying 10 he'd whack Met pitching for in 1968 (Willie Stargell also had 10 vs. the Mets, in 1966) — to win it for Philadelphia, 4-3. Taking the nightcap, thus, became imperative if the Mets wanted to savor their overall progress sans bad taste during the All-Star break.

Their opponent was Larry Jackson, a Metkiller of Allenian proportions as a pitcher. Jackson, a fine if not outstanding pitcher most of the time, morphed into a monster when he was facing Mets batters. His record against New York, dating to the very first game the Mets played in 1962: 20-1. Yet 1968 was to be Jackson's final season and this was, hands down, the best Mets team so far. Win or lose this game, they were headed to the All-Star break nearer to .500 than ever before and farther above tenth place than ever before. The nearer and farther they got, respectively, the happier everybody in Metsdom would be.

Jackson turned out not to be his usual problem. Phil Linz, starting at second for the Mets, singled in a pair of runs in the second to put the Mets out in front, 2-1. The Phillies tied it off starter Danny Frisella in the fourth, but the Mets put together another rally off their old nemesis in the eighth: doubles by J.C. Martin and Ed Kranepool built the lead run and a one-out error by Phillie shortstop Roberto Peña provided insurance. Larry Jackson left trailing, 4-2, after giving up 11 hits to his traditionally easy marks.

Hodges had Frisella go eight innings and he kept the score 4-2. For the ninth, though, the manager realized the All-Star break allowed him some extraordinary flexibility. He could fill his bullpen with starting pitchers, get them a little extra work and not do any damage to his rotation since there'd be nothing to rotate for another four days. Plus, since he had some awfully good starters, they were likely to help secure this win. Out went Frisella and into begin the ninth came Jerry Koosman. Kooz was building a strong case for himself as Rookie of the Year, having gone 11-4 in the first half and earning a slot on the National League All-Star team. Here, Hodges looked to his stellar lefty to get out lefty hitter Tony Gonzalez.

Instead, Koosman hit Gonzalez with a 2-2 pitch, meaning the tying run was coming to bat with nobody on...and it was a righty...Richie Allen. So Hodges pulled his lefty specialist *du jour* and inserted his right-hand man, Tom Seaver.

This was Seaver's second career relief appearance. Wes Westrum used Tom out of the pen in his rookie year of 1967 in an odd circumstance. It was another doubleheader, this one in August at Pittsburgh. Seaver started the first game and was knocked around badly enough to be gone after two innings. The Mets rallied to beat the Bucs, 6-5, and went for the sweep in the nightcap, which also got off poorly for the Mets. Starter Billy Wynne didn't last two innings, and Westrum had to keep dipping into his relief corps: Hal Reniff, Selma, Taylor, Joe Grzenda and, in the twelfth, with two out and the dangerous Donn Clendenon up, Seaver.

Yes, Tom Seaver started one end of a doubleheader and was brought in to hopefully close the other end. For a moment there, Wes Westrum was a genius. Seaver retired Clendenon and then pitched a scoreless thirteenth. Alas, Tom wasn't so fortunate in the fourteenth, loading the bases and giving up the game-winning single to Manny Mota for a 6-5 loss.

It didn't affect the kid too badly. He went on to win the Rookie of the Year award in '67 and pitch the first half of '68 well enough to merit his second All-Star selection alongside Koosman and their catcher, Jerry Grote (the first time the Mets rated multiple All-Star representatives). And now, in Philadelphia, Hodges was asking Seaver to make a one-day return to relief, all in the name of quelling Richie Allen.

Tom, good Marine that he was, followed Hodges's orders and struck out Allen on three pitches. Seaver then got fly balls out of Callison and Tony Taylor to preserve the 4-2 victory, giving Frisella his second win of the season, dealing Larry Jackson his second loss ever against the Mets (he'd finish his career versus New York at 21-2) and earning for himself the first save of his career.

Make that the only save of Tom Seaver's career...not counting the one he earned for pitching the 15th inning of the 1967 All-Star Game.

The save wasn't a universally recognized statistic during the 1968 season; it would take an offseason Rules Committee edict to make saves an official part of the box score forever more. As the Associated Press reported that December, saves previously "had only been kept by scorekeepers on an unofficial basis." But look through the records maintained by the likes of Retrosheet and Baseball-Reference, and you'll see saves documented going back many decades, not just from 1969 forward. As the B-R Bullpen explains, "Baseball researchers have worked through the official statistics retroactively to calculate saves for all major league seasons prior to 1969."

In any event, Seaver had one and only one regular-season save, though Hodges would parachute him into a couple of more pre-break ninth innings. In 1970, two days before starting him in the All-Star Game, Gil called on Tom to strike out Bob Bailey of the Expos with two out in the ninth. Unfortunately for the Mets, Seaver's role that day was to slam the barn door after the horse — in the form of a pair of ninth-inning runs off starter Ray Sadecki — had already gotten loose in what became a 5-3 Met loss (Hodges used Seaver in a similar losing ninth inning versus the Cubs in April 1969).

In 1971, with one out and one on and the Mets up by one over the Reds, Tom played fireman again, but the situation was too hot even for a pitcher as Terrific as him. Seaver gave up a single to Lee May and a three-run homer to Tony Perez, winding up the losing pitcher in Jon Matlack's first major league start. It goes down in the books as Tom Seaver's only blown save.

All told, Seaver made six relief appearances as a Met, to go with his team-high 395 starts. The last of them came during arguably the most star-studded pitching inning in Mets history, in the last game before the break in 1976. Matlack began the bottom of the seventh that Sunday at Atlanta-Fulton County Stadium up 4-1; he got in trouble, so manager Joe Frazier brought in Koosman, who deepened the trouble enough to put the Mets into a 6-4 hole; Frazier replaced him with Seaver, who got out of the inning with no further runs scored. The Mets pounced on former Cy Young winner (and future Met) Mike Marshall in the eighth to retake the lead, positioning Seaver for his only relief win as a Met...but Bob Apodaca surrendered a three-run homer in the bottom of the eighth to Braves cleanup hitter (and another future Met) Willie Montañez, and the Mets — despite using Matlack, Koosman and Seaver in rapid succession — lost, 9-8.

Tom Seaver had three relief appearances left in his career, but they wouldn't come until he was with the White Sox in 1984 and 1985. The first of them was downright historic. The White Sox and Brewers played 17 innings at Comiskey Park on May 8, 1984. At 3-3, the contest was suspended, to be picked up before the next night's game. Yet this one wasn't so easily dispensed with. The Brewers scored three in the top of the 21st inning on a Ben Oglivie home run...but the White Sox answered back with three in their half of the 21st. On it went, at 6-6 through 24. Sox skipper Tony La Russa, having gone through seven pitchers already, had no choice but to insert his starter for the regularly scheduled May 9 game in relief for the remainder of the suspended game from May 8 — Tom Seaver. Seaver pitched two scoreless frames, holding the fort long enough for Harold Baines to hit a walkoff (or a dragoff) home run, allowing the White Sox to prevail, 7-6, in 25 innings.

With that, Tom Seaver not only recorded the sole relief win of his career, but won the longest game ever played to a decision in major league history. Then he went out and pitched into the ninth inning of the regularly scheduled game, beating Milwaukee, 5-4, giving him, depending on how you read these things, wins on consecutive days or two wins in the same night.

More proof, as if Mets fans needed any, that Tom Seaver could do just about anything whenever he was handed the ball.

SEPTEMBER 11, 1968
METS 1 CUBS 0
WRIGLEY FIELD

55

A promising young pitcher was learning what life on the Mets could be like, particularly during a year notorious for pitching, pitching and nothing but pitching.

Which pretty well describes the 1968 Mets' offense.

When it came to run support, Jim McAndrew of Lost Nation, Ia., consistently found himself on the mound figuratively naked...though Jim might read into that characterization, given that he studied psychology at the University of Iowa. His earliest Met experience was practically a recurring nightmare. He'd stand in the middle of the field, pitch his heart (and everything else) out and have nothing to show for it. Consider McAndrew's first four starts as a midseason callup:

- 2 earned runs
- 2 earned runs
- 1 earned run
- 1 earned run

With results like that, the righty could expect...well, nothing. The Mets scored the following for McAndrew in those first four starts:

- 0 runs
- 0 runs
- 0 runs
- 0 runs

Four starts into his major league career, the hard-throwing 24-year-old had an ERA of 1.82 — and a won-lost record of 0-4. Then Jim had the nerve to have a bad outing in San Francisco, hiking his earned run average to 3.38 and dropping his mark to 0-5.

Not, by all indications, the luckiest man on the face of the earth.

Deliverance came on August 26, in his sixth start, against formidable competition. Taking on the pennant-bound Cardinals at Busch Stadium and facing off against emerging lefty star Steve Carlton, McAndrew figured out that the only way to win was to give up absolutely nothing, and then hope against hope that his batting teammates — on a team that hit a league-worst .228 for the year — would give him just a little something with which to operate.

The plan worked. Tommie Agee scored on Cleon Jones's eighth-inning sacrifice fly to give Jim a 1-0 lead, and Jim made it stand up by retiring the final six Redbirds of the night. McAndrew's first major league shutout lowered his ERA to 2.58, and raised his record to 1-5.

Then he went out, pitched eight and seven innings in his next two starts, gave up two runs in each of them, and — as the Mets continued to not score behind him — saw his record plunge to 1-7 even as his ERA dipped some more.

Tough league.

To "salvage" his career, Jim McAndrew revisited his August 26 formula on September 11, a Wednesday afternoon in Chicago. First, he made sure to oppose yet another future Hall of Famer, Ferguson Jenkins. Then he decided he would give up nothing all day, which in Jim's case constituted 8 1/3 innings. And he trusted his teammates to do the least they could do for him: score one lousy run. That occurred in the top of the fourth, when two Mets catchers (who could presumably come closest among all position players to understanding a run-starved pitcher's mental anguish) doubled. Jerry Grote's two-base hit drove in J.C. Martin, that day's first baseman, from second to provide Jim with a 1-0 lead.

He took it to one out in the ninth, when a Don Kessinger single and a Ken Boswell error on Glenn Beckert's ground ball convinced Gil Hodges that McAndrew had given all he could. Jim was removed after striking out seven and allowing only two hits and two walks. Relievers Billy Short and Cal Koonce each recorded an out and McAndrew was a winner again.

The Met victory — their 66th of the pitching-rich/hitting-impoverished season, or as many as they'd ever accumulated in one year to date — brought Jim McAndrew's record to 2-7, yet his ERA to 2.19. He'd started nine games to that point; the Mets scored six runs for him and five times they decided to not score at all. The only way he could win was by a) prevailing 1-0 and b) besting all-time greats just as they were getting good.

Hard to imagine they covered that kind of stress in psychology class.

I n a sense, the Mets couldn't have asked for a better way to wind down their season. Jerry Koosman pitched yet another gem this Saturday at Shea, a three-hitter that gave him 19 wins, three more than Tom Seaver totaled to set the franchise standard in 1967 (and three more

56

SEPTEMBER 28, 1968
METS 3 PHILLIES 1
SHEA STADIUM

than Tom recorded in '68). With his earned run average at 2.08 and seven shutouts, Kooz was at least a co-favorite for Rookie of the Year honors alongside Cincinnati catcher Johnny Bench.

And just as Jerry won more games than any Met pitcher before, the Mets had piled up more wins as a team than at any time in their history, breaking the 70 barrier and landing on 73. Two years earlier it was significant that the Mets came in not last and didn't lose 100 games. This time, ninth place — clinched the next day when Houston lost — was nice, but even more pleasing to the trained eye was the Mets' "failure" to accumulate 90 defeats. 73-89 wasn't going to win the Mets a pennant...or a division title, which was what would be at stake in the expanded National League of 1969...but it provided hard evidence that the Mets were on the rise.

Yet the Mets were in no way ending 1968 as they would have liked because they had to do it without their leader. Manager Gil Hodges suffered a heart attack while the Mets were in Atlanta on September 24. Pitching coach Rube Walker took the reins while Hodges, a heavy smoker, began his long, uncertain recuperation.

A beloved figure from his days in the middle of the Brooklyn Dodgers order and an Original Met, Hodges honed his managerial skills in the American League, shepherding the Washington Senators to slow, steady improvement from 1963 until 1967. His New York homecoming was too good an idea for the Mets to pass up. When they had the chance to nab him, they took it, even though they had to compensate the Senators with pitcher Bill Denehy and cash to obtain his services.

It was the best investment the Mets ever made.

Ninth place or not, the Mets of 1968 were a team apart from their predecessors. Under Gil, Jerry Grote made his first All-Star team — starting ahead of Bench — and Cleon Jones flourished as the everyday left fielder, hitting .297, sixth-best in the league. Newly acquired Tommie Agee struggled at bat (mostly the result of an exhibition game beaning at the ornery right hand of Bob Gibson) but established himself as a fixture in center, a position that had long eluded permanence. Rookie Ken Boswell earned a foothold at second base, forming a double play combination with shortstop Bud Harrelson, while a right field platoon of Ron Swoboda and former Red Art Shamsky took shape. Ed Charles gave the Mets respectable production at traditionally troublesome third base. The Met bench was fortified by the likes of Al Weis, who came with Agee from the White Sox for Tommy Davis and Jack Fisher, and another former Pale Hoser, catcher J.C. Martin. Ed Kranepool's development took a step back, but even if he'd been around long enough to have been a Polo Grounds teammate of Hodges, he was still only 23. Besides, it was a tough offensive season for everybody in baseball.

In the Year of the Pitcher, Met pitchers were among the best around, ranking fourth in the N.L. with a collective 2.72 ERA. Koosman at 19-12 and Seaver at 16-12 were the stars of the show, but the rotation's supporting cast — veteran Don Cardwell and rookies Jim McAndrew and Nolan Ryan (the latter a flamethrower given to bouts of wildness) — was pretty stellar, too. They were backed up ably by a bullpen corps whose featured arms belonged to Ron Taylor and Cal Koonce.

Individually, they were all pieces of an intriguing and increasingly professional puzzle. Hodges was the man in the midst of putting them together. Barring a disastrous turn, Mets fans would look to Gil to recover from what had been termed a "mild" cardiac episode and continue doing the job in 1969 he'd begun so promisingly in 1968.

1969

OH, HAPPY DAY

How often does a home run leave a mark that requires a full demolition crew to remove? There was one in particular whose aftermath you couldn't help but notice nearly four decades after it occurred.

Tommie Agee crushed a Larry Jaster pitch in the second inning of the third game of the 1969 season.

Crushed it? Mashed it.

Mashed it? Pulverized it.

Whatever he did to it, two things were immediately apparent:

1) Tommie Agee was emerging from his miserable 1968 (.217 batting average, 5 home runs, 17 runs batted in) and setting the tone for a different kind of season for him, and, hopefully, the Mets, in 1969.

2) Tommie Agee had struck the first fair home run to ever land in the Upper Deck of Shea Stadium — and the first of two home runs on the day as the Mets captured their first series of the year.

Few were there to witness it, not even 9,000 on this April afternoon (when Gary Gentry made his major league debut), and nobody was sitting anywhere near the area it smashed into way above left field. Yet everybody who was on hand swore it traveled to where no other ball had dared to soar.

"That one today," Ron Swoboda admired, "would have gone over the third fence and hit the bus in the parking lot if it hadn't hit the seats."

Funny Rocky put it that way, because other sluggers would go on to dent buses and the like, but never again in the life of Shea would a home run make it fair to the Upper Deck. If it wasn't immediately clear how significant a wallop Agee unleashed that Thursday, it came to be understood as something unmatched in the quarter-century to follow. Come 1994, at Mets Extra host Howie Rose's urging, the Mets commemorated the approximate spot where Tommie's homer touched down. A generation of Sheagoers would make pilgrimages up to Section 48 to check it out and gasp in awe. That marker — listing the batter's name, his uniform number (20) and the date — stayed painted in place clear through to Shea's demolition in 2008.

This was a big deal in the eyes of some, yet a complete non-event to those responsible for its execution. There was no denying something was going on that was worth capturing for the ages, but not for the reason those doing the capturing thought.

That, however, was impossible to know at the time. It usually is.

What was undeniable was Tom Seaver had just fired a complete game three-hitter past the Atlanta Braves in Georgia and won a 5-0 decision over Phil Niekro. Tommie Agee and Ken Boswell each doubled, Buddy Harrelson tripled, Ed Kranepool stole a base (the eighth of his eight-year career) and Cleon Jones drove in two runs as he raised his batting average to .391. The bottom line to the pack of Mets beat reporters was what happened in the standings because of the Wednesday night victory: the Mets were now a .500 ballclub.

To the scribes, and to many following the doings back in New York, it was no trifling feat. The Mets' cachet for so long was their losing. It was their bête noire, too. What was long framed as adorable, thanks to the efforts of correspondents who had to keep finding ways to make grinding, redundant defeat sound colorful, had become tedious. Mostly it was the norm. The Mets, from 1962 through 1968, went a combined 343 games under .500...and that was after achieving an uplifting mark of 73-89 (a.k.a. not losing 90 games) in 1968.

Their fate was cast early every season, never escaping the first week of a new year above the break-even point, never even sustaining a win-one/lose-one pace beyond eight games, which happened once, in 1967. It was all downhill from there. It was always downhill from there.

So of course when the Mets made it deep into May, all the way to their 36th game of the year with a .500 mark — 18 wins, 18 losses — there was bound to be excitement. What didn't figure into the calculation was the people least excited by the "achievement" were the New York Mets themselves.

Reporters rushed into the visitors' clubhouse and looked for a sign of celebration, for the presence of a party, for as much as a toast to provisional good fortune. They found none.

Jack Lang of the *Long Island Press*, one of the original Met writers, inquired of Seaver why there was no self-congratulations in the air. "You're a .500 ballclub," Lang reminded him. "Aren't you going to celebrate?"

Why, no. Tom had no intention of getting charged up about breaking even. "What's so good about .500?" he asked the media men. "That's only mediocre. We didn't come into this season to play .500 ball. I'm tired of the jokes about the old Mets. Let Rod Kanehl and Marvelous Marv laugh about the Mets. We're out here to win."

And to emphasize the point, Seaver added the champagne would be on ice "when we win the pennant".

This sudden outburst of youthful hubris struck the reporters as amusing if inappropriate. They knew the Mets were always abysmal. They knew every victory better be savored. They knew Seaver had stuck his foot in it when the Mets promptly went out and lost their next five and fell to 18-23.

Turned out they didn't know a damn thing.

MAY 28, 1969
METS 1 PADRES 0 (11)
SHEA STADIUM

Someday, Mets fans would be prompted by a mammoth video board planted beyond Shea Stadium's left field fence to sing along with Neil Diamond's 1969 Top Five single "Sweet Caroline," no matter that it was a staple of another fan base in another city. But at Shea, on the last Wednesday night in May, it was as if the first line to the song Fenway Park would make immortal was being composed.

"Where it began" could only be known with hindsight — let alone that something had indeed begun. All any of the 11,860 on hand could reasonably be concerned about was ending.

When would the current Met losing streak end? And, as they looked at the night, when would the game end?

Fresh off Tom Seaver's declaration that the Mets reaching .500 was no big deal, the Mets went right out and, as if on cue, dropped their next five. Longtime Metwatchers snickered. The club was heading in its traditional direction. In other seasons, a five-game losing streak might have been prelude to something much longer.

But in a theme that would get quite a workout before 1969 was over, this was a season like no other.

The Mets had pitching like few others, so how long could a losing streak go? Also, they had opponents they hadn't had before. They had the San Diego Padres, brand new to the National League in 1969. Like the Expos — the only team currently trailing the Mets in the N.L. East — the Padres were scuffling in a fashion familiar to fans of previous expansion teams. True, the Mets lost their first-ever game to the Padres the night before (same as they lost on Opening Day to Montreal), yet even caught in a momentary downward trajectory, it was nice to have neophytes to try to break a losing streak against.

And it was even nicer to have a lefty like Jerry Koosman to take the Mets' best shot at getting back to winning. Koosman's best shot was particularly on target against the Padres. He mowed them down inning after inning, piling up strikeout after strikeout. Kooz struck out the side in the eighth, increasing his total to fourteen on the night. By then, he'd given up two hits and no runs. His opposite number, Clay Kirby, was doing similar good work for San Diego, thus when Kooz got through the ninth with his shutout intact, the Mets still had to bat in the bottom of the inning.

Kirby kept us his end of the nothing-nothing bargain, shutting out the Mets for a ninth consecutive inning himself. Gil Hodges sent Koosman to the mound for the tenth, and he maintained his masterpiece. When he was done pitching this Wednesday, Jerry had struck out fifteen batters, a new Met record. But he had no run support, not even after Padre manager Preston Gomez had removed Kirby. The Mets didn't score in the tenth, so Kooz had to hit the showers with ten brilliant four-hit innings in his back pocket, but no win on the table.

And the Mets still hadn't won in the week since Seaver insisted the Mets would win more often than they lost.

Tug McGraw had to overcome wildness in the top of the eleventh (and get help from a double play), but he kept the game 0-0. In the bottom of the inning, against Billy McCool, the Mets received a break when shortstop Tommy Dean made a wayward throw to first on Cleon Jones's leadoff grounder. Cleon was safe. After Ed Kranepool struck out, another reliever, Frank Reberger, entered and allowed a single to Ron Swoboda. With Jones taking third, Gomez opted to walk Jerry Grote to load the bases. Bud Harrelson, however, foiled the Padre pilot's strategy when he singled to left. Jones scored and the Mets won, 1-0.

It didn't do anything for Koosman's mark, but it snapped that nettlesome five-game skid. Something better took its place as spring was about to become the summer.

Mass production? Overrated. The Mets chose instead to hand-craft their winning run the old-fashioned way: one base at a time, eschewing modern contrivances like hits.

60 JUNE 1, 1969
METS 5 GIANTS 4
SHEA STADIUM

Their Sunday game at Shea against the Giants boiled down to the bottom of the ninth, the score tied at four. The Mets took on reliever Joe Gibbon in a very stealthy manner. Buddy Harrelson led off with a walk. Tommie Agee bunted him to second. A Wayne Garrett grounder to the right side moved Harrelson to third. Cleon Jones (batting .364) was intentionally walked. Jones crossed up San Francisco manager Clyde King's best-laid plans by taking off for second, stealing it safely. Rookie Amos Otis (batting .141) then walked, loading the bases. Ron Swoboda heroically kept his bat on his bat on his shoulder long enough to accept ball four from Gibbon, and the Mets won, 5-4.

It was their fourth consecutive victory and their third in a row over the Giants, encompassing their first sweep ever against the team that previously wore the mantle of New York (N.L.).

61 JUNE 4, 1969
METS 1 DODGERS 0 (15)
SHEA STADIUM

There was Jackson Heights. There was Brooklyn Heights. There was Washington Heights. But nobody was scaling the heights in New York like the Mets suddenly were in 1969. With one increasingly characteristic thrilling victory, they reached all kinds of new peaks and didn't appear intent on stopping their climb anytime soon.

It had already been a homestand unprecedented in Mets history. After salvaging a split of a two-game set with the expansion Padres, the Mets swept three from the Giants for the first time in their relatively young lives. Then the Dodgers came to Shea and the Mets beat them twice. On getaway night, they attempted to fully eradicate the ghosts of their other ancestral oppressor.

Gil Hodges assigned this task to 26-year-old lefthanded rookie Jack DiLauro, making his first start that Wednesday evening after a handful of relief stints. "Gil told me I'd be starting two or three days in advance," the former Tiger farmhand recalled for author Stanley Cohen nearly twenty years later in *A Magic Summer*, "but it felt more like a month. I was really nervous, and it took me a couple of innings to calm down." Yet DiLauro appeared every bit the serene veteran across nine innings as he fired shutout ball against Los Angeles. Jack struck out five, walked two and, aided by some slick defense, allowed only two hits.

Bill Russell reached DiLauro for a first-inning double, "and I came within a couple of inches of giving up more. Buddy Harrelson saved a run with a great play at short" on a liner by Wes Parker, "and Cleon caught a drive at the wall that held up" in the second. When Jones hauled in that fly ball from Russell, DiLauro "took a deep breath; from that point on, I was all right." Better than all right — after walking Andy Kosco with two out in the third, the rookie retired the next sixteen batters he faced, taking him through nine.

DiLauro received a standing ovation after Bill Sudakis flied out to end the top of the ninth. "That was the biggest thrill of my career," Jack told Cohen. Only problem for the Mets was Bill Singer, who would win twenty for the Dodgers that season, was just as effective and a lot more overpowering. Singer struck out ten Mets while walking no one and giving up no hits through six innings. Harrelson became the first Met baserunner by singling to open the home seventh. A sacrifice bunt, a hit batsman and a fielder's choice grounder landed the Mets runners on first and third with Ed Kranepool up to give the Mets a chance to take the lead. But Dodger catcher Tom Haller picked Buddy off third to end the threat. An Art Shamsky single with one out in the ninth was the only other offense the Mets generated versus Singer.

The starting pitchers exited and extra innings arrived. Tug McGraw held off L.A. in the top of the tenth as fellow screwballer Jim Brewer did the same to the Mets. McGraw and Brewer would give way to teammates Ron Taylor and Al McBean, respectively, and the zeroes would continue to flow. In the top of the fifteenth, however, things got very sticky for the Mets. With pinch-runner Billy Grabarkewitz on third (after a Jim Lefebvre double) and Russell on first, Willie Davis chopped a ball up that seemed headed up the middle for a run-scoring base hit. Taylor, luckily, stood in the way.

"It hit the back of my glove," the reliever said after the game. "When it did, I thought it was by far a hit." But the deflection altered the course of events long enough for second baseman Al Weis to lunge for the ball and make an off-balance throw to the plate. Jerry Grote took it on a short hop and tagged Grabarkewitz for the second out of the inning.

"It was the greatest play I've ever seen on any team I've ever played for," the Mets' catcher marveled.

After escaping the top of the fifteenth when Parker fouled out to third (L.A. batters had left a dozen men on base and had gone 0-for-14 with runners in scoring position), it was the Mets' turn to make the Dodgers sweat. Walt Alston's new pitcher, Pete Mikkelsen, made things difficult on himself immediately by walking Harrelson. A Tommie Agee grounder forced Buddy at second. Up stepped rookie third baseman Wayne Garrett, who stroked a single to center. Davis — who had three Gold Gloves in his future — charged the ball... but the ball charged right past him. As it rolled toward Shea's center field wall, Agee came all the way around from first to score the winning run, as the Mets beat the Dodgers in fifteen innings, 1-0.

It was a great win by any measure, but what made it extra special was all the ways it could be measured:

- The Mets had won their seventh consecutive game, matching the franchise record previously achieved in 1966 and ending this eight-game homestand 7-1.
- The Mets had engineered what Leonard Koppett referred to as "the longed-for

double sweep of the Giants and Dodgers". How longed-for? Consider that the former New York City representatives of the National League teamed to slap around the baby Metsies 58 times in 72 opportunities in 1962 and '63 and had never been fully avenged...not until late May and early June of 1969, that is.

- The Mets raised their record to 25-23, two games above .500, a modest apogee to the naked eye, but one the Mets had never seen in nearly seven and one-third seasons of playing baseball. And as they jetted to the Coast to take on the California teams on their turf, the Mets would do so as sole proprietor of second place in the National League East — another first.

More than a plane took off for the West Coast after that win over the Dodgers. Hope flew like crazy.

That five-game losing streak after the Mets finally reached .500 may as well have taken place in 1962. The debate over whether .500 was much of a milestone was practically ancient history, too. The Mets were off in another dimension by now.

JUNE 10, 1969
METS 9 GIANTS 4
CANDLESTICK PARK

Streaks were all about winning for these 1969 Mets, and on this Tuesday night in San Francisco, the winning streak was topping out at eleven.

Eleven wins in a row. By the Mets.

Amazin'.

This one, which followed a three-game sweep in San Diego, was a 9-4 victory over the Giants at Candlestick Park featuring a two-homer, four-hit outburst from Tommie Agee and three RBIs from his Mobile, Ala., running mate Cleon Jones (now batting .351). Don Cardwell gave up five hits in pitching to one out in the ninth before giving way to Ron Taylor. After all their streaking, the Mets were six games over the break-even point, seven games behind the Cubs and ensconced in second place, comfortably ahead of the Pirates and Cardinals.

To repeat in the context of all that had preceded it, Amazin'.

JUNE 29, 1969
METS 7 PIRATES 3
SHEA STADIUM

Tom Seaver spent his Sunday doing something as he did everything in his young career: quietly, professionally, methodically. In doing so, he established a standard that — once he took it and ran with it — no Met would come anywhere near.

By throwing a six-hit complete game 7-3 victory against the Pittsburgh Pirates at Shea Stadium — striking out ten Bucs along the way — Tom raised his season record to 12-3...and in doing *that*, he collected the 44th win of his major league career, all with the Mets. Before the midpoint of his third big league season, he had set a new mark: most wins by any Mets pitcher, 44.

It was as much a commentary on Seaver's immediate excellence as it was on the difficulty even above-average pitchers encountered in getting anywhere in the win column for the Mets before 1969. Al Jackson, pretty darn good as top lefty starter for the Mets from 1962 through 1965, was the previous record-holder, with 43 wins. Those were counterbalanced, however, by 80 losses. The L's had a way of having their way with the W's on Met pitching ledgers in the team's first few years. Jackson actually had a second go-round as a Met, in 1968 and 1969, compiling a 3-7 mark mostly in relief. He was a teammate of Seaver's then, but not when Tom passed Little Al on the win charts; the Mets sold his contract to Cincinnati a couple of weeks earlier.

Seaver, meanwhile, was not going to stop winning for a very long time. The all-time record for most wins by a Mets pitcher would grow to 198, and it is still very much Seaver's. Nobody's come within forty victories of it yet.

They don't throw Bar Mitzvahs for baseball teams, but if ever a franchise noticeably came of age, it was the 1969 Mets on a Tuesday afternoon in July. When it was over, 25 men could collectively declare, *"Today, we are a contender."*

JULY 8, 1969
METS 4 CUBS 3
SHEA STADIUM

Maybe they already were when the brilliant summer day at Shea commenced. After all, they were well above .500, in second place and a mere 5 1/2 games out of first. There was a hurdle that had to be cleared, though, and it could be found in the 25 men wearing gray uniforms, the division-leading Chicago Cubs. At no point in the previous seven seasons of Mets baseball was there a sense that something beyond the "time of your life" was at stake when a baseball game was played at Shea. This here...this would be something different. This would be the time of the Mets' lives, the time for them to step up in class, the time to make a statement, the time to bring an essential truth to Cliché Stadium.

It was time to tell the Cubs and everybody else that a pennant race was, for the first time ever, going to include the New York Mets. Gone as of July 8, 1969, were all traces of the old Mets. The roster may not have transformed in the dead of night, but then again, it didn't have to. Throughout the first half of 1969, Mets fans figured out they had the team they needed. They were only waiting for their moment to arise.

Prior to their first date with destiny, when you spoke about the Mets, it was the Mets whose birthright was loss and last place. Those Mets shed that unwanted skin in April and May and June of '69. Those Mets ceased to exist somewhere between Spring Training, when Gil Hodges suggested 85 wins was doable for a team that had never lost fewer than 89, and July 8, when the Mets laid out the not-so-welcome mat for the Cubs.

It was a whole new ballgame, and it had the good fortune to be monitored minute-by-minute by 17 different writers contributing notes, observations and asides to editors Dick

Schaap and Paul Zimmerman for a book called *The Year The Mets Lost Last Place.* The book put a microscope to "nine crucial days" in the life of the franchise, starting with July 8. You couldn't ask for a better opening chapter in baseball or literary terms.

On "the day the Mets became a contender," as *TYTMLLP* put it, the world was ready and waiting. New York sat at the kitchen table with a knife in one hand, a fork in the other and a napkin tied around its neck, famished for the piping hot baseball that had been baking in Hodges's oven over the previous three months.

"Ever since 1965, when they outdrew the Yankees by half a million spectators, the Mets have been the baseball team in New York, and the Yankees have been the other team," the book said in real time. Problem was the Mets were locally pre-eminent without portfolio. National League baseball was the Metropolitan Area's preferred variety, but what the people really wanted was *winning* National League baseball, a commodity absent since the heyday of Don Newcombe and Dusty Rhodes. Now they were getting it. "For the first time in at least five years," *TYTMLLP* reported that summer, "New Yorkers by the millions were talking baseball."

Mets baseball. Talking about it, relishing it, mainlining it. The laughs were of the "with us" rather than "at us" nature. Everybody was in on the joke that the Mets were no longer a joke.

Everybody included Joseph Ignac of Elizabeth, N.J., 65 and without a team to take seriously since the Giants won in '54. He took two hours of buses and subways to be first in line at Gate E for a general admission seat the morning of July 8. "*As he heads for the park, Ignac is looking forward for the first time to watching his team fight to become a pennant contender.*" The boxscore says 55,095 other Mets fans had the same notion that Tuesday afternoon.

Everybody included Jerry Koosman of Morris, Minn., summering at a rented house near LaGuardia Airport. He stepped into his backyard and was gratified that it would be "*a beautiful day for a ball game. Just the way I like it — not too hot, not too cool.*" Thirty-seven years later, in the runup to the 2006 playoffs, Matt Yallof of SNY asked Kooz to reflect on what it was like to pitch in New York in October 1969. I always liked pitching in cool weather, Kooz answered literally and practically. Over four decades, whatever the season, Jerry Koosman always kept his cool.

Everybody included Frank Graddock, settled in front of his television in Ridgewood, Queens. Graddock stayed put there throughout the game, one that commenced at 2:05 PM. The action on Channel 9 was far along by 4 o'clock (this was 1969; nine innings took only 129 minutes), but it wasn't over. Mrs. Graddock — Margaret — only knew 4 o'clock meant the serial *Dark Shadows* was coming on on Channel 7. *Dark Shadows* was a huge show then. Frank Graddock's wife watched it every afternoon.

This, however, wasn't just any afternoon in 1969. There were no VCRs, no DVRs and apparently Frank did not consider radio an option. As *TYTMLLP* chronicles, a screaming match over which channel the Graddock TV would be tuned to ensued. It would turn fatal. While the Mets were maturing, Frank Graddock had been drinking… drinking enough to lose all sense and perspective.

The Graddocks' domestic dispute yielded dark shadows of its own. Of course

Frank Graddock deserved to be charged, as he would be the next day, with the first-degree murder of his wife after literally beating the life out of her. Of course it was a heinous response to something as silly as what would appear on the TV screen.

Jerry Koosman kept his cool while the passions of the Metropolitan Area heated up: 8 hits and 4 walks, but only 3 runs against the most dangerous lineup the N.L. had to offer through 9 innings. Cub ace Ferguson Jenkins, though, was coolest of all. Cleon Jones reached on an Ernie Banks error in the fourth. Ed Kranepool touched him for a solo home run in the fifth. And that was it. For eight innings, Fergie Jenkins, on track for his third consecutive 20-win season, was almost perfect. The Mets trailed by two against a pitcher emerging as one of the best of his generation.

Then they didn't.

Ken Boswell pinch-hits for Koosman to start the bottom of the ninth and lofts a ball that is catchable in a devil's triangle among the shortstop Don Kessinger, the second baseman Glenn Beckert and an unaccomplished center fielder named Don Young. Young would have had it had he seen it. He didn't. Because Beckert and Kessinger had backpedaled on the ball, no one covered second. Boswell acts quickly enough to stand there with a gift double.

Tommie Agee fouls out. One out. Donn Clendenon steps up. Donn Clendenon stepped up in mid-June as the righty first baseman Gil Hodges required for his platoon with Kranepool. He's gotten a slew of big hits since he was traded here from Montreal. Now Donn's batting for Bobby Pfeil. Clendenon steps up for real: a long shot to left-center. Young's got this one in the webbing of his glove.

Then he doesn't.

He hits the fence and the ball squirts loose. Three months later, Agee would have the opportunity to make a similar play against another allegedly unbeatable Metsian foe and make a better showing for himself than Young. Nobody could know that on July 8, just as Boswell couldn't know whether Don would maintain control of Donn's ball. Ken thinks carefully before proceeding and goes only as far as third on the Clendenon double.

Cleon Jones, one of two Mets baserunners during the first eight innings, is up next. Cleon, two weeks from starting for the National League All-Star team, entered this contest batting .354. He's 0-for-3, including reaching on that earlier error. He will end today at .352, 1-for-4, because he shoots a liner to left. Don Young has nothing to do with this play on which Boswell and then Clendenon score. It is 3-3. The Mets have tied the Cubs.

Jones on second. Art Shamsky up. Leo Durocher orders an intentional pass. Wayne Garrett, the youngest of the mostly young Mets, grounds to second, a second out that moves the runners up. Durocher could walk the next batter, Kranepool, to face light-hitting J.C. Martin. Martin's starting because he's a lefty and Jenkins is a righty. It's not like Jerry Grote, a righty, is a better option for Gil. It's not like there's another Clendenon waiting in the wings. (And it's not like Leo's making a call to the bullpen; again, this is 1969 when your best matchup almost always involves your ace.) Leo tells Fergie to face Ed.

Ed Kranepool's a Met from just after the Mets were born in 1962. Ed has not overly distinguished himself across the eight seasons he's been a Met. A famous banner a few years earlier asked, "Is Ed Kranepool over the hill?" Ed isn't old — he's 24 — yet he's already somehow ancient.

But Ed Kranepool did hit a home run off Ferguson Jenkins in the fifth inning, the only hit the Mets had most of Tuesday. And Ed Kranepool collects their fifth and final hit, a bloop single to left that scores Cleon from third. The Mets win, 4-3.

Ed Kranepool was an eternal disappointment and .227 hitter when the afternoon began. He is a hero when it ends.

Jerry Koosman was the winner, but so were the millions who had invested themselves in his team. Joseph Ignac, 65, of Elizabeth, for example. He had a two-hour trip home on the subway and the bus. So what? He could have soared. "Never once, in his eight seasons of cheering for the Mets," it was written in *The Year The Mets Lost Last Place*, "has he felt so good. For the first time, he doesn't miss Willie Mays quite so much."

Less than seven hours later, the early edition of the *Times* is on the streets. "The story of the Mets' rally is on the front page of the newspaper," *TYTMLLP* reports. "The Mets have been on the front page before, but only once for winning a ball game, way back in 1962, when, after nine consecutive defeats, they scored the first victory of their existence."

That existence was now from another time. The Mets existed on a different plane, in a different context, for different stakes starting July 8. The news was the stuff of the front page of the *New York Times*, but Don Young didn't have to wait until eleven that night to read it. He hears it immediately from captain Ron Santo and skipper Leo Durocher. He absorbs the blame for the first-place Cubs losing to the second-place Mets — and he's facing a benching the next day for sure. The Mets are a team coming together. The Cubs are individuals falling apart at the first sign of stress, the first instant they dip from 5 1/2 to 4 1/2 ahead of the team that couldn't have possibly beaten them but did.

"Now it is 1969," Mark Mulvoy wrote that July in *Sports Illustrated* as the dust settled from the Mets encountering the Cubs, "and in the fairyland of Shea Stadium, the toad has turned into a prince."

The transformation was official as of July 8. The Mets were reborn and rebranded as an honest-to-goodness baseball team that was likely to beat any other baseball team any day of the week. Nothing would ever be the same. In the short-term of 1969, that (save for the tragic fate of the late Margaret Graddock) was all for the best.

JULY 9, 1969
METS 4 CUBS 0
SHEA STADIUM

It's known as the Imperfect Game, which is ironic in that it may be the most perfect regular-season game the New York Mets have ever played. The "imperfect" aspect refers to a base hit leaving an indelible blot on the otherwise sparkling ledger of the Mets' starting pitcher.

As if every Mets starting pitcher in the franchise's first 50 years hadn't experienced such a smudge every time he had started as a Met..

The base hit that lingers as this game's imperfection — a clean single off the preternaturally obscure bat of Jimmy Qualls that fell between Cleon Jones in left and Tommie Agee in center — has come to define the Wednesday night in question. As convenient a shorthand as it makes, Qualls's ninth-inning, one-out safety shouldn't. Everything that preceded it was too perfect.

Still is.

The perfection associated with the Imperfect Game peaked the inning before Tom Seaver lost his claim to universal baseball immortality. That was in the eighth inning, mere minutes before Qualls, playing center only because Don Young failed at fielding the prior afternoon, became not so much the answer to a trivia question, but as a phrase only Mets fans could truly understand when a no-hit bid grew serious en route to its inevitable evaporation.

For decades after July 9, 1969, everyone from icons like Ernie Banks and Wade Boggs to relative nonentities like Benny DiStefano and Paul Hoover did some version of what Jimmy Qualls did. It's a cast that wrecked Met no-hitters when they felt within the grasp of possibility, but includes nobody else who ever became "Jimmy Qualls". That's because the role had been filled to — if you'll excuse the expression — perfection.

But we know that. We also know that the Imperfect Game was, in actuality, a rousing 4-0 victory by the second-place Mets over the first-place Cubs, pulling the unlikely contenders to within 3 1/2 of the suddenly vulnerable N.L. East frontrunners. We know that 59,083 (50,709 paid) jammed into Shea Stadium to see what Seaver and the Mets could do to the Cubs and that they witnessed more than they probably dared to imagine. That they didn't necessarily imagine a perfect game speaks to the limits of the Metsopotamian imagination after seven seasons when not losing 90 games seemed as good as anything could possibly get.

We know, too, if we've done our reading (*The Perfect Game: Tom Seaver and the Mets* by Tom Seaver with Dick Schaap) that Seaver threw Qualls a sinker and it sank Tom's heart:

"I didn't want to believe that I'd come so close to a perfect game and lost it."

And that it sank Nancy Seaver's heart as well, at least until her husband cheered her up with incredibly wise words for a 24-year-old:

"What are you crying for? We won, 4-0."

To which, Nancy added her own hard-earned wisdom:

"I guess a one-hit shutout is better than nothing."

What we might really want to keep in mind about this one-hit, eleven-strikeout masterpiece in the heat of a burgeoning pennant race against the team the Mets were aiming to catch was how divinely, absolutely, unceasingly perfect it was before Jimmy Qualls got in its way. And we can do that thanks to the magic of the recording technology that captured Lindsey Nelson's call of the top of the eighth inning over WJRZ-AM:

Tom Seaver on the mound for the New York Mets. Through seven innings he has retired twenty-one consecutive batters, and Ron Santo, who leads the National League in runs batted in with seventy-four, is up to lead off. He has struck out and flied to center.

Rod Gaspar has come in in right field now in place of Ron Swoboda for the New York Mets. Rod Gaspar, that's a defensive move by manager Gil Hodges.

Wayne Garrett comes in at second base now and Bobby Pfeil moves over to third as Charles comes out of the ballgame.

Here's the pitch to Ron Santo. Swung on — hit in the air to deep centerfield, Agee going back, he has a bead on it, he's there, and he makes the catch.

Listen to the crowd, riding on every pitch of the ballgame now, riding on every play as Tom Seaver has retired twenty-two consecutive batters at the start of the ballgame.

Wayne Garrett is playing second base. Bobby Pfeil is playing third.

In the history of the Mets, the longest that any Met pitcher has ever gone without allowing a hit, seven-and-one-third innings, by Al Jackson, in Pittsburgh against the Pirates. Seaver has gone seven-and-one-third here.

The pitch to Ernie Banks is high for a ball.

The crowd is humming.

Here is the one-oh pitch now to Ernie Banks. Swung on and missed, it's one-and-one. Seaver has struck out nine and he's walked none in this game tonight.

This will be a one-one delivery, it's on the way — curveball, swung on and missed, GOOD curveball. One-and-two now to Ernie Banks, as Seaver faces the heart of the batting order of the Chicago Cubs.

Santo opening up with a LONG fly to center, Banks is at the plate and Al Spangler's on deck.

Here's a one-two pitch — swung on and fouled back, he's still alive at one-and-two.

In the first inning, Kessinger struck out, Beckert lined out, Williams struck out. In the second inning, Santo struck out, Banks struck out, Spangler struck out. In the third, Hundley flied out, Qualls flied out, Holtzman struck out. In the fourth, Kessinger struck out, Beckert grounded out, Williams grounded out. In the fifth, Santo flied out,

Banks grounded out and Spangler struck out.

There's a swing and a foul ball back and out of play.

In the sixth, Hundley grounded out, Qualls grounded out and Abernathy struck out. In the seventh, Kessinger lined out, Beckert flied out, Williams grounded out. Here in the eighth, Santo has flied to center.

The count is one-and-two to Ernie Banks and Seaver's pitch is on the way — curveball misses WAY outside, caught in the webbing of the glove by catcher Jerry Grote, who leaned WAY out. Count goes to two balls and two strikes now.

Here is a two-two delivery to Ernie Banks. Swung on, fouled back, it's out of play, the count HOLDS at two-two, as thirty-eighty year-old Ernie Banks continues to foul that ball off.

The Mets lead by a score of four to nothing. Here's the two-two pitch — swung on and missed, he struck him out! Listen to the CROWD! Strikeout number TEN for Tom Seaver.

He has retired twenty-three consecutive batters from the start of the ballgame.

Left-hand batter Al Spangler's coming up. He's been up twice and he struck out swinging both times. The Cubs are batting in the top half of the eighth inning here at Shea Stadium.

There's a swing and a miss at strike one!

Seaver again takes the sign from Jerry Grote, two men out and nobody on base. He's into the motion again and here's the strike one delivery.

It's in there for a called strike two!

Oh-and-two the count now, to Al Spangler. Seaver again takes the sign. Here is the two-strike delivery — it's high and away for a ball, one-and-two.

Nancy Seaver, Tom's wife, seated in one of the lower field boxes, on the EDGE of her seat, RIDING with every pitch of this ballgame. Here's a pitch now — swung on and missed, he struck him out!

The side is retired. Seaver has gone through EIGHT innings; he has retired TWENTY-FOUR consecutive batters; he has not allowed a HIT or a BASERUNNER; he's getting a STANDING OVATION; he's gone LONGER…without allowing a hit than any MET pitcher in the history of the New York Mets.

That was his ELEVENTH strikeout.

No runs, no hits, no errors and none left. In the middle of the eighth inning, the score IS the Mets FOUR and the Cubs nothing.

See? Perfect.

Leo Durocher didn't establish his "nice guys finish last" legend based on good sportsmanship. No wonder, then, that when asked, after the Cubs salvaged the third game of their series with the Mets on July 10 if those were "the real Cubs" on display, he bristled, nope, those were "the real Mets".

A chance to force-feed Leo the Lip his words presented itself almost immediately. One week after the showdown at Shea, the two teams renewed acquaintances at Wrigley Field. The Real Mets vs. The Real Cubs.

66 JULY 15, 1969
METS 5 CUBS 4
WRIGLEY FIELD

For the Lip, reality bit, with the biggest chomp taken by the notable non-power hitter Al Weis. Weis — who required a recent hot streak to boost his batting average above .200 — entered the second of this North Side trio of games with all of four home runs in a major league career that dated back to 1962. The infielder was a White Sock from then through 1968, yet had never homered in the city of Chicago.

The Windy City drought ended when Weis took the measure of ex-Met Dick Selma (lost to San Diego in the expansion draft, not long after dealt to the Cubs for Joe Niekro) with a three-run, fourth-inning blast over the ivy, giving Gary Gentry a 4-1 lead he would not surrender. Weis's double play partner, Ken Boswell, also went deep off Selma, giving Gentry enough breathing room — with help from Ron Taylor — to secure a 5-4 Mets win.

Compared to Weis, Boswell was a bona fide slugger. He now had three home runs on the year. But as the Bleacher Bums and Cubs fans everywhere were figuring out this Tuesday afternoon, these Mets were more than the sum of their parts. Weis was a perfect example of how Gil Hodges moved his pieces around. Al normally platooned with Ken at second, but when Bud Harrelson was called away on military duty, Weis became the everyday shortstop and Boswell would be spelled as necessary by rookies Wayne Garrett and Bobby Pfeil. The five infielders together didn't bring to the fore the starpower of any one of the Cubs who manned the diamond (Ernie Banks, Glenn Beckert, Don Kessinger and Ron Santo, every one of them a 1969 All-Star selection), but they gelled as necessary, just like all of Hodges's charges were doing to everyone's surprise.

To definitively demonstrate to Durocher that he wasn't seeing anything inauthentic out of his sudden rivals, the Mets took the rubber game of the series the next day, 9-5, to pull within four games of the Cubs. One of the nine New York runs was accounted for by Al Weis...with his second home run in as many days.

Unreal.

67 JULY 20, 1969 (2ND)
METS 4 EXPOS 3 (10)
JARRY PARK

At 10:56 PM Eastern Daylight Time, on a Sunday night nowhere near Montreal — where the Mets had just split a doubleheader with the Expos — the prevailing wisdom of the 1960s was confirmed.

Man walked on the moon before the Mets won the pennant.

President John F. Kennedy might have wanted to trump the Soviets in the space race when, on May 25, 1961, he declared the nation's business "before this decade is out" should be dedicated to "landing a man on the moon and returning him safely to the earth". Yet as America moved ever closer to the late president's goal, it couldn't help but be noticed that man was nearing the moon with greater alacrity than the Mets were zeroing in on the first division. As late as the May 26, 1969, splashdown of Apollo 10, NASA's final pre-moon mission, the Mets were fourth of out of sixth in the N.L. East, four games below the surface of .500, their liftoff in the standings still the stuff of celestial dreams.

Now, on July 20, as Neil Armstrong was astonishing an entire planet with one small step for a man, one giant leap for mankind, the Mets were at least in the orbit of first place. They were second to the Cubs, five games from the top. They had never set foot so high in any standings. Their launch into the stratosphere of an honest-to-goodness pennant race was, in its baseball way, nearly as breathtaking as what the crew of Apollo 11 was accomplishing far from their little slice of earth...which was, unfortunately for them, an airport lounge in Montreal. On the night man landed on the moon, the Mets' charter home to New York was grounded due to mechanical difficulties.

The space program had had its misfires, too, but the moon eventually got reached. Perhaps the unwillingly earthbound Mets were just receiving a reminder that soaring toward the heavens never amounts to a smooth ride.

Or as Ron Swoboda put it impatiently at Dorval Airport, "How come we can send a rocket to the moon, but we can't get our plane off the ground?"

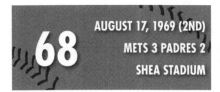

AUGUST 17, 1969 (2ND)

68

METS 3 PADRES 2

SHEA STADIUM

Some 84 miles north of Flushing, 3 Days of Peace & Music had been promised. At Shea Stadium, the draw was 4 Games of Pitching & Triumph. Both festivals delivered memorably.

The big story in New York this third weekend in August was taking place on Max Yasgur's farm in upstate Bethel: the Woodstock Music and Art Fair, arguably the most extraordinary pop culture event ever staged. It began on Friday night and wound through mud, storm and traffic to Monday morning. By Sunday afternoon, 400,000 would-be Age-of-Aquarians were encamped to listen to, among others, Joe Cocker, Country Joe and the Fish, Ten Years After and the Band.

Down in Flushing, the performers of note were Tom Seaver, Jim McAndrew, Jerry Koosman and Don Cardwell, and they were on the brink of creating a legend that, like Woodstock's, would extend well into the 21st century. Just as there was nothing like Woodstock before Woodstock, the 1969 Mets as they were about to be understood were truly taking shape at the very same time.

The Mets of 1969 were already the best Mets team ever, but by the middle of August, few were the hints that they were destined for transcendence. Since jarring the Cubs by taking four of six in two July series, the Mets had gone a very mortal 11-14, including six losses in six tries against Houston. Their young pitchers' arms ached, their heads-up play diminished (as evidenced by Gil Hodges's removal of Cleon Jones for not hustling after a ball in left field against the Astros) and their distance from first place lengthened. Heading into Woodstock weekend, the Mets had slipped into third place behind St. Louis and trailed Chicago by a daunting margin of 9 1/2 games. On top of it all, the same rains that softened the ground at Yasgur's farm forced a postponement of the Mets' Friday night opener versus the Padres. Thus, while the music played upstate (and the festival grew so memorably festive), the Mets would have to get in tune with back-to-back doubleheaders.

The concert got underway with more than a few hitches, but it fast took on a life of its own. The local *Times Herald-Record* headlined the affair a buffet of **FREEDOM, POT, SKINNY-DIPPING**, and that was after only the first night. As word from Woodstock reached the five boroughs, the tarp was being rolled up at Shea for Saturday's twinbill. While Country Joe fired up the masses in Bethel, the Mets were fixin' to sweep San Diego. Seaver fired a four-hit shutout in the opener, McAndrew and Tug McGraw combined on a four-hitter in the nightcap. The Mets won, 2-0 and 2-1.

Sunday, while everybody at Woodstock was recovering from the Grateful Dead, Creedence Clearwater Revival, Janis Joplin, Sly & the Family Stone, the Who and the Jefferson Airplane all in a row — not to mention everything else (**HIPPIES MIRED IN A SEA OF MUD**, the *Daily News* blared) — the team that played a few IRT stops from Woodside prepared for its second consecutive doubleheader. Even better at this moment of unprecedented enthusiasm for free expression, it was Banner Day. After the opener, won 3-2 on a Jerry Koosman five-hitter, bedsheets unfurled in Flushing, a good 3,612 of them. The winning entry celebrated "One Small Step for Hodges, One Giant Leap for Met-kind," reminding the 35,711 who skipped Woodstock that there was plenty going on among all worlds that summer.

The Mets, no squares, trotted out after the last of the fan banners breezed by with their annual placards of appreciation, spelling out for the fans that "You Turn Us On!"

So as not to disappoint those grooving on the Mets, the Amazins served notice they would not be dropping out of the pennant race anytime soon. Thirty-three year-old Don Cardwell, clearly of the pre-Woodstock generation (he once grabbed Ron Swoboda's love beads on a team flight and stuffed them in the trash; talk about a bad trip), spread good vibes nonetheless, giving up no runs while scattering eight hits over seven innings to hang tough in a scoreless duel with Clay Kirby. Cardwell finally received a little help from his friends once Buddy Harrelson tripled in two runs in the bottom of the seventh, and J.C. Martin, pinch-hitting for the pitcher, tacked on a sac fly. Though the Padres would manage a pair of runs off Cal Koonce and Ron Taylor, the Mets hung on to sweep their second doubleheader in two days with another 3-2 win, Cardwell's first since the Fourth of July.

If it wasn't exactly the "breakfast in bed for 400,000" Wavy Gravy and his Please Force were passing around, it was revelation enough for the crowd in Queens to chew on. The Mets who had stumbled through late July and early August were straightening up and about to fly right. By the time Jimi Hendrix was reinventing "The Star-Spangled Banner" early Monday morning in Bethel, the Mets had taken themselves higher in the N.L. East, flying over the Cardinals and edging to within eight games of the Cubs. Soon enough, they'd put the weight of a full-blown pennant race on Chicago — that four-game winning streak mounted at the expense of the Padres was on the verge of becoming a movement of Woodstock Nation proportions.

O ne of the best pitchers of his generation shut out the Mets for 13 1/3 innings and still couldn't beat them. Juan Marichal may have been on his way to the Hall of Fame, but the '69 Mets were on their way to a whole other level.

AUGUST 19, 1969
METS 1 GIANTS 0 (14)
SHEA STADIUM

Marichal was typically brilliant this Tuesday night at Shea, not allowing the Mets two baserunners in any one inning until the tenth and facing serious danger only through a fielding mishap in the twelfth, an episode that came to naught when Cleon Jones was thrown out at the plate. Gary Gentry was no piker, either, throwing ten scoreless frames. Tug McGraw took over in the eleventh, keeping the zeroes flowing, though you'd have to give an assist to his manager. With two out and nobody on in the top of the thirteenth, lethal lefty slugger Willie McCovey came up. Gil Hodges, truly protecting against the extra-base hit, convened a four-man outfield by moving third baseman Bobby Pfeil to the far left field corner and positioning Jones in the left-center power alley.

Hodges wasn't concerned with Stretch singling and he couldn't do much about him homering. But anything else that could be prevented the skipper was determined to prevent. And wouldn't you know it, mighty Willie swung and belted a ball to the fence — not quite high enough to be gone maybe, but plenty deep enough to be trouble if only three men had been patrolling Shea's outer pastures. Yet because Gil sent Cleon to left-center, it wasn't trouble. It wasn't easy, mind you: Jones had to leap and grab the ball backhanded, but he made the catch and got the Mets out of the inning.

The scoreless duel continued apace, Marichal setting down the next three Mets, McGraw retiring the next three Giants. Then, in the bottom of the fourteenth, after grounding Rod Gaspar back to the mound, Marichal finally proved human. He got a pitch up to Tommie Agee and Agee sent it where no outfielder — no matter how many you might have stuck out there — could stop it. Tommie's homer into the left field bullpen shattered Marichal's shutout and gave the Mets a 1-0 win for their fifth victory in a row.

70

AUGUST 30, 1969
METS 3 GIANTS 2 (10)
CANDLESTICK PARK

Y ou don't get out of the tangles the Mets found themselves in this Saturday afternoon at Candlestick Park. You just don't.

But the Mets did. That'll happen, apparently, when it's 1969.

Here's how the bottom of the eighth of this 2-2 game ended and how it stayed 2-2, per Retrosheet:

> [Ken] Boswell caught popup and threw toward home, but [Ken] Henderson was retreating to third. Throw hit first base coach [Wes] Westrum and [Donn] Clendenon retrieved it to throw out Henderson who crashed into catcher [Jerry] Grote.

You got that?

Ken Henderson was on third as a pinch-runner and go-ahead run with one out. Jim Davenport hit a popup behind second. Boswell caught it in the outfield. His throw home was not a good one — it indeed hit Westrum, former manager of the Mets, then coaching first base for San Fran. Henderson was scurrying back to third at that instant. Seeing Wes inadvertently get in the way of the play, Ken reversed his scurry and dashed for home. But Clendenon saw what was going on, picked up the ball and threw it to Grote to complete a sudden 4-3-8 double play.

You ain't seen nothing yet, however, because you ain't seen the bottom of the ninth, when it was still 2-2, with one out:

> *Big shift against [Willie] McCovey who sliced double down left field line. Grote waited casually at plate, pretending no throw was coming, then lunged at last moment to tag [Bob] Burda. Grote rolled the ball to the mound, thinking there were 3 outs. Clendenon retrieved ball and threw to [Bobby] Pfeil for out.*

Where to start?

Let's see...Gil Hodges had put a modified version of his McCovey shift into effect. Ol' Stretch crossed it up and hit it the other way.

As Gaspar chased the ball down (he had just been inserted for defense in the eighth; Art Shamsky got the start that day), Bob Burda, who had been on first, decided to try to score.

Gaspar heaved to Grote.

Grote pulled the DEAD MAN play, acting as if absolutely nothing of interest was taking shape. But the throw came, allowing him to tag the surprised Burda for the second out of the inning.

It was such a supreme moment of deception that Grote stayed in character and continued to portray a clueless catcher. In other words, he casually rolled the ball to the mound because he forgot that THERE WERE ONLY TWO OUT.

Dead man, indeed.

McCovey saw this incredible faux pas unfold and, from second, started steaming toward third. It was Clendenon to the rescue again. Donn grabbed the ball and threw it to third baseman Bobby Pfeil who tagged McCovey for...the...uh...7-2-3-5 double play.

Then Clendenon homered in the top of the tenth off starter Gaylord Perry. And, in the bottom of the tenth, with two out, Swoboda lost Bobby Etheridge's fly ball in the sun...but found it at the last second so the Mets could hold on to win, 3-2. They snapped the Giants' nine-game winning streak and, presumably, broke their spirit (San Francisco was in an N.L. West dogfight, and their divisional lead had just been reduced to one game).

As for the Mets...well, geez, they're the 1969 Mets for a reason.

It was a milestone that, before 1967, seemed out of the Mets' grasp for at least another generation. Come 1967, you knew it was only a matter of time.

Three years' time, as it turned out.

Tom Seaver was a break with all that had gone on before in Metsdom, won-lost records included. Mets fans saw it when he racked up 16 wins in 1967 and another 16 in 1968. His ownership of the franchise record for most wins by a starting pitcher in one year was eclipsed during his sophomore campaign when Jerry Koosman attained a spectacular 19 of his own, but Seaver was still the yardstick for what a Met pitcher — and what the Mets — could be.

In early September of 1969, the Mets were aiming higher than ever, including Seaver, who came into this first game of a Friday doubleheader at Shea against the Phillies with a 19-7 record, having already matched Koosman's '68 number with a month to go, not having lost since the middle of July. The team was in second place, five games behind the Cubs. That the Mets were bearing down on first-place Chicago was the most accurate barometer of how far the Mets had come in such a short time, but the fact that they possessed a starting pitcher on the precipice of a heretofore unthinkable Met milestone...just chalk it up as another Amazin' element of a season whose most magical properties were yet to be revealed.

Seaver was never much for magic. He was skill and competitiveness, so why shouldn't he be 19-7? Better yet, why shouldn't he be 20-7?

A second-inning leadoff single to Johnny Callison and an RBI triple to Deron Johnson would provide a momentary impediment to Tom's provisional aspirations, but the Phillies didn't score anything else and their 1-0 lead was short-lived. In the bottom of the second, two Grant Jackson walks (to Ron Swoboda and Rod Gaspar) sandwiched a Richie Allen error (on a Grote grounder) to load the bases for Al Weis. Weis singled off Jackson's glove to put one on the board for the Mets, and Seaver's subsequent infield groundout, thanks to Weis's tough takeout slide at second, became two unearned runs as Gaspar hustled home behind Grote.

With a two-run advantage, Seaver's businesslike instincts kicked in. He was perfect in four of the next six innings and allowed two unrelated hits in the two other frames. When Grote added a two-run homer off John Boozer in the bottom of the eighth, that matter of time was reduced to only three outs.

Allen grounded out. Callison struck out. Johnson was all that stood between a Met and a milestone. A one-two count set the stage. Ralph Kiner calls it:

> "No pitcher for the Mets has won twenty ballgames in their history. Seaver's one strike away. Here's the one-two pitch...swung on and missed, strike three! So Tom Seaver becomes the first twenty-game winner in Mets history, the first twenty-game winner in the National League, and the Mets win it by a score of five to one."

An economy of words for an economic effort. Though Mets fans had waited nearly eight years for such a moment, Seaver expended a mere one hour and fifty-two minutes capturing it. Five hits, one walk, seven strikeouts...yes, very much a vintage Tom Terrific effort in the kind of year an older Seaver would not hesitate to bottle, pour and savor.

His work in the pitching vineyard was just that sublime.

SEPTEMBER 8, 1969
METS 3 CUBS 2
SHEA STADIUM

The first-place Chicago Cubs were ready to take a historic tumble. All they needed was a little nudge.

The New York Mets were more than happy to provide it.

While the Mets were gaining steam in the second half of August and the first week of September, the Cub juggernaut had begun to take on water. Every hint of righting the ship was negated by an undeniably wrong turn. The latest evidence that the 1969 Cubs weren't quite what they were cracked up to be came via the four-game losing streak with which they were saddled as they made their way to New York for a two-game showdown with the Mets. There was never supposed to be a showdown with the Mets. As recently as September 2, the Cubs had won their fifth in a row, allowing them to reopen a five-game lead on the Flushing upstarts. It may not have been the nine by which they led the pack as late as August 16, but it was still pretty formidable.

Besides, who was chasing them? The Mets. The same team manager Leo Durocher derided as "the real Mets" after a July loss. Durocher surely knew more about baseball than the mayor of New York City, yet it was John Lindsay — clinging to the speeding Mets' express as he sought unlikely re-election — who read the landscape more accurately when he sent a message to the Cubs' skipper via Gil Hodges:

"Tell Leo Chicago is still the second city."

Durocher offered a response unprintable for the family newspapers of 1969, but the Lip was never afraid to speak his mind or incite an opponent. Almost two months to the day since sparring with the mayor and the Mets, Durocher returned to New York to discover "second" was part of his immediate future.

Chicago's nine-game lead that became a five-game lead was now down to 2 1/2. The real Mets were proving unstoppable of late, winning 18 of 24. One of Leo's minions thought he had the answer to their relentless upward trajectory.

Knock them down.

That was what Cub starter Bill Hands attempted to do to Mets leadoff hitter Tommie Agee in the bottom of the first this cool, rainy Monday night. Hands came up, high and tight with chin music aimed at Agee's coconut (a head that had absorbed a pitch from Bob Gibson to commence his first Spring Training as a Met in 1968). Agee was dusted. Hands was pleased. "I was not *told* to do it," Bill insisted to Rick Talley, author of *The Cubs of '69*, nearly two decades later. "I just *did* it."

If Hands's strong-arm tactics were supposed to send the Mets a message, the wires got crossed en route to home plate. True, Agee grounded out in that first plate appearance, but the Mets weren't scared off. If anything, they were ready to retaliate. The first batter Jerry Koosman saw in the top of the second was Ron Santo, he who irked Mets and Mets fans alike earlier in the year with his post-victory heel-clicking. No heel-clicking here. Maybe just some furtive wrist-rubbing after Kooz let Hands (and Santo) know that "just *doing* it" would come with payback.

"I don't mind getting knocked down," Agee said later. "As long as my pitcher retaliates."

Nobody ordered Jerry to take out Ron. It was just what needed to be done, and he did it. "Our pitchers," Gil Hodges advised, "know all about taking care of our people."

Hands would try to get even by coming inside at Koosman in a later at-bat, but the most effective response of the evening came a batter later when Agee let Hands know he was just fine. Tommie homered with Bud Harrelson on base to give the Mets a 2-0 lead in the third. The Cubs answered with a pair of runs in the sixth, but once again, Agee's bat got very talkative in the bottom of the inning. He led off against Hands with a hustle double to left. When Wayne Garrett singled to right, Agee took off for third and just kept going. There was a play at the plate...a very close play. Cubs catcher Randy Hundley applied a swipe tag to the thinnest of air that separated his mitt from Agee's body.

Tommie was safe. The Mets led three to two...no matter Hundley's endless stream of objections. They began the instant after Satch Davidson ruled in the Mets' favor — Randy jumped high enough to match his dudgeon — and they never really stopped. Twenty years later, Hundley was still complaining that Davidson got the call wrong.

"I tagged him so hard I almost dropped the ball," Hundley swore to Talley. "Right up his bloomin' side. It wasn't just a little tag: I swept him right up the uniform. I was really afraid I would drop the bloomin' ball."

For all of Randy Hundley's protestations, the only thing bloomin' that frenzied night in New York was Koosman's strikeout total. Jerry had fanned seven through six, and added five over the next three to give him thirteen on the night. When it was over, Koosman had a complete game 3-2 victory and the Mets were within 1 1/2 of the Cubs. The baker's dozen worth of K's were dandy, all right, but what meant the most to the Mets was Koosman standing up for Agee — and all his teammates — when he let Leo know that those knockdown tactics of Hands's were a nonstarter.

"He tried to run us out of the ballpark on the very first pitch," one Met said of the opposing skipper, "and he found out that he couldn't do it."

T uesday night. Shea Stadium. A black cat appears.

Is that all she wrote?

With apologies to Polo Grounds resident beagle Homer and 1979 mascot Mettle the Mule (and, for that matter, George "The Stork"

73

SEPTEMBER 9, 1969
METS 7 CUBS 1
SHEA STADIUM

Theodore), the unnamed black cat that crossed in front of the visitors' dugout when it was full of Chicago Cubs is the most famous animal in New York Mets history. He was plainly working for the home team when he seemingly sought out — depending on whose version you believe — Glenn Beckert, Ron Santo or Leo Durocher, and irreversibly altered the luck quotient of the 1969 pennant race. The Cubs who came to town as the holders of the longest-lived lead the National League East had ever seen (in, granted, the first year there was a National League East), would be leaving with their proverbial tails tucked between their hind legs.

And the Mets were clearing their collective throat to roar the roar of a fresh, new frontrunner.

It was a night to say hello to one legend and bid a derisive adieu to another.

Foregoing the question of where that cat came from anyway, who was he intending to spook? The whole Cubs team, broadly, but specifically? A wire-service photo that appeared in papers nationwide the next day identified the Cub in the on-deck circle past whom the Flushing feline of foreboding padded as second baseman Beckert; his face and uniform number were obscured, but he was the second batter in the visitors' lineup, and since the episode is generally recalled as occurring as the game got underway, Glenn was a logical candidate. Later accounts, however, fingered the victim of furry misfortune as Santo, and, indeed, the third baseman turned announcer definitely created a lucrative sideline from autographing copies of the image.

Rick Talley, in *The Cubs of '69*, meanwhile, deduced the kitty had another target in mind, observing that as the cat "ran back and forth in front of the bench as if trained, Leo the Lion stared straight ahead."

Nobody ever accused that cat Durocher of not being hip to what was going on around him.

On whomever he set his gaze, the black cat was recognized immediately as bad luck for one team, and not the other. Richard Dozer in the next day's *Chicago Tribune* described a first inning in which "the frightened feline reversed his course and dashed under the stands to safety on the other side, next to the Mets' dugout." And years later, Shea's head groundskeeper Pete Flynn recalled in the book, *Moments in the Sun,* "He looked in the dugout and gave them the jinx. The cat came from behind home plate and went in front of the Cubs dugout. It was a bizarre moment."

Most bizarre of all, at least from the perspective of past performance, was how the Mets had been making their own luck dating back to August 16. They'd won 21 of 27 entering the Night of the Cat, while the Cubs didn't need any superstitions gone awry to tell them things weren't going their way any longer. Since August 20, they'd lost 12 of 19. The table-turning had placed the Mets only a game-and-half-back before the cat reared its (depending on your allegiance) adorable or ominous head.

Once the cat had his say, it was the Cubs who were put out. In the bottom of the first, after Chicago had gone down in order, two Ferguson Jenkins walks set the stage for Ken Boswell to double home two runs and give Tom Seaver as much lead as he'd need. Seaver was money by this point in the 1969 season. Certainly his manager thought so. As Bob Sales of the *Boston Globe* noted, Gil Hodges neatly printed on his lineup card, as the Mets' ninth-place hitter, "$eaver – P".

Tom didn't give up anything for three innings, long enough for the Mets to increase their margin, thanks to a botched Cubs pickoff attempt that didn't erase leadfooted Art Shamsky at second and a succeeding two-run homer from Donn Clendenon. The Cubs manufactured one run in the top of the fourth, but Seaver personally got it back when he doubled in the bottom of the inning and came around on a fielder's choice and sacrifice fly. A Shamsky home run and a Jerry Grote RBI double eventually elevated the Mets' advantage to 7-1.

Which wasn't enough to bring out the cat for an encore but was plenty of cue for the 58,436 in attendance (51,448 paid) to serve as *Hallelujah!* chorus behind Seaver. They took out handkerchiefs, they waved them in the general direction of the third base dugout and they serenaded the Chicago manager with a new twist on an old favorite.

> *Goodbye Leo!*
> *Goodbye Leo!*
> *Goodbye Leo!*
> *We hate to see you go!*

It was splendid accompaniment to Seaver's 21st win of the season, as was Karl Ehrhardt's extraordinarily topical sign held aloft in the box seats not far from where the serenadee sat and fumed:

TOOTHLESS CUBS — JUST A LOTTA LIP

"These fans," Durocher was heard to grumble as he was heckled en route to the team bus, "they're not goin' after any maiden." Yet in other, seemingly distant lifetimes, Durocher was one of them. He had been a New Yorker. He played (albeit without distinction) with Babe Ruth on the Yankees. He cajoled the Dodgers to the 1941 pennant, Brooklyn's first in 21 years. His guile was behind the miraculous Giant comeback of 1951 and front and center for New York's last National League world champions in 1954. Now, however, Leo the Lip was on the wrong side of the field and the wrong end of a miracle in the making. The usually garrulous manager had only this to say to reporters after Seaver completed the 7-1 defanging of the once proud Lion and sliced what was left of the Cubs' divisional lead to a fragile half-game:

"No comment. No [bleeping] comment."

74 SEPTEMBER 10, 1969 (1ST)
METS 3 EXPOS 2 (12)
SHEA STADIUM

The Mets were going to ascend into first place sooner or later. It's just that nobody would have ever bet on sooner.

Ever...at least not the ever that started in 1962 and rolled on until a few weeks before, when the Mets were improved, but still a light year or two from first. But that was all prehistoric times now. The New York Mets who couldn't be mentioned in the same sentence with first place no longer existed. They'd been replaced with a couple of dozen fellows who wore uniforms eerily similar to those of their predecessors, but the resemblance ended once these Mets took the field and deposited their results in the standings.

This was a franchise for whom finishes above last place were news, and there were only two of those in seven seasons. Precedent indicated that would be a reasonable Met goal again. In 1969, the birth of the first expansion team in their time zone since then figured to guarantee the newly created six-team National League East's basement would be furnished with Montreal Expos paraphernalia. Sure enough, the Mets didn't spend any time in sixth.

More aspiration? The Philadelphia Phillies — featuring a disgruntled Richie Allen and little else — loomed as pretty crummy; the Mets finished only three games behind them in 1968. The Phils fell into fifth to stay by late May. That meant last *and* next-to-last were occupied by teams who weren't the Mets.

Higher up the food chain were the Pittsburgh Pirates, a sub-.500 team the year before and, despite the dangerous bats belonging to Roberto Clemente and Willie Stargell, not considered pitching-laden enough to be a serious contender heading into '69. By June, the Mets had put the Pirates in their rearview mirror.

The St. Louis Cardinals were a heavy favorite to contend for their third consecutive league championship — or divisional championship, anyway. But the Redbirds were grounded early. Save for a brief Cards resurgence in mid-August that coincided with the Mets groping to find themselves, St. Louis was not a direct challenger to ascendant New York. The Mets spent the bulk of 1969 ahead of the once-threatening Cardinals.

Let's review:
Sixth place? Not the Mets.
Fifth place? Not the Mets.
Fourth place? Not the Mets.
Third place? Not the Mets.

Second place? That was the Mets most every day from June 3 through September 9. It was a hellacious accomplishment considering the humble beginnings that never completely shook off their humility for seven years. The Mets were better than everybody in their immediate sphere except for one team: the mighty Chicago Cubs.

But the Cubs, as the Mets had just witnessed, were no longer mighty by September. Leo Durocher had brought them to Shea for two games and they left town with two losses. The separation between Chicago and New York in the standings — which, when the Cubs were running away with the division, felt like the 789.4 miles measured by Rand McNally — was down to a half-game.

A half-game? That's a day's work as baseball math goes. You win and your prey loses, you've got it. You've got first place. The Mets couldn't take on the Cubs directly, but they could make a pretty significant push on their own, as they were playing the last-place Expos twice this Wednesday evening at Shea. True, the Cubs were down in Philadelphia, taking on the next-to-last place Phillies, but in their case, other teams' positions hardly mattered.

The Cubs had met the enemy, and it was as much them as it was whomever they were playing. They were also going up against the specter of the Mets, who suddenly couldn't lose, and the surging relentlessness of the schedule. That the Cubs had to play anybody was bad news for them. That the Mets would have two shots at the Expos... let's just say moving day loomed.

The Mets made their move first. Their doubleheader started well ahead of the Cubs' single night game at Connie Mack Stadium. To add a little drama to the prevailing trends, the Mets and Expos — knotted at two from the fifth inning on — needed to go to extra innings in their opener. Until they had a final, the standings couldn't budge even temporarily...no matter how much they were plainly dying to.

In the bottom of the twelfth, after Bill Stoneman got two quick outs, Cleon Jones singled and Rod Gaspar walked. Ken Boswell came to the plate. Here is how Ralph Kiner described the climactic swing:

> *"The pitch is hit through the middle, it's gonna go into center field, a base hit and the Mets will win it! Coming around to score is Cleon Jones, and the Mets have won the ballgame, three to two, on the base hit.*
> *"So for the first time in the history of the New York Mets, they have gone into first place!"*

The standings, as of September 10, 1969, 8:43 PM Eastern Daylight Time, couldn't have been more provisional. The Mets and Expos had another game to play, while the Cubs and Phillies were still in progress down the New Jersey Turnpike. Nevertheless, the fans knew they were in on an unprecedented moment, declaring, in case anybody missed it...

WE'RE NUMBER ONE!
WE'RE NUMBER ONE!
WE'RE NUMBER ONE!

Their assertion was confirmed by the Shea scoreboard:

LOOK WHO'S NO. 1

It wasn't the Cubs anymore. The NY METS were listed as having WON 83 and LOST 57. That information was posted one line above the record of the CHI CUBS, who had WON 84 and LOST 58. The all-important PCT. was included to let every Sheagoer and the entirety of the free world know the Mets held an advantage of .593 to .592.

That was it. It would be referred to as one percentage point, but technically it was one one-thousandth of one percent. In the jargon of Chesterfield Cigarette ads of the era, the Mets' winning percentage was no more than a silly millimeter longer than the Cubs'. But it was longer. And larger. And bigger. And better.

The Mets were No. 1. By the end of the night, the Phillies downed the Cubs, 6-2, and the Mets (behind Nolan Ryan's complete game, eleven-strikeout, three-hitter in the nightcap) swept Montreal, 3-2 and 7-1. That translated to a full one-game lead for the Mets.

The first-place Mets, that is.

The Mets had just made the cover of *Time* magazine as "Baseball's Wunderkinder", and now they were set to keep making the kind of news that would capture an underdog-loving nation's fancy.

Though Mets players might have disputed the notion that talent and ability weren't responsible for their headlines, nobody with a grip on basic baseball statistics would contend they were winning because of offense. Defense? Solid. Pitching? Outstanding. Hitting?

On this Friday at Forbes Field, hitting would have to be filed under "pitching".

Against the Pirates in the first game of a twinight doubleheader, Jerry Koosman pitched a characteristic gem: a three-hitter that carried the day, 1-0. What made it unique was the lone run the Mets managed was driven in by...Jerry Koosman. A notoriously unskilled hitter (he finished the game batting .056), Jerry singled to right with Bobby Pfeil on third in the fifth against Bob Moose. When the game went final, it could be said Kooz did something no Met pitcher had ever done: win a 1-0 game in which he drove in the only run.

That distinction would grow not nearly so distinct in the second game of the doubleheader. This time, the Mets' starter was Don Cardwell, crafty on the mound and competent at the plate. Don was a veritable slugger among hurlers, having blasted 15 homers since 1957, including one a year in each of the three years he had been a Met. So it couldn't have been too shocking to Pittsburgh starter Dock Ellis that Cardwell reached him for a run-scoring single in the second to put New York up, 1-0. And the eight innings of four-hit ball registered by Cardwell wasn't wholly surprising, either.

The Amazin' part is that when Don drove in Ron Swoboda from second in the second, that was all the scoring anybody would see in this nightcap. Ellis was brilliant the rest of the way, striking out eleven over eight, giving way to Chuck Hartenstein, who pitched a scoreless ninth. Tug McGraw succeeded Cardwell and closed out the Bucs for the 1-0 win...which meant the Mets won a 1-0 game in which their starting pitcher drove in the only run.

Again.

It had never happened in any Mets game before and suddenly it was happening twice in the same doubleheader.

Koosman's and Cardwell's feat would remain iconic in all future retellings of 1969, but it should be given its due as an overall Met rarity as well. Only three other pitchers turned the same trick, if that's what it can be called: Buzz Capra, in 1972; Ray Sadecki, in 1974; and Nino Espinosa, in 1977. It hasn't happened since.

Neither has 1969.

H e would go down as one of the all-time greats. And he threw one of the most overpowering games of his life. And it did him absolutely no good.

Meet Steve Carlton: 24, hard-throwing, ultracompetitive and getting better all the time. One of the real southpaw comers in the National League. Won 27 games total in his first two full seasons and pitched in consecutive World Series for St. Louis. Named to a pair of All-Star teams. Already had 16 wins in the bank and an ERA under two entering a Monday night at Busch Stadium where Carlton would show his stuff like he'd never shown it before.

But it would still do him absolutely no good, because Steve Carlton would be meeting the Mets.

Not good acquaintances to make in the midst of September 1969.

The Mets had just come off a ten-game winning streak and stood 3 1/2 games ahead of the Cubs in the National League East. A Sunday loss in Pittsburgh leveled them off at 30 games above .500, yet even in a 5-3 defeat, they banged out 11 hits off Pirate starter Steve Blass. The Mets could pitch and the Mets could field...if the Mets were to suddenly start hitting with any consistency, then there'd be no chance of anybody stopping them — not even a talented lefty like Carlton.

Gil Hodges called on those who could swing from the right side to ignite a new winning streak: Al Weis at second; Ed Charles at third; Donn Clendenon at first; Amos Otis in for an injured Cleon Jones in left; and Ron Swoboda in right to go with regulars Bud Harrelson, Tommie Agee and Jerry Grote. Factor in starter Gary Gentry, and that was seven righties and two switch-hitters. Hodges, an old Marine, believed in platoons.

This night, however, he would have needed a battalion to halt Carlton, for it didn't matter from which side of the plate the Mets swung. Everybody was taking a turn at missing what Steve threw. Harrelson struck out to start the game. Otis struck out looking behind him. An error and a base hit followed, but Swoboda struck out to end the frame. Steve Carlton wasn't perfect in the first, but he had struck out the side.

A pattern was established. Weis would single in the second, but the other three Mets who came up all struck out. Agee struck out to end the third, giving Carlton seven K's in three innings. It was a record-setting pace.

Down 1-0 in the fourth, the Mets rallied by way of a Clendenon walk and a Swoboda swing that connected: a two-run homer to give Gentry the lead. Unrattled, Carlton handled the next four batters as such: strikeout, strikeout, single, strikeout. That made it ten whiffs in four innings. His pace was still record-setting.

In the fifth, two more. In the sixth — after the Cards took a 3-2 lead — another. And in the seventh, with two on and two out, Otis went down looking. Fourteen strikeouts after seven innings, or four from tying the major league record for most in a nine-inning game. Bob Feller struck out 18 in a loss to Detroit in 1938; Sandy Koufax punched out 18 twice, in 1959 and 1962; and Don Wilson of the Astros tied the mark during 1968's Year of the Pitcher.

One Met in Hodges's lineup had experienced a night very much like this before. Ron Swoboda struck out three times against Cincinnati's Jim Maloney in 1965 as Maloney no-hit the Mets for ten innings en route to losing to New York, 1-0, on Johnny Lewis's leadoff home run in the top of the eleventh. Swoboda was the batter up directly after Lewis and became Maloney's 18th victim. It was Rocky's third strikeout of that game.

Here, in St. Louis, the 25-year-old outfielder, who was one of the handful of '69 Mets to commence his career under Casey Stengel, represented two of Carlton's 14 strikeouts. But he was also responsible for the only two Met runs on the board through seven. Thus, after Agee singled to lead off the eighth, and Clendenon became strikeout victim No. 15, there was precedent for what Swoboda was about to do.

Though that didn't make it any less mind-boggling when Swoboda swung not through a Carlton pitch but right at it, belting it out of Busch for his second two-run homer of the night. The Mets now led, 4-3. There was little for Carlton to do but rear back and finish the inning with one more strikeout — No. 16 — and then set down the Mets on three consecutive strikeouts in the ninth. When he fanned reliever Tug McGraw, Harrelson and Otis (the fourth time the rookie left fielder whiffed), Carlton had the record: Nineteen strikeouts in nine innings.

What he didn't have was an opportunity to win his overpowering start unless the Redbirds rallied in the bottom of the ninth. Two runners reached against McGraw, but Tug had an idea about not besmirching a story that seemed too good to be true. He didn't give up any runs and the Mets came away 4-3 winners on the night they were struck out 19 times...more than any team had ever been struck out in regulation.

Every Met starter, plus McGraw, had fanned at least once. And the Mets won anyway.

What could Carlton say? Back in the days when Lefty wasn't so reticent to speak to the media, he explained he came to the ballpark late because of a fever, yet found himself on the mound with "the best stuff I ever had".

Swoboda, on the other hand, was on a team enjoying a season cooked up in a Mets fan's fevered dream, and it countered anything a future Hall of Famer could bring. "He'd throw a pitch so good," the improbable star of the game attested, "that I'd say to myself, 'if he throws two more like it, there's no way I can touch him.'"

Yet he laid two pretty good hands on him, marinating the tone that the Mets had set for improbable outcomes in September 1969 and perhaps foreshadowing what was to come for Carlton down the road. Steve started 76 games against the Mets in a National League tenure that lasted until 1986. He put up impressive numbers against them: a 3.12 ERA, a WHIP of 1.222 and more strikeouts against the Mets — 464 — than he had versus any other team. But nobody beat Steve Carlton more often than did the Mets, just as the Mets beat Steve Carlton more than they did any other pitcher in their first half-century of baseball. In a career that was put into the books at 329-244, Carlton's record against New York finished a pedestrian 30-36.

And he'd be sharing his strikeout record with a Met by the following April.

"Tonight the New York Mets and the Saint Louis Cardinals. The Mets have a magic number of one. This afternoon, the Chicago Cubs won their ballgame from Montreal by a score of six to three

SEPTEMBER 24, 1969
METS 6 CARDINALS 0
SHEA STADIUM

to keep alive their chance for a tie for the championship. So the Mets' magic number is one; a Met victory here tonight would clinch the championship in the Eastern Division of the National League. So we have a big, big crowd on hand for this concluding game of the series."
—Lindsey Nelson, pregame

Seven years removed from the humblest beginnings imaginable. Two years removed from 101 losses. One year removed from a place so low that the standings didn't include it anymore. Light years removed from what the human imagination could have conjured six months before. The longest of long shots six weeks earlier. Yet for two weeks, nobody couldn't have known this was coming.

It was still beyond the realm of the imagination, but there was no stopping it. The New York Mets were about to become champions. Champions of the National League's Eastern Division, but it might as well have been the universe. Just by arriving on the edge of clinching, they were the champions of possibility. They were the champions of wishing and hoping and praying, if not necessarily thinking, because thinking would have guided any sane person away from this scenario. They were the champions of faith.

And this Wednesday night, the final scheduled home game of 1969, may merit the title of champion of all regular-season games in Mets history. Considering where the Mets had come from and where they would go shortly thereafter, no Mets win in the first half-century the team existed — or maybe ever — could possibly mean quite as much.

"Hello everybody, it's Lou Brock coming around to lead off now for the Saint Louis Cardinals in what is, for the Mets and Mets fans, the biggest baseball game ever played in this stadium."
—Lindsey Nelson, top of the first

Was there any way the Mets were going to lose this game? Putting aside whatever latter-day metrics might tell us retroactively about win probability; and the factors that might have influenced this matchup — Steve Carlton was 17-10, Gary Gentry was 11-12, the Mets were 11-6 vs. the Cards; and the eternal truth that it's anybody's ballgame, particularly before one starts...no, the Mets were not going to lose this ballgame.

The Mets were going to use this ballgame as the template for all celebratory events to come. They and the 54,928 on hand needed the practice. They'd never had anything concrete to celebrate before other than themselves. Mets fans led the league in mere happiness to be here — that there were Mets to root for and that they were the ones doing it.

Even Leo Durocher's Cubs cooperated. The former frontrunners had lost nine of fourteen coming into their afternoon action. Had they dropped their matinee to sixth-/

last-place Montreal, the Mets would have been in Anticlimax City. But they beat the Expos, less keeping their own chances alive than making sure the party in Flushing would be more than hugs and hearty handshakes.

> *"Carlton strikes out Jones. First strikeout for Carlton. Donn Clendenon's coming up. Clendenon's hitting Two Forty-Six, he has thirteen homers and forty-five runs batted in. Lefthander Steve Carlton checks the runners, here's the pitch to Clendenon, swung on and hit DEEP to center! Way back, Flood goes back into the track, it's going, going, it's gone, it's a home run! A home run for Clendenon! Donn Clendenon hit a three-run homer over the center field fence. The Mets are out in front by a score of three to nothing, one man out, nobody on and Ron Swoboda coming up."*
> *—Lindsey Nelson, bottom of the first*

Donn Clendenon, 34, was acquired for nights like these. Not that there were nights like these in the Mets' past, but GM Johnny Murphy and manager Gil Hodges were intent on making sure there'd be a few in the near future when they pulled the trigger on a four-for-one deal with Montreal at the June 15 trading deadline. They had to give up a quartet of youngsters. One of them, Kevin Collins, had been a Met on and off since 1965 — he pinch-hit on Opening Day against the Expos. One of them, Steve Renko, had pitched at Wrigley Field that very afternoon of September 24, taking the well-timed loss in front of 52,711 fewer people than would be at Shea Stadium this night. The other two fellows, Bill Carden and Dave Colon, never reached the majors. Collins played in the bigs until 1971. Renko had a representative career, winning 134 games (while losing 146) from 1969 until 1983.

Steve Renko was still pitching and occasionally winning more than a decade after Donn Clendenon retired. Renko theoretically could have helped the Mets throughout the 1970s and into the 1980s. But that didn't matter. The distant future, that time toward which the Youth of America had been mythically developing since Shea Stadium was under construction, was no longer the Mets' nebulous aim. The Mets in the middle of June 1969 decided they were a "now" team. They now needed a power-hitting first baseman, a veteran righty complement to the prematurely ancient if technically 24-year-old Ed Kranepool.

Clendenon's three-run homer off Carlton marked the instant "now" arrived. Four prospects were a scant price to pay for that 3-0 lead.

> *"Low and away for a ball, it's two-two. I got a letter this week from an army chaplain in Korea saying that the United States servicemen there were pulling for and following the fortunes of the New York Mets day by day. Here's a swing, a fly ball to deep right field, Flood going back into the track, he's way back there, and he leaps up, can't get it! Home run! A home run for Ed Charles! A two-run homer! Ed Charles hit his third home run of the year over the right field fence, the right-center field fence, a two-run homer that scored Swoboda ahead of him,*

the New York Mets are leading five-nothing, and that is all for Steve
Carlton! The sign has gone to the bullpen now for Dave Giusti."
                                        —*Lindsey Nelson, bottom of the first*

Ed Kranepool, born in November 1944, made his major league debut in 1962. Ed Charles, born in April 1933, made his major league debut in 1962.

Something was wrong with this picture, and it had nothing to do with the high hopes and big bonus applied to the 17-year-old Kranepool. Charles should have been a major league infielder in the 1950s. He was a .300 hitter in Class C ball at age 18. He maintained that level his next couple of seasons as he climbed the Braves chain before and after a stint in the military. He reached Triple-A for the first time in 1956 and put all the lower minors behind him by 1958.

And there, it seemed, Ed Charles was left, an experienced, skilled minor leaguer in his sixth...seventh...eighth...ninth year in the pros. The Braves never brought him up from Triple-A.

Couldn't have anything to do with a quota system that informally limited the number of black players on any given roster, could it?

Charles thought so. Prevailing evidence doesn't suggest otherwise. Ed Charles may not have been a player the caliber of incumbent Braves third baseman Eddie Mathews, but he certainly should have been given a shot long before Eddie Kranepool got one. Charles was a native of the Jim Crow South, Daytona Beach, Fla. His inspiration was the sight of Jackie Robinson playing Spring Training baseball in 1946, the year before he broke the major league color line (another "informal" obstacle) with Brooklyn. Jackie may have integrated baseball, but he didn't make the business end of it color-blind.

Ed didn't get his break until Milwaukee traded him to the Kansas City A's, where he put up respectable numbers for a hopeless organization. As he established himself in the American League, the Glider, as he was known, became intent on making his own luck as much as he could, displaying "a discipline and humility that is rarely seen in the clubhouse," by George Vecsey's *Joy in Mudville* reckoning. "He began attending college in his late twenties and wrote inspirational poetry, paying for the printing and mailing it to young fans who asked for autographs."

When the Mets traded Larry Elliot (and cash) to Kansas City in May 1967 to get Charles, they got more than a third baseman. They got a man who, per Vecsey, "drew the Met players closer together with his warmth and maturity." In July 1969, Charles took it upon himself to pen a team song. The Mets had just taken two of three at Wrigley Field, and the man who personified perseverance adapted new lyrics to an old standard:

> *East Side, West Side*
> *Word is goin' round*
> *When late October comes*
> *The Mets will wear the crown*

Two months later, as the righthanded half of a third base platoon on a first-place team, Ed drew them two runs closer to a championship.

"In case you joined us along the way, the New York Mets got five runs in the bottom of the first. Harrelson singled and Agee walked. After Jones struck out, Clendenon hit a three-run homer. Swoboda walked and Charles hit a two-run homer, and that was all for the starter Steve Carlton. Dave Giusti came in to relieve him, here's Giusti's pitch. Hit DEEP to right, that's WAY back there, it's going, going...and it is GONE for a home run for Clendenon, his second home run of the night! The Mets are leading six to nothing. Home run number fifteen for Donn Clendenon, over the right field wall and into the Met bullpen."
—Lindsey Nelson, bottom of the fifth

Has any in-season trade in Mets history paid the immediate dividends that the Donn Clendenon deal did? They got him in the middle of June and well before September was over, they had a single-digit magic number. Who else effected that kind of result? Even Keith Hernandez, acquired exactly 14 years later, didn't make that quick a difference.

In Stanley Cohen's 1988 retrospective, *A Magic Summer*, it is instructive to reread how Donn Clendenon's teammates recalled him almost twenty years on. "The catalyst," according to Art Shamsky; "a take-the-pressure-off kind of guy," said Tug McGraw; "probably the key to our whole season," in Wayne Garrett's mind — "the ingredient we needed."

Were 35 RBIs ever as important as those Donn Clendenon collected between June 22 and September 24, up to and including the bottom of the fifth when his second home run of the night increased the Mets' lead to six? He played in only 72 games for New York in '69 because he platooned with Kranepool. Think about that for a moment. The fates of a franchise, a city and maybe a sagging sport searching for a scintillating storyline pivoted on the presence of a man whose manager deemed he split time with, well, Eddie Kranepool. But Kranepool plus Clendenon, along with Ken Boswell plus Al Weis, Wayne Garrett plus Ed Charles, and Art Shamsky plus Ron Swoboda added up to the sum of Gil Hodges's parts. Their generally slight individual numbers may have matched their middling reputations, but their collective contribution was co-authoring a fairy tale.

Clendenon was clearly the most accomplished of the 1969 Mets' irregulars. He'd had two seasons of better than 90 RBIs as a Pirate, and in '68, the Year of the Pitcher, drove in 87.. The Mets didn't have anybody with those credentials. The expansion draft made him an Expo. Good sense — Clink's no-BS threat to retire — prevented him from becoming an Astro despite Montreal's attempt to trade him to Houston. A college education and off-season planning gave him a path outside baseball, working for the Scripto pen company (as a VP, no less). Foresight and fortune, though, had a different script in mind. Commissioner Bowie Kuhn convinced him to play in Quebec. Johnny Murphy convinced his employers to send him to Queens.

It's no wonder Donn Clendenon stood out as a veteran, accomplished, professional power hitter on the New York Mets. He was that good and they hadn't had anybody quite like him before. Yet he meshed as well as he mashed. Consider Tom Seaver's recollection of the Mets' first home game after Donn joined their ranks. It involved his wife, Nancy, introducing herself to hubby's new teammate, and Donn "putting on a little show" in return, suavely charming the ace's better half as only a veteran, accomplished, professional power hitter might.

"Hi Donn," Tom greeted him after perhaps enjoying the show enough. "What are you kissing my wife's arm for?"

"It's great to be a Met," Donn replied.

It was even better to be up 6-0 with 14 outs to go for a divisional flag.

> *"So two cast aside by Gary Gentry here in the seventh inning, it brings up Tim McCarver. The Cardinals' talented backstop has fouled to third and fouled out to first, nothing for two. In the Astrodome tonight, the Atlanta Braves will call on Pat Jarvis and Houston will pitch Tom Griffin. Over the inside corner, strike one called. Tom Griffin of Houston and Gary Gentry of the Mets the two top rookie pitchers in the league this year. Interestingly enough, both are trying for their twelfth win tonight. Ground ball hit hard, but right at Al Weis, he has it. Throws to Clendenon and the side is out. No runs, no hits, no errors, none left. Now seventh-inning stretch time for the huge crowd at Shea Stadium. At the end of six-and-a-half innings, the New York Mets six and the Saint Louis Cardinals nothing."*
>
> *—Bob Murphy, middle of the seventh.*

How did they do it? How did the Mets keep churning out hard-throwing young arms? Seaver in '67, Koosman and Ryan and McAndrew in '68, now this year Gary Gentry? You could piece together lineups from what others would consider spare parts if you could pitch like the Mets. And boy could the Mets pitch.

Gary Gentry sure could. He was drafted out of Arizona State in June 1967. It was off to Double-A Williamsport, where his ERA sat under two and his strikeout-per-inning rate was nearly nine. Promoted for a full year at Triple-A Jacksonville, he threw 198 innings in 1968 and won 12 games.

Gentry was ready. In his first start, on April 10, he came within one out of a complete game, giving up two runs to the Expos. Tommie Agee hit a home run to Shea Stadium's highest fair perch and the Mets were a game over .500. The team was 2-1. The rookie was 1-0. Gary Gentry slotted in nicely behind Seaver and Koosman. He may not have been quite at the level in his rookie year that they had been in theirs — Seaver was Rookie of the Year, Koosman finished a hair behind Johnny Bench — but there was no shame in holding down the third spot every five days with this crew. He had the stuff and he had the self-confidence to fill an important role on a team that didn't necessarily think it was making a miracle. Gentry was just doing what he had always done.

"I never played on a team that didn't expect to win," Gary told Stanley Cohen, recounting his squads' successes through college and the minors. "So when I came up with the Mets in '69, I never thought about anything except winning. I didn't know much about the team's history."

Yet here he was, 33 games into his big league career, emphatically rewriting it. Through seven visiting innings, the Cardinals landed only three baserunners, and two of those were erased on double plays. The Mets of this new era, of these days of Gentryfication when winning was the norm and losing was for the other guys, had their eyes on the finish line. They were going the distance, and Gentry would be damned if he wasn't going to be the one to take them there.

Gentry, as befit a pitcher pitching behind Seaver and Koosman, liked completing games, even if he wasn't given that many opportunities relative to his more-established teammates. In 1969, pitchers were geared to finish what they started. Met starters completed 51 of their starts and that was good for only sixth in the National League. Just as Gil Hodges wasn't shy about platooning, he didn't hesitate to deploy an effective bullpen led by the likes of righty Ron Taylor and lefty Tug McGraw. It was all about the team winning.

Nevertheless, Gentry preferred to complete games. He finished five entering the action of September 24: a number stellar in modern terms (as many as N.L. Cy Young winner Clayton Kershaw would compile in 2011, for example), a total that didn't even register on the radar in 1969. In retirement, Gentry would rue that he was a victim of "the relief syndrome," the budding pattern in baseball that didn't demand nine innings out of every starter. Gentry wanted that demand made of him. He wanted Hodges and pitching coach Rube Walker to leave him in. "That was my style of baseball," he told Cohen. "I always felt that I got to the majors ten years too late."

Actually, after he worked the eighth and prepared to take the ball in the ninth, the Mets still out front by a half-dozen runs, it was clear Gary Gentry was right on time.

"Lou Brock will lead off against Gary Gentry. The crowd is standing, waving and cheering. The Mets are three outs away from a divisional crown. Fouled back to the screen, strike one. This is the moment Mets fans have waited for. Ed Charles in close at third against Lou Brock. Brock has one of the two hits given up by Gary Gentry, who has turned in an absolutely magnificent performance with the pressure on. Now the lean righthander stands and pitches. Call strike on the outside corner! It is two strikes. And the standing room crowd will be roaring with each delivery."
—Bob Murphy, top of the ninth

Brock produced a grounder up the middle that Harrelson made a play on, but Buddy couldn't throw out the speedy Redbird. St. Louis had a man on first. Vic Davalillo was up next.

"Not a soul is leaving the stadium. Everybody just jamming the aisles and standing right by the exits. Now the Glider comes over from third to

have a word with his young pitcher. This has to be a huge moment in the life of Ed Charles. He has known about as much hard times as anybody. Ground ball hit toward the middle, Harrelson can't get it. It's a base hit to center for Davalillo, and the Cardinals are slowing things up on back-to-back base hits by Brock and Davalillo."

Gentry had hoped for an "easy game," and that it had been for the longest time. The confident rookie was nervous for the first four or five innings and then was "just more or less in a hurry to get the game over with so that everyone could enjoy what was happening."

The nerve of those Cardinals to delay such a well-planned party. But Gentry got two quick strikes on the next batter, Vada Pinson, before the St. Louis right fielder fouled one off.

"Now Gentry up in pitching position. And the pitch on the way… swing and a miss, he struck him out! The Mets are two outs away. Strikeout number five for Gary Gentry. Now the hitter is Joe Torre. The infield is set at double play depth."

Joe Torre grew up in Brooklyn before there were Mets. In the borough of Dodgers, he was a Giants fan. Then he left to become a Milwaukee Brave. There was talk through the spring that the kid who had grown into a five-time All-Star catcher might come home. The Braves were looking to trade him in the aftermath of his role during the Spring Training player job action (more a boycott than a formal strike). Torre was sitting out camp — "sulking" in Manhasset, by George Vecsey's account — waiting for resolution. In March, the Mets still needed a power-hitting first baseman, and Joe could certainly fit that bill. He'd played the position intermittently since the Braves had moved to Atlanta in 1966. With a hitter of Torre's caliber, Hodges wouldn't have to platoon at first.

What would it take to make it so New Yorkers could come see what this Brooklyn kid could do in Queens? A lot, Joe Durso recounted in *Amazing*. The first request filed by Atlanta GM Paul Richards was for Ryan, outfield prospect Amos Otis and Jerry Grote (which would have sent Torre back behind the plate). After Johnny Murphy presumably stopped laughing at the audacity of the proposal, he countered with something less Met-onerous: Grote's backup J.C. Martin, Kranepool, *either* Ryan or Jim McAndrew, and somebody else for Torre and third baseman Bob Aspromonte. This time it was Richards who demurred.

Murphy held on to all his young players until Clendenon became available in June and then stayed in possession of the ones he really liked. Richards, meanwhile, swapped Torre to St. Louis for Orlando Cepeda. If the division leads held over the next week, the Mets and Braves would meet not at the trading table but in the first National League Championship Series. Atlanta had just the night before wrested control of the wild West from San Francisco by winning their fifth in a row.

The Mets, meanwhile, were still looking at Joe Torre, but in a very different context than they did six months prior.

"Torre, the cleanup batter, has lined out, bounced out and popped up, nothing-for-three. Al Weis shaded toward the middle of the diamond. And the pitch on the way…low and outside, it's ball one. The crowd chanting We're Number One. The Mets made up fifteen-and-a-half games since the thirteenth of August. And the pitch thrown…fouled into the air, back toward the crowd. It's one ball and one strike to Joe Torre. Tim McCarver is the on-deck hitter. Mets have the infield hoping for a chance to make a double play that would end it. Tommie Agee just a stride to left-center. Now the ballboy brings out some balls for umpire Al Barlick. Lou Brock is on second and Vic Davalillo is the runner on first with one man out. Ninth inning, six-nothing New York, and the pitch… ground ball foul, down the third base line. He went after a curve from Gary Gentry."

Ralph Kiner, Bob Murphy reported over Mets flagship WJRZ-AM and affiliates like WKAJ-FM in Saratoga Springs, was down in the clubhouse waiting to "talk with the players as they come in". Lindsey Nelson was handling play-by-play duties on Channel 9. The three men had been Original Mets, chronicling every move Casey Stengel made, dating back to St. Petersburg in the runup to 1962, and following the fortunes of his successors Wes Westrum, Salty Parker and now Gil Hodges. They weren't "we" announcers, though. They were even-handed — complimentary to the other side when the other side deserved it, which was most of the time from 1962 through 1968. Life was different now. The Mets were the heart of the story Murphy and Kiner and Nelson told. The Mets were the story everywhere. They had been on the covers of *Time* and *Life* that September. They would dominate the front page of the *New York Times* the next day. And the Mets fans were the story every bit as much as the Mets team.

"[T]he roar that is going to come out of this stadium on the final out, if the Mets are still in front," Murphy predicted in the seventh, "is going to be something to hear. After seven agonizing years and many frustrations, the Mets fans, the best and most loyal baseball fans to be found in this land, are really going to have something to cheer about."

It's easy enough to butter up your listeners, but Murph wasn't saying anything that wasn't easily verifiable. The Mets opened for business in a crumbling Polo Grounds with a roster that was every bit as dilapidated, and the best and most loyal baseball fans were born. They accepted the Mets and their flaws. They took them to their heart and didn't let them go. The 40-120 Mets drew 922,530 to a neighborhood most (including the erstwhile New York Giants) were bent on avoiding. This was in an age when a million fans was not a given for any team and nearly a million for a historically horrendous team was as laughable as the idea of trading Ryan, Otis and Grote all at once.

In 1963, the Mets barely improved to 51-111, the Polo Grounds crumbled a little more and attendance leapt to over a million. Those fans, identified immediately by Metsologists as the New Breed, made noise, made banners, and made a pledge of undying love with no evidence their ardor would be rewarded with anything but more losing.

The love affair continued in a new ballpark in another borough. The Mets drew 1,732,597 to beautiful Shea Stadium in 1964. The facility sparkled. The team (53-109) was mostly grim as ever. Novelty? The Mets were a shade worse in 1965 (50-112) yet they drew a shade more. They showed the slightest sign of forward progress in 1966 — not finishing last, not losing a hundred games (66-95) — and attendance soared toward 2 million. The gate leveled off in 1967 and 1968, but the Mets were still bringing more fans through the turnstiles for tenth- (61-101) and ninth-place (73-89) baseball than just about anybody in the National League was attracting for outfits sporting better records. And if Mets attendance didn't lead one and all in sheer body count, nobody beat it for enthusiasm generated.

Why? Why were Mets fans so giving of affection when the Mets couldn't possibly reciprocate in the win column? Theories abounded from the first day Ol' Case set to putting the most human face in captivity on what could have been a very dismal enterprise. Mets fans were the way they were because they were imps...or ironists... or inveterate optimists...or enthralled by being in on the ground floor (or basement) of what was brand spanking new — at a moment in time when Camelot was in full swing and the Beatles were first tuning their instruments...or reassured by a well-orchestrated throwback to what had recently departed (senior circuit successors to the Giants and Dodgers, the Mets held an Old Timers Day during their very first year of existence)...or underdogs in life, so therefore they couldn't help but identify with the most clearly identifiable underdogs in baseball.

"The Metophile," the *Times*'s Robert Lipsyte wrote with tongue a touch in cheek as he attempted to explore what made Mets fans tick in 1963, "is a dreamer," someone whose life was devoted to yearning to reach unreachable stars: like punching "that arrogant foreman at the plant square on his fat nose"; like getting in "the last word with his wife"; like believing "the Mets will start a winning streak."

Ouch — that one had to hurt more than even the theoretical sock to foreman's schnozz.

Early in that second season, Lipsyte predicted the Met Mystique would wear thin soon enough. "As the Mets progress from incompetency to mediocrity," he appraised, "their psychological pull will be gone."

The Mets, however, breezed right by mediocrity and bulleted to overwhelming success. Their appeal required little analysis now. As the franchise's top executive, M. Donald Grant, would put it with the kind of grace and accuracy with which he wouldn't forever be associated, "Our team finally caught up with our fans. Our fans were winners long ago."

"This," Bob Murphy assured his listeners in the seventh inning on September 24, 1969, "has truly been an amazing year for the New York Mets."

What else was left to say?

"*It's two-and-two on Joe Torre with one out in the ninth. The pitch by Gentry is...fouled, out of play behind the third base dugout to the crowd. Everybody right on the edge of their seat. I'll bet Cleon Jones sets a track record getting to that dugout from left field when that final out is made.*

"*Gentry, working hard here against Joe Torre, now in the set position, here's the pitch. GROUND BALL HIT TO SHORTSTOP. HARRELSON TO WEIS, THERE'S ONE, FIRST BASE, DOUBLE PLAY! THE METS WIN! IT'S ALL OVER! OH, THE ROAR GOING UP FROM THIS CROWD! An unbelievable scene on the field. Fans are POURING onto the field, the ballplayers trying to get to the dugout. A six-four-three double play, and it's all over. Congratulations to Gil Hodges, the coaches and the ballplayers — what a year! It's hard to believe.*

"*The Mets are on their way into the clubhouse, final score, the New York Mets six and the Saint Louis Cardinals nothing, they knocked Steve Carlton out in the first inning, Donn Clendenon hit a three-run homer, Ed Charles hit a two-run homer, later in the game, Clendenon hit another home run, and Gary Gentry, the rookie righthander from Phoenix, Arizona, pitched a marvelous FOUR-hit shutout.*

"*THOUSANDS and THOUSANDS of fans are out on the playing field. Banners are being paraded. The Mets are IN the clubhouse. And in just a very few moments, we'll be joining Ralph Kiner as he picks up the comments from the players.*

"*Ah, it's almost too much to believe. Imagine finishing ninth a year ago, one game out of tenth, although it was a vastly improved club... Gil Hodges, who a year ago today suffered a heart attack in Atlanta, Georgia, fighting back from a heart attack to take his ballclub in his second year and MOLD a championship team.*

"*Well, we'll be back with the locker room show now in just one moment.*"

But first, after a commercial break, and as the microphones picked up Jane Jarvis's happy organ accompanying the nonstop elation in the background, Bob Murphy offered a coda from the booth that would eventually bear his name:

"*THOUSANDS and THOUSANDS of Mets fans are out on the field, all shouting We're Number One, We're Number One. You have to see this scene to believe it. All the happiness comes pouring out.*

"*For the first six years of their lives, the Mets were laughed at, kicked around. They were the ballclub that was the big joke. They never believed it themselves, they knew they were going to be a ballclub.*

"George Weiss, the first president of the Mets, had put together a good organization. The SCOUTS, the best he could get his hands on, turned out to be exactly that, the very best. They started signing GREAT young pitchers. It took a short time to develop them in the farm system. It took the guiding hand of a Gil Hodges to put it all together. And now THIS is the climax, a scene that Mets fans, I'm sure, since that first day eight years ago, have longed for."

On July 31, 1994, Bob Murphy stood at a podium in Cooperstown accepting the Ford C. Frick Award for baseball broadcasting. In his acceptance speech, Bob singled out his favorite Mets team of them all.

"They were my boys of summer," the Hall of Fame announcer said. "You'll never enjoy a year any more than following the 1969 Mets."

Though he never used his signature phrase that Wednesday night at Shea Stadium when Clendenon, Charles and Gentry starred and first place was clinched, chances are pretty good that September 24, 1969, endures as Bob Murphy's Happiest Recap of them all.

78   OCTOBER 1, 1969
METS 6 CUBS 5 (12)
WRIGLEY FIELD

Las Vegas took one look at the New York Mets before the 1969 campaign commenced and labeled them 100-to-1 long shots to win a pennant.

They got the "100" part right, anyway.

The Mets weren't pennant-winners — yet. For the first time, a regularly scheduled playoff series would decide the National League flag. But the Mets would be part of that playoff, and they'd go there having turned math on its head. The team that lost at least 100 games five times in its first seven years stopped off in Chicago on a Wednesday afternoon to win No. 100. Only a month earlier, the date loomed as a monster matchup that might determine the division. But no, the Mets were way past that now. Not only had they already clinched a week before, but they hadn't lost since doing so.

After making Shea roar on September 24, the Mets' pitching staff made like a lair of librarians and *shushed* enemy bats to a dead quiet. The N.L. East champs threw four consecutive shutouts, including one apiece from Tom Seaver (finishing out the season at 25-7) and Jerry Koosman (17-9). Overall, the staff strung together 42 consecutive scoreless innings, a streak that remains unmatched after fifty years of Mets baseball.

The Cubs snapped the Mets' stingy ways in the very first inning of their little get-together, but that was all the solace Chicago would derive from Game 161 of their respective seasons. It would take a dozen innings — with Art Shamsky driving in the go-ahead run — but the Mets would shove their erstwhile nemeses one more car lane back with a 6-5 victory. The Mets were 100-61: on a nine-game winning streak and nine games ahead of the Cubs.

Perhaps so as not to tempt fate heading into their very first postseason, the Mets cooled off ever so slightly the next day, allowing the Cubs one face-saving win to take with them into winter. The Mets' final regular-season record was thus inscribed for the ages as 100-62, the fourth-best mark in the National League since 162-game seasons became the standard in the Mets' first year of 1962. They accomplished it via a load of pitching, suspiciously light hitting (Cleon Jones finished third in the N.L. batting race with a .340 average but the team as a whole hit a mere .242) and tons of what millions swore was Mets magic.

But was the rise from 73 wins to an even hundred really magic? Members of the 1969 Mets have been known to scoff at the supernatural as a direct cause for their unforeseen success. They were plenty good, they insist; they won 100 games, after all, including 38 of their final 49. The Cubs, like Las Vegas, underestimated their capabilities and see where it got them. Vegas, however, couldn't resist not learning its lesson and installed the N.L. West champion Atlanta Braves as 11-to-10 favorites to beat the Mets and win the National League pennant.

Even though those 100-to-1 wagers were three wins from paying off.

POSTSEASON

The New York Mets placed one toe into the Promised Land's anteroom. Then another. Then another. Soon enough, they had all ten within its playing field.

79

OCTOBER 4, 1969
METS 9 BRAVES 5
ATLANTA STADIUM

And nine runs to boot.

Welcome to the first Met postseason and, in a sense, Major League Baseball's first postseason. There had been World Series since 1903, but never a tournament like that which MLB set up to accommodate its 1969 expansion. With twelve teams in each league, two divisions of six squads apiece made logistical sense. Thus, for the first time, the Eastern winner and its Western counterpart would have to face off to resolve the league title once schedules concluded. What were commonly called "pennant races" were really now misnomers. The pennant was about to become a playoff prize. The team with the best record in the circuit might not even be its champion when these newfangled playoffs were said and done. The World Series wouldn't necessarily be that team's reward. A ticket home might be its fate if it couldn't capture the three of five wins that decided ownership of the flag.

Leave it to the Mets, whose entire existence to date was comprised of historic losing and, of late, historic winning, to show up for this "postseason" with the league's best record. Outpacing the N.L. West champ Atlanta Braves (who emerged from a four-team September scrum) by seven games won them nothing more than a shot at moving on. They would be granted home field advantage in this best three-of-five, but that was just by predetermined rotation. Winning 100 games versus Atlanta's 93 didn't mean a thing in terms of where the series would start. As it happened, it would start in Atlanta.

The road didn't exactly frighten the Mets. Away from Shea, they went a tidy 48-32, including a nifty 4-2 at Atlanta Stadium. It may not have been home sweet home, with its Sign Man, its LaGuardia flight path and its occasional burst of feline fury, but it would do as well as any alien ballpark for the duration.

If nobody saw the Mets making the first-ever NLCS, it's doubtful anyone would have predicted how they'd go about making the first game their own: by performing against form. They sent their ace, Tom Seaver, against the Braves' ace, Phil Niekro, and neither behaved quite like the aces they'd been in the regular season. Seaver won 25 games in 1969, Niekro 23. Though each battled gamely (Seaver for seven innings, Niekro for eight), they combined to surrender nine earned runs on thirteen hits and seven walks. The knuckleballing Niekro struck out more batters (four) than fireballing Tom Terrific (two).

Yet in the end, with the Mets' strongest weapon nullified, they won by four this Saturday afternoon. How? By scoring more in a single game than they'd managed in almost a month. The Mets hadn't put nine runs on the board since September 7, against the Phillies. They did it here, finishing with a necessary flourish of five in the eighth to overcome the 5-4 lead the Braves took in the seventh when Henry Aaron homered off Seaver. The crowning Met blow belonged to J.C. Martin, batting for Tom. He singled with the bases loaded to bring home all three runners. The Mets went up, 9-5, and Ron Taylor held the Braves in check the rest of the way to give Seaver his first postseason win.

These Mets had been winning everything in sight for quite a while. They'd won the hearts of unaligned baseball fans everywhere. By succeeding when their best pitcher struggled, they were winning over the minds of the baseball experts who doubted them.

Winning a playoff game? Apparently, it was just one of those things these Mets knew how to do.

OCTOBER 5, 1969
METS 11 BRAVES 6
ATLANTA STADIUM

All-hit, not-so-much pitch? The Mets? *These* Mets? It wasn't how they managed to win games that made them the 1969 Mets. It was that they won them. So never mind the wan offensive stats from the regular season and the pitching that registered as the N.L.'s second-best by earned run average. Just know the Mets found ways to win; one part of their game was on the fritz, the other kicked into high gear.

A day after pounding the Braves as necessary, 9-5, the Mets kept their war clubs handy. Ron Reed was Sunday's victim, despite beating the Mets twice during the regular season. Ed Kranepool reached Reed for an RBI single in the first. Tommie Agee added a two-run homer in the second. Once the bases cleared, Reed found trouble again, allowing a two-out double to Cleon Jones, then a run-scoring single to Art Shamsky. Down 4-0, Atlanta skipper Lum Harris removed his starter to get out of the second.

It was to no avail, for in the third, the Mets went on the rampage once more: Bud Harrelson followed an error with a double to score Jerry Grote, and Buddy came around on a Wayne Garrett single. The Mets were up, 6-0, through three. Harris went to a starter, Milt Pappas, but the story continued apace in the fourth when Ken Boswell sent a two-run homer out of the place they called the Launching Pad. The Braves gained one run back in the bottom of the inning, but the Mets answered via Cleon Jones's RBI single in the fifth.

What a bounty for Jerry Koosman! Staked to a 9-1 lead, the lefty who pitched to a 2.28 ERA during the regular season could relax, throw strikes and...

Not so fast. With two out, Kooz surrendered a single to Felix Millan, a walk to Tony Gonzalez and the second home run of the series to Hank Aaron. His edge trimmed to 9-4, Jerry walked Rico Carty, gave up a double to Orlando Cepeda and a two-run single to Clete Boyer. Now it was 9-6.

And now it was time for Gil Hodges to act. Koosman was one out shy of being positioned for the win, but the manager, a veteran of multiple Octobers in Brooklyn, understood the bottom line trumped individual concerns this time of year. Saturday's closer, Ron Taylor, was called on to get the final out of the fifth.

If there could be insurance runs in a 9-6 game, the Mets got them in the seventh on Jones's two-run homer. His cushion clout followed an attempted steal of home by Agee. Cleon nearly took Tommie's head off as a sign went missing. Better to come around by more conventional means and live to play another day.

Taylor gave way to Tug McGraw, who assured the Mets that their next day would be rife with possibility. Nothing else was launched from the Braves' pad as the Mets took their second playoff game, 11-6. Shea Stadium would be both teams' next stop, and the pennant the offensively potent, starting pitching-shaky Mets' immediate goal.

The starting rotation may have been the featured unit on the 1969 Mets and the lefthanded platoon Gil Hodges was employing against the righty-laden Braves may have been putting up the big numbers in the first two games of the 1969 NLCS, but the most quiet

OCTOBER 6, 1969
METS 7 BRAVES 4
SHEA STADIUM

aspect of the Met success story, even as the volume grew on the playoffs' arrival in New York, was the team's outstanding relief pitching. The bullpen was easy to miss in the wake of 51 complete games from Tom Seaver, Jerry Koosman and the rest of the strong-armed gang of starters, but its corps was getting the job done on a regular basis. The Braves certainly saw it from Ron Taylor in Games One and Two of the pennant series and Tug McGraw in Game Two. Six-and-a-third innings from the duo had yielded only zeroes on the Atlanta Stadium scoreboard.

Gary Gentry would have preferred his teammates stay put in Shea's right field bullpen, perhaps trading gardening tips with tomato-growing coach Joe Pignatano. Gentry's last start at Shea produced a complete game shutout that assured the Mets' participation in this postseason. A dozen days later, he had the chance to be at the center of another celebration. All he had to do was go the route the way he did against the Cardinals on September 24.

It wasn't to be. The Braves put a dent in Gary's Monday immediately when Henry Aaron, author of 554 regular-season long balls in a sixteen-year career, socked a two-run homer. It was his third in three days. Hammerin' Hank, absent from October baseball since the 1958 World Series, was making the most of what proved to be his final playoff appearance. This was one Brave determined to make those 100-to-1 odds against a Met pennant stand up.

He was at it again in the third, doubling on the heels of Tony Gonzalez's leadoff single. With a 2-0 lead and runners on second and third, Gentry's many miles of bad road were suddenly curtailed. Out went one young fireballer, in came another.

Hodges brought in Nolan Ryan, the fastest-throwing Met he had, and also the least predictable. During the season, as a spot starter and long reliever, he struck out 9.3 batters per nine innings, which was sensational. He also averaged 5.3 walks in the same span, which was worrisome. Yet everything about the Mets in 1969 had been about what could go right. If Ryan could control his undeniably great stuff, the Mets still had a very good chance of having an undeniably great day.

First thing Nolan did was strike out the dangerous Rico Carty. After Hodges ordered the lethal Orlando Cepeda walked, the 22-year-old righty from Alvin, Tex., struck out Clete Boyer and flied Bob Didier to Cleon Jones in left. With a palpable sigh of relief, Ryan left the bases loaded in the third. And as the Mets and all of Shea were exhaling, Tommie Agee came up in the bottom of the inning and blasted a solo homer off Pat Jarvis to halve the Braves' lead to 2-1.

Ryan's top of the fourth was blissfully uneventful. The Mets' bottom of the inning was happily active, starting with Art Shamsky's single and Ken Boswell's homer to give Nolan a lead. Shamsky, getting every start in this series because the Braves were throwing righties, was thriving. He'd end the NLCS batting .538. Boswell was also having the time of his life, driving in five runs to lead all batters not named Henry Aaron.

Nolan took care of Aaron for the second out of the fifth, but then he walked Carty and gave up a homer to Cepeda. The Mets were behind again, 4-3. Nevertheless, Hodges stuck with Ryan and let him lead off the bottom of the inning. Faith paid off: the pitcher singled and, one out later, another of Gil's lefthanded platoonists, Wayne Garrett, homered. The redheaded rookie, who'd bat a cool .385 for the series, put the Mets up, 5-4. Jarvis lasted one more batter, surrendering a double to Jones. Pat was pulled and George Stone took his place. By inning's end, Stone gave up another run-scoring hit to Boswell.

It was a 6-4 Met lead with four innings to go. Ryan had been periodically plagued by blisters (soaked, to reporters' delight, in pickle brine secured by Met trainer Gus Mauch) and had his development derailed by calls to duty in the military reserves. But Hodges was giving the kid every chance to end what now loomed as Mets Flag Day. Nolan grounded out Didier and Gil Garrido and struck out Stone.

Nine outs to go until the Mets won the pennant.

In the bottom of the sixth, with Jerry Grote on second, Agee (.357 in the series) singled to make the score 7-4. Ryan, getting stronger the longer he stayed in, lined out Felix Millan, struck out Gonzalez and popped the great Aaron to Bud Harrelson at short to make quick work of the seventh.

Six outs to go until the Mets won the pennant.

Carty led off the Brave eighth with a single, but Ryan recovered to catch Cepeda and Boyer looking at strike three. Pinch-hitter Mike Lum singled to put runners on first and second, but Lum Harris's next pinch-hitter, Felipe Alou, lined to short to end the threat.

Three outs to go until the Mets won the pennant.

Ryan batted for himself in a scoreless Met eighth, so it was he who was charged with clinching the first National League pennant within the five boroughs of New York City since the New York Giants traveled to Ebbets Field and beat the Brooklyn Dodgers, 7-1, on September 20, 1954. A year later, the Dodgers would capture the flag while on the road in Milwaukee, playing the Braves. Barely two years later, neither the Giants nor Dodgers would be New York City teams. They each headed west after 1957, inspired by the smart business move those Braves had made when they bolted Boston for Wisconsin in 1953. Yet before another generation could pass, the Braves would give up on Milwaukee and seek permanent shelter in Atlanta, while New York would welcome the homely, hopeless Mets into its boroughs and its heart, partly to win back the affections of abandoned Giants and Dodgers fans, partly to create a New Breed loyal first, foremost and forever to something all their own. A dozen years removed from a league and, really, a world that was unrecognizable to the contemporary citizen of 1969, the Mets were beautiful and they were on the cusp of achieving something almost unthinkable.

Almost.

Bob Aspromonte pinch-hit to lead off the top of the ninth for the Atlanta Braves. Ryan flied him to center field. One out.

Millan was up next. Ryan grounded him to Harrelson, who threw to Ed Kranepool at first. Two out.

Tony Gonzalez was the next batter. Ryan got him to ground to Garrett at third. Garrett threw to Kranepool.

"And," Ralph Kiner confirmed, "the Mets are the National League champions!"

The Mets, on the strength of an unyielding offensive attack (27 runs scored in 26 innings) and three sturdy relievers (2 runs allowed in 13 1/3 innings), were indeed owners of the pennant in the oldest, established, permanent baseball league in New York. They'd finished 59 1/2 games behind the Los Angeles Dodgers and 60 1/2 games behind the San Francisco Giants the year they were born. They'd finished eighteen games behind the team nearest their nascent reach, and that team, a sorry band of pre-Durocher Chicago Cubs, lost 103 games. Everybody in the National League had been exponentially better than the 40-120 Mets of 1962. With the exceptions of 1966 and 1968, everybody in the National League had always been better than the New

York Mets before 1969. It was just the way it always was.

But "always" had a funny way of evaporating when talent, confidence and perhaps magic were added to the atmosphere. The Mets made up hundreds of games in the cumulative loss column over the balance of the 1960s. New York filled its Giantless, Dodgerless void and then some. And those fans who crowded Shea Stadium this festive Monday, however they got there, whatever their roots...

Well, they took over the field, just as they had when the Eastern Division was won. As the champagne poured in the home clubhouse — electioneering Mayor Lindsay insinuating himself into the soirée as if he and not Nolan Ryan (7 IP, 2 R, 3 H, 2 BB, 7 SO) had earned the victory — the party from the night of September 24 resumed in broad daylight. Grass was grabbed, paper streamed about, the incredibly accurate statement "WE'RE NUMBER ONE" rang out and, as an AP reporter observed, a "mini 'Woodstock Pop Festival' set in on the infield."

It was October 6. The music was still playing. So were the 1969 Mets.

Next gig: the World Series.

OCTOBER 12, 1969
METS 2 ORIOLES 1
MEMORIAL STADIUM

So much fuss over so spare a part. If the Mets' 25-man World Series roster was viewed as a depth chart, Rod Gaspar would probably rank no higher than 22nd. Although no player was unimportant in Gil Hodges's scheme of things, by any objective measure, Gaspar — who started exactly two games during the Mets' stretch drive — didn't figure to be the focus of any opponent's planning.

But he sure got the attention of the Baltimore Orioles. The 23-year-old rookie fifth outfielder batted .228 in 1969 yet snuck under the mighty Birds' skin when, in the giddiness of the Mets' pennant-clinching festivities, he predicted the Mets would sweep the World Series in four straight.

To turn such cheeky boldness into fact, the American League champion O's would have be steamrolled by the increasingly miraculous Mets. To the Orioles' thinking, no miracle of any proportion had a chance to stop them...nor did the Mets.

The National League believed, clear up to Henry Aaron, whose monster NLCS left him emptyhanded in terms of a World Series date. "They are Amazin'," the Hammer conceded. But Frank Robinson, about as great a player as Aaron, had yet to be impressed. When he last saw the Mets in action, as a Cincinnati Red, it was 1965, and the Mets were amazing only in their awfulness. Perhaps the perennial All-Star right fielder hadn't kept up since leaving for Baltimore and leading his team to its second pennant in four years.

After being apprised of Rod Gaspar's comments, Frank Robinson's reaction, per instant legend, was a dismissive, "Bring on Ron Gaspar!"

It's Rod, stupid, a playful teammate interjected.

Then, "Bring on Rod Stupid!" which he clarified immediately: "Bring on Rod

Gaspar, whoever the hell he is! He said he wanted us."

False modesty wasn't a problem from either side of this 66th Fall Classic, though most were sure only the Orioles had a good reason to be dripping confidence. These were the Orioles of 109 victories, the Orioles who rampaged over the American League East by nineteen games, the Orioles who outlasted the A.L. West champ Twins in two extra-inning nailbiters before spanking them, 11-2, in their playoff finale. These were the Orioles whose talent dotted the A.L. All-Stars (six members) and whose weaknesses were unapparent enough to be understood as nonexistent.

These were the Orioles of two Robinsons — Frank and Brooks — on the road to immortality; of three pitchers — Mike Cuellar, Dave McNally and Jim Palmer — who combined to go 59-22; of dangerous power (Boog Powell hit 37 homers); of sterling defense (Paul Blair, Mark Belanger and Brooks Robinson earned Gold Gloves); of more than enough speed (Belanger, Blair and Don Buford each collected double-digit steals); of a manager, Earl Weaver, quickly establishing himself as some kind of genius.

How smart was Weaver? Smart enough to not outwardly doubt the team that would be visiting Baltimore for the first two games of the World Series. "The Mets are as worthy an adversary as any team the National League could put up," he said. It was bland boilerplate, but it worked better on a bulletin board than Frank Robinson's statement that the Orioles were good for "seven in a row". The O's had taken down the Twins in three. Why shouldn't they make minimal work of the Mets? He would have found an ally in Las Vegas, where oddsmakers stuck with their 1969 script. The Mets had been 100-to-1 underdogs from the outset of the season, 11-to-10 underdogs against the Braves and were now installed as — what else? — underdogs in the World Series, at a price of 8-to-5.

The Mets were a worthy adversary. The Orioles were a daunting obstacle. The Mets won 100 games. The Orioles won 109. The last time the margin between pennant winners was greater was fifteen years earlier, when the Cleveland Indians (111-43) were overwhelming favorites to cut the New York Giants (97-57) down to size.

New York's National League representative pulled a stunning upset then — beat the Tribe in four straight, actually. New Yorkers didn't have to look back that far for inspiration, either. The Baltimore Colts were supposed to be a lock in the previous January's Super Bowl. Vegas put the spread in the neighborhood of eighteen points; the New York Jets, the Mets' stadium co-tenants, won anyway, 16-7.

So there was a New York precedent and a Shea precedent. There was also a Rod, two Rons, a Don, a Donn and, oh yes, a Tom Terrific among the names Orioles may not have felt compelled to memorize. Finally, there was a wave of Met magic.

Yet in the first game of the World Series, it crashed into an Oriole-sized wall. Tom Seaver wasn't so terrific that Saturday afternoon, giving up a home run to leadoff batter Don Buford. Ron Swoboda almost nabbed it as it cleared the right field fence at Memorial Stadium...but he didn't. The Mets trailed, 1-0. The Mets trailed all day. Seaver left after six innings. Don Cardwell and Ron Taylor were effective in relief, but by then the Birds were out of the barn. Mike Cuellar struck out eight Mets en route to a 4-1 victory.

And Rod Gaspar grounded out as a pinch-hitter.

If the World Series looked easy to the Orioles after besting the Mets' ace, they might not have noticed the full deck at Hodges's disposal. He dealt another ace on Sunday afternoon for Game Two. Jerry Koosman set about making Baltimore's life extremely difficult.

For three innings, nobody scored. Koosman and McNally exchanged walks in the second, but allowed no hits. Al Weis notched the first safety of the game in the visitors' third, leading off with a single, but he was left at second base. The zero-zero tie wasn't broken until the fourth, when Donn Clendenon belted a McNally delivery over the right field wall to start the inning. The Mets were up, 1-0, and stayed there for a very long time.

Nobody else reached base in the fourth. Or the fifth. Or the sixth. McNally had recovered nicely, holding the Mets to that one run on two hits. Kooz was positively historic. After six innings, his performance had summoned the ghost of Don Larsen. Larsen, an original Oriole from when the St. Louis Browns moved to town in 1954, created an immortal identity as a Yankee on October 8, 1956, when he threw a perfect game against the Brooklyn Dodgers in the fifth game of the last of the old-time Subway Series. Nobody had ever done that before in World Series play. Nobody had done it since. Nobody had thrown as much as a no-hitter in the World Series, either. Yet here was Koosman, nine outs from achieving a Fall Classic second and a New York Met first.

It was still 1-0 in the bottom of the seventh inning when those ancillary aspects of Mets magic disappeared. Paul Blair lined a single to left to end the no-hitter. Two outs later, he stole second and then scored when Brooks Robinson singled. Koosman had pitched a whale of the game, but it was now a 1-1 tie.

Mound brilliance continued at Memorial Stadium. McNally set down the Mets, 1-2-3, in the eighth. Except for an Ed Charles double and an intentional walk to Weis (ahead of Koosman) in the seventh, McNally had permitted no baserunners since Clendenon's homer. Once Kooz retired the Orioles in order in the eighth, his ledger was essentially just as spotless.

Having bashed the Braves into elimination and put the Cubs in their rearview mirror in a veritable blur, it might have seemed the Mets hadn't nipped an opponent in a must-win game for several weeks. But the Mets still knew how to do that. The ninth inning reminded those with short memories how lethal they could be when the score was tight and the hour was late.

Clendenon and Swoboda made outs but Charles singled, Jerry Grote singled him to third and then, finally, Weis — Weis! — singled the Glider home. The Mets led, 2-1. Koosman, like McNally, recorded his first two outs immediately, but then ran into a bit of self-imposed trouble: a walk to Frank Robinson, then another to Boog Powell.

A complete game victory would elude Kooz, as Hodges pulled him after what loomed as 8 2/3 Series-saving innings. Jerry had given up only the one run and the two hits. Whether those walks would be crucial was now up to Taylor.

They weren't. Ron grounded Brooks Robinson to his opposite number, Charles. The third baseman threw to Clendenon to seal the Mets' first World Series win, 2-1. The

Series was tied at a game apiece. A player from each team had promised a sweep. Neither was right. Predictions weren't working, but at least one rallying cry seemed apropos:

Bring on Shea Stadium!

Among all the ways one could measure what was swirling adjacent to the waters of Flushing Bay, consider Shea Stadium and its almost exactly five-and-a-half years of multipurpose activity, from the day it opened on April 17, 1964, to the raising of its gates

for business this second Tuesday in October 1969. Shea had hosted soccer, boxing, college football, professional football and the Ice Capades (amid June swelter, no less). In consecutive Augusts, with its de facto house band playing road dates, it provided the grandest stage imaginable for the Beatles.

But Shea's primary purpose was baseball. Setting aside four Mayor's Trophy exhibitions put on to benefit city sandlotters (the most recent of them, on September 29, a 7-6 Mets win over the afterthought Yankees) and the 1964 All-Star Game (which involved only one Met, Ron Hunt), there had been 488 professional baseball games that counted at Shea Stadium. The first 400-plus, spanning the beginning of '64 to early '69, gave absolutely no indication — none — that in the 487th Mets game that mattered, their final regular-season home game of the current year, the Mets would be crowned champions of their division...and that in the 488th, the third and final game of the NLCS, they'd add the title of league champion to their résumé.

Now here was William A. Shea Municipal Stadium, not quite 500 baseball games old, about to roll out the most regal red carpet a ballpark could. An operations staff whose autumnal weekdays were usually pretty quiet by this time of year had its marching orders: Haul out the bunting, take care of the swells (Jackie Onassis, Jerry Lewis, Pearl Bailey, Ed Sullivan and Governor Nelson Rockefeller would all make appearances in the Field Level boxes), find space for the out-of-town press and keep the Jets off the grass.

The World Series was arriving in Flushing.

Thanks to the recurring excellence of the Yankees, the Giants and the Dodgers, New York had seen part or all of 39 World Series take place within its borders between 1905 and 1964. The event became old (if lately out of style) hat for the Bronx. However cherished it might have been in Manhattan and Brooklyn, it was never going to come back there for an encore. 1969 was Queens's turn in the spotlight. For three days, 123-01 Roosevelt Avenue was going to be the sporting capital of the universe. Shea Stadium was ready for its closeup.

The new kid on the block was not utterly unfamiliar with the championship concept, even before Gentry clipped the Cardinals and Ryan beat the Braves. There were Joe Namath and the Jets back in December, defeating the Raiders and earning the American Football League title. There were fighters Jose "Chegui" Torres and Emil Griffith leaving the park wearing light heavyweight and middleweight title belts, respectively. And there was no doubting John, Paul, George & Ringo were the heavyweight champs of rock 'n' roll. But before 1969, the only time championships crossed paths with the Mets at Shea was when judges handed out prizes to fans parading the best and the brightest of the bedsheets on Banner Day.

Nobody dreamed the Mets would be closing in on the kind of banner that gets run up underneath the Stars and Stripes, the kind of banner your team can wave when it's won the World Series. Nobody except the flightiest of Banner Day entrants promoted the notion of a World Series at Shea Stadium...not before the summer of '69 and the autumn that nobody saw succeeding it.

No matter how detailed the blueprints drawn by architects Prager-Kavanagh-Waterbury, it's doubtful the firm's plans included a World Series within 500 games of Shea's first Opening Day. Ground was broken on the stadium on October 28, 1961. Myriad construction delays meant it took almost half as long to build the darn thing as it did to usher the Fall Classic inside its sea-green walls. Yet here it was, the World Series at Shea Stadium. If the Mets could take full home field advantage of the Orioles over the next three days, their 1969 would end at Shea, impossibly happily ever after.

Gary Gentry, starter in the division- and playoff-clinching wins at Shea (it had gotten so that preliminary championships now existed in the plural), had the ball once more. His last outing, against Atlanta, was troubled and short. This one seemed on a more promising track when all that the Orioles notched off him in the first was a walk. Then the bottom of the first foretold great fortune when Tommie Agee led off the Mets' half of the inning against Jim Palmer with a home run. Agee had jolted pitchers four times with sudden wakeup calls during the regular season. He picked a fine time for a fifth.

This World Series stuff really seemed to suit Shea. Gentry enjoyed an easy inning in the second and then made Palmer's life difficult when he came to bat with two on and two out in the bottom of the frame. Gary batted a comical .081 in 1969, yet he was about to be a 1.000 hitter in World Series play. He smashed a two-run double into the center-right gap and gave himself a 3-0 lead.

Gentry came perilously close to giving it back in the fourth. Singles to Frank Robinson and Boog Powell gave the Orioles runners at first and third. With two out, catcher Elrod Hendricks, considered one of Earl Weaver's lesser lights, roped a ball to very deep left center, a shot bound for the fence. With the runners in motion, a 3-2 score seemed seconds away.

But just a little bit closer was Tommie Agee, who moved in on the ball with characteristic speed. He attempted a backhanded stab with his gloved hand, breaking his momentum against the wall with his bare hand and...he caught it. Tommie Agee made one of the most incredible catches in World Series history. Then, just as remarkably, he maintained its integrity by gripping the ball in his glove's webbing. From the Upper Deck, it looked like the most delightful scoop of vanilla a counterman ever served up at a Baskin-Robbins.

Tommie Agee kept 56,335 who screamed for the Mets in very good humor.

Jerry Grote doubled Ken Boswell home in the sixth to increase Gentry's cushion to 4-0. For the second game in a row, a Met was carrying a shutout deep into World Series competition. Once again, however, Gary couldn't avoid a brush with catastrophe. Two outs in the Oriole seventh were recorded before the creeping black and orange terror made its presence felt.

Mark Belanger walked. Dave May walked. Don Buford walked. Paul Blair was up. So was Nolan Ryan in the Mets bullpen. And so was Gil Hodges from the Mets bench, striding to the mound to remove Gentry. The occasionally wild Ryan was the skipper's choice to enter a fray in which three men had just reached via bases on balls. Counterintuitive thinking, perhaps, but they weren't Ryan's batters.

Control wasn't exactly Ryan's problem here. He got two strikes on Blair — a Met farmhand in 1962 until Baltimore drafted him away under the minor league rules of the day — before Blair got ahold of one of his deliveries. It was, as with Hendricks's threat in the fourth, laced with disturbing implications. Blair's ball headed for the right-center gap. This one, like the feeling in 56,000 or so stomachs, was sinking fast. If it fell in...and it appeared fated to do so...the Orioles were suddenly back in the game at 4-3. With the wrong kind of bounce, Blair was capable of coming all the way around.

Of course he was hardly the only capable center fielder at Shea Stadium that afternoon. Tommie Agee was still on patrol and he was still allowing nothing to get by him. This time, Agee went into a dive; a "skidding sprawl," Curt Gowdy called it on NBC.

Like last time, he made the catch.

It appeared to the naked eye the more flamboyant of his two retrievals. Tommie was on his belly, his left arm extended with ball in glove. Replays and in-house testimony (Agee's and Hodges's, in particular) ranked the first catch above the second in terms of difficulty. However you stacked the two grabs, they added up to five runs the Orioles didn't score.

"The homer," the defensive wizard said of his relatively low-key contribution to the Met cause, "meant only one run. The catches saved more than that."

Ryan benefited from another home run, this one from Ed Kranepool in the eighth. Armed with a 5-0 lead, Nolan attempted to finish off the Orioles. Following a familiar Game Three theme, he got two quick outs but then encountered peril. The reliever waked Belanger, gave up a single to pinch-hitter Clay Dalrymple and walked Buford. The bases were loaded once more and the Orioles were still imposing.

Hodges let Ryan have one more shot to finish it. He struck out the beleaguered Blair to confirm the 5-0 win that gave the Mets a 2-1 World Series edge in the 489th baseball game Shea Stadium had ever hosted. Things looked bright for the Mets and fairly bleak for the Birds, no matter how much Frank Robinson objected to that interpretation of what Gentry, Ryan and especially Agee had wrought. The Mets, he snorted to reporters, were "not Supermen".

But just maybe Shea Stadium was the Orioles' Kryptonite.

If the Orioles protested that they were not nearly done in the 1969 World Series, they were not alone — at least where protesting was concerned. Most of New York was wrapped up in the ascent of the undeniably, unironically Amazin' Mets, but

OCTOBER 15, 1969

84 METS 2 ORIOLES 1 (10)

SHEA STADIUM

world affairs were nonetheless capable of intruding on the World Series.

To Mets fans, baseball fans and a nation of mesmerized rubberneckers, the story in Queens was the primary focus of Wednesday afternoon attention. How could it not be? The Mets were two wins from completing the final chapter of the most uplifting story imaginable (save for the imaginations of Baltimoreans). Goodness knows 1969 could use some uplift given that the Vietnam War dragged on and on and the split between its supporters and its opponents grew wider and deeper.

Throughout America, New York very much included, October 15 represented more than the fourth game of the World Series. It was Moratorium Day, encompassing rallies, demonstrations and vigils from coast to coast. Americans gathered by the hundreds and by the thousands for peace. Other Americans gathered in vast numbers to voice their disapproval of their fellow citizens' disapproval of their government's actions. To one side, the war itself was the crime. To the other, not standing behind the President of the United States during a time of military hostilities was unacceptable. This debate provided the drumbeat of public discourse as the divisive decade drew toward a close. Even the roar that went up at Shea Stadium couldn't drown it out.

Moratorium Day touched Shea in its own way. For proof, you had to look no further than the center field flag pole where, in accordance with the peace demonstrators' wishes, the American flag was going to fly at half-mast to honor those Americans who lost their lives in Vietnam. That was Mayor John Lindsay's decision, which was within his purview given that Shea was municipal property. Except the military honor guard on hand as part and parcel of the usual World Series pomp let it be known it would not participate in pregame ceremonies if the flag didn't fly high over Shea. Baseball commissioner Bowie Kuhn and Lindsay opted to avoid a confrontation in the middle of the sport's and the city's big week and let the flag be raised to its usual height.

On college campuses where the peace movement took off, the World Series got students' attention, though — per the divisions of the day — it was processed differently depending on the school. From Clark University in Worcester, Mass., came a request that Game Four be postponed in deference to the cause the Moratorium represented. At the University of South Carolina, a dorm window sign was spotted representing an opposing viewpoint: "Go Mets. Win In Vietnam. To Hell With The Hippies." At the University of Toledo, the student union drew its own standing room crowd...to watch the Mets and the Orioles.

The center of the action at Shea wasn't political, it was athletic, personified by Mets starter Tom Seaver. But even Seaver wasn't immune to controversy unrelated to the national pastime. The young man's picture, usually found on baseball cards and the like, appeared on the cover of a pamphlet titled "Mets Fans For Peace". It included a quote from the 25-game winner: "If the Mets can win the World Series, then we can get out of Vietnam." Seaver later said he wasn't unwilling to endorse those sentiments (copy for an ad the Moratorium Day Committee wished to run in the *New York Times*), but he hadn't given his permission for his picture to be printed in this rogue pamphlet and, more importantly to him, this day wasn't a day for him to climb atop a soapbox.

His cause awaited on the pitcher's mound.

Game Four was a rematch of Game One, with Seaver hoping to avenge Mike Cuellar. Tom took the loss in the first World Series contest, his only loss stretching back to August 5. Over his final eleven regular-season starts, Seaver posted a 10-0 record with a sparkling 1.34 ERA. He wasn't nearly as sharp against Atlanta, but the Mets' offense rescued him. In Baltimore, the Mets couldn't do anything with Cuellar and Seaver couldn't do what he wanted against the Orioles. For the Mets to truly take command of this World Series, Seaver would have to be Seaver.

He was, from the outset. Two scoreless frames set the tone. When Donn Clendenon homered to lead off the bottom of the second, Tom had a 1-0 lead with which to work, and he guarded it zealously. There were stray Bird baserunners, but as the game wore on, nothing that caused a fuss. Between Seaver and an equally tough Cuellar, the only non-pitching ruckus raised was courtesy of Earl Weaver, who in the third committed a no-no: he disputed a ball/strike call with home plate umpire Shag Crawford as Mark Belanger batted. Weaver picked the wrong authority to figure to demonstrate vociferously against, as Crawford ejected him. It was the first managerial tossing in a World Series since 1935.

"I told him to shut his damned mouth," Crawford elaborated afterwards. "If he didn't hear me, then his ears are as bad as he thinks my eyes are."

Sideshow elbowed aside, the focus returned to how good the right arm of Seaver and the left arm of Cuellar were. Baltimore's starter gave the in-absentia Weaver seven solid innings, the homer to Clendenon his only blemish. Seaver mowed down O after O through the eighth. The Mets didn't do anything against reliever Eddie Watt to pad their margin, so Seaver would enter the ninth defending the same skinny 1-0 lead that had held so firmly since the second.

After retiring Paul Blair, Frank Robinson singled to left, producing the first hit Seaver had given up since the third. Boog Powell's single to right sent one Robinson to third and brought the other, Brooks, to the plate with a chance to, at the very least, tie the game.

Brooks Robinson had more than the very least in mind when he belted a sinking liner to right, a certain RBI extra-base hit if right fielder Ron Swoboda could cut it off, probably an RBI double that might very well bring Powell around from first to give the Orioles the lead. And if Ron — whose Rocky defense wasn't exactly considered an asset — did anything reckless, who knew where Robinson's ball might roll?

But Swoboda wouldn't do anything crazy like attempt to desperately dive for an uncatchable ball that would surely scoot right by him if he was unsuccessful.

Or would he?

He would. And he did. Swoboda — not replaced by Rod Gaspar for defense with a one-run lead — pulled an Agee of his own. A righthanded fielder, he dove across his body, stuck his left gloved hand out in the general direction of center field and absolutely robbed Brooks Robinson of the big hit the Orioles needed. His backhanded grab was every bit as breathtaking as what Tommie Agee had accomplished the day before, and given the timing in the game, even more dramatic.

The Mets had struck again.

"It wasn't a gamble," Swoboda explained to his satisfaction, reasoning, "There's one chance in a thousand that I'm going to catch it, but I had to go for it. If I don't get to it, two runs score."

Frank Robinson did tag up from third, which was a big deal on the scoreboard. Seaver was no longer ahead. He still had one more out to get and even if he got it, the Mets would have to try and find another run in the bottom of the ninth or hope their dormant offensive generator would be recharged by extra innings.

The scoreboard said that, but between the light bulbs, you could read the whole episode as another feather plucked from the Orioles' hopes. Three surefire game-changing hits in two games from the powerhouse of the American League had turned into outs that dashed Baltimore's momentum one day and sapped it the next. The tying run rearranged the numbers, but it was little more than consolation. The Mets were still making magic...and Seaver got Elrod Hendricks to line to Swoboda (who stayed on his feet this time) to end the top of the ninth.

The Mets threatened in the bottom of the ninth, as Cleon Jones and Swoboda — three hits on the day — each singled, but Watt grounded out pinch-hitter Art Shamsky to escape, so the Mets entered their first postseason extra inning. An error and a pinch-hit gave the Orioles runners on first and second with one out, but Seaver kept Don Buford — his Game One nemesis — in the park with a fly to deep right and then struck out Blair.

That marked ten innings of work for Tom, who knew he had just thrown his last pitch. His line against the toughest lineup baseball had to offer: 6 hits, 2 walks, 1 run. He'd be pitcher of record only if the Mets could help him out in the bottom of the tenth to make him a World Series winner. "Let's get a run," Seaver told his teammates upon his final return to the dugout. "No use fooling around any longer."

Righty Dick Hall was the new Oriole pitcher, facing Jerry Grote to lead off the bottom of the tenth. Grote seemed to make the 39-year-old reliever's life easy by lofting an unassuming fly ball to left field. But with the 1969 Mets, you could assume nothing. Glare from the late-afternoon sun and the sound coming off the Met catcher's bat played havoc with the defense. Buford broke away from the ball before he reversed course. Belanger rushed back from short. Nobody got to it. Grote, running all the way, landed on second with a double. The Mets were 180 feet from a two-game lead in the Series.

Gaspar pinch-ran for Grote. Third base coach Billy Hunter, managing in Weaver's stead, gave the order for the next batter, Al Weis, to be intentionally passed. With lefty-swinging J.C. Martin batting for Seaver, the Oriole brain trust opted for southpaw Pete Richert.

One pitch, one toss and one wrist decided the matter in an instant. Martin laid down his expected bunt. Richert fielded it and fired to first. Except it never made first. The ball hit Martin in the wrist and bounded away in the direction of second baseman Dave Johnson. Gaspar, who had already advanced to third, just kept going. He scored the winning run from second.

"I'm not the best bunter in the world," Martin demurred after the ten-inning, 2-1 victory, "but I think I'm pretty good." Nobody among a jubilant attendance of 57,367 was going to argue. The Orioles themselves didn't object. Perhaps they were too stunned to squawk at J.C.'s placement within the baseline as he raced for first and inadvertently got in the way of Richert's fling. Later looks at the play indicated an interference argument could have been made — and nobody liked to argue more than Earl Weaver. Yet a day that began enveloped in controversy regarding peace would be deprived of any more substantive baseball conflict.

When the United States would get out of Vietnam was long from being resolved. But that pamphlet Seaver disavowed contained one irrefutable fact: the Mets could win the World Series.

They were only a day away.

The word preceding the Mets to this moment seemed as appropriate as it did alliterative. These weren't just the New York Mets. These were the Miracle Mets. Everybody said it. Everybody knew it.

85   OCTOBER 16, 1969
METS 5 ORIOLES 3
SHEA STADIUM

But at this point, following the events of the past three games let alone so much of the last six months, the miracle would have been the Mets not winning the World Series. Such a reversal of contemporary fortune was not out of the question in theory. Teams had blown 3-1 Series leads before. It had happened three times in seven-game sets, including a year earlier, when St. Louis surrendered a supposedly insurmountable edge to Detroit. Yet without discounting whatever the 1968 Cardinals, the 1958 Braves and the 1925 Senators had going for them before succumbing to the worst of seven-game fates, they weren't a happening the way these 1969 Mets were. They did not represent a rise from hopelessness, a lesson in perseverance, an advertisement for surpassing self-confidence in the face of derision.

Nobody was ever the 1969 Mets besides the 1969 Mets. To stop them one game from a world championship would take a whole other kind of miracle...the darkest of miracles.

The baseball gods had shown no inclination toward such ill humor. The Orioles would have scratched out an extra run against Jerry Koosman and Ron Taylor in Game Two if that were the case. Elrod Hendricks and Paul Blair would have hit their balls a few inches away from the grasp of Tommie Agee in Game Three. Brooks Robinson would have confounded Ron Swoboda, Jerry Grote wouldn't have confounded Don Buford, and J.C. Martin's wrist would have found a less serendipitous slice of airspace.

The Mets mustered all the pitching, all the defense and, per usual, just enough of the offense they needed. They clearly didn't want for breaks, and there was no question they remained their usual upbeat selves. Agee, for example, wasn't shy about what he expected to take place inevitably if not imminently, telling reporters shortly after Rod Gaspar crossed home plate to end Game Four, "We've got it in the bag now. We'd like to win tomorrow, but we're going to win it one way or the other." Central California native Tom Seaver was a touch more impatient, urging Game Five starter Koosman to put it away ASAP:

"I don't want to go back to Baltimore. That place makes Fresno look like Paris."

Shea Stadium was seeing its last baseball of 1969 this Thursday. Kooz was determined to end the Mets' extended engagement in style. He told Seaver he wasn't interested in visiting Maryland again so soon, either. The Birds, however, wanted to flock home with whatever chance remained, and made a compelling case to avoid extinction in the third inning. With no runs on the board and one runner on first, Koosman's opposite number, Dave McNally, surprised him with a home run. The Mets trailed, 2-0, falling behind for the first time since Game One. Frank Robinson increased Jerry's deficit with a homer of his own. It was only the previous week that Robinson wondered aloud who the hell "Ron Gaspar" was. Since then, it was the two-time MVP who didn't resemble himself. Frank's shot was his first RBI of the Series.

It was also the last run scored by the Orioles.

Koosman endured a rough third, but shook it off, stymieing the big, bad Birds following Robinson's blast. Next time Frank batted, in the sixth, he was sure he'd been hit by one of Kooz's pitches, but home plate ump Lou DiMuro took exception to his — and Earl Weaver's — presumption and told him to get back in the box. Koosman proceeded to strike him out.

Slugger McNally shut the Mets down for five innings, but one more break was coming New York's way. Cleon Jones led off the inning and...what happened? That was the question. Jones indicated he'd been hit. DiMuro was no more sympathetic to Cleon's conclusion than he had been to Robinson's. The ump said no way to Jones and told him to continue his at-bat.

Not so fast there, countered Gil Hodges, pacing slowly toward home plate. Just over eleven weeks earlier, Hodges took another deliberate walk to where Cleon Jones stood. Then it was to calmly yet forcefully remove Jones from left field when he was sure Jones didn't hustle after a ball. It would be cited as proof that Hodges was serious about winning and the Mets had best follow his lead. Today, in the fifth game of the World Series, the destination Gil had in mind as he departed the dugout wasn't Jones, but DiMuro. He was out to disagree with the non-HBP call...and he had evidence to back him up. The ball Cleon said hit him *had* to have hit him, the Mets' manager assured DiMuro, because, look: shoe polish. There's a smudge of shoe polish on the ball. You don't get shoe polish on a ball unless it makes contact with a hitter's shoe. And if it does that, well, that puts the runner on first.

DiMuro, an American League umpire who knew Hodges as the straightest of shooters from when Gil helmed the Washington Senators, saw the ball, saw the polish, saw the man who brought it to him and had no choice.

Cleon Jones went to first base.

Gil Hodges went back to the dugout.

Earl Weaver went ballistic.

Donn Clendenon, after Weaver's protestations were dismissed, went deep over the left field wall with a McNally pitch for his third home run of the Series.

The Mets trailed, 3-2, yet more or less made clear to the 57,397 on hand and everybody listening on radio and watching on television that they were bound for glory sooner than later.

Sooner was the seventh. Al Weis, he whose only two home runs of 1969 came in consecutive wins over the Cubs at Wrigley Field in July...he who had never hit a home run at Shea Stadium in two years as a Met...Al Weis homered off McNally to tie the game at three. All the Mets needed now was a go-ahead run to confirm that they were technically on top in this game.

Spiritually, the rout was already on.

The eighth inning sealed the deal. Jones's leadoff double was matched an out later by a Swoboda double. The Mets went ahead, 4-3. Another out later, Boog Powell failed to corral a Grote grounder and Rocky rumbled home. The Mets led, 5-3, with three outs to go.

In the temporary bleachers the Mets constructed in left field to accommodate wounded servicemen, a small placard was visible. The day before, on Moratorium Day, counterdemonstrators expressed their dismay by driving with their lights on, they said, to support the Vietnam War. The vets the *New York Times* spoke to in those bleachers during Game Four — men who had fought in Southeast Asia — were opposed to the Moratorium organizers' call for American flags being lowered to half-mast, particularly at Shea. One told the *Times* anyone looking to lower the flag over the ballpark "would have to fight us first". That was the mood in the city and the country as the 1960s ended. The war divided people. Politics divided people. Race divided people. Items as trivial as music and hair-length divided people. In 1968, Don Cardwell and Ron Swoboda had a brief in-flight falling out over Swoboda's choice to wear love beads. These were divisive times that tore everybody apart, even teammates.

But the 1969 Mets were a unifying antidote to viral dissension. All you had to do was read that placard displayed by those veterans in those bleachers to get an idea of how New Yorkers chose to coalesce around their pennant-winners:

LIGHTS ON FOR KOOSMAN

In '68, presidential candidate Richard Nixon made electoral hay out of a sign he swore he saw on the campaign trail, one that plead for somebody (Nixon, presumably) to "bring us together". A year later, in a stadium where thoughts were regularly expressed on poster board, oak tag and bedsheet, the Mets were a rallying point for a disparate city and a desperate nation. The Mets brought people together and lit up the outlook of all willing to be touched by them.

Unless you counted the Orioles, who by the ninth inning of the fifth game of the 1969 World Series had to be some of the loneliest souls in America. Their last chance for a pseudomiracle of their own began with a walk by Frank Robinson to lead off the ninth. A grounder off the bat of Powell rolled to Weis, who flipped to Bud Harrelson at second to cut down Robinson for the first out. Brooks Robinson revisited his bad habit of hitting fly balls to right. Swoboda didn't have to do anything extraordinary on this one, unless you consider catching a ball to bring the Mets within one out of winning the World Series extraordinary. In which case, Swoboda did just that and the

Mets were one out shy of winning the World Series.

Shy was for another day, another era. These Mets, up 5-3 in the game and 3-1 in the Series, had nothing to be bashful about. Together they were a single, solitary step from the mountaintop: Grote behind the plate; Clendenon at first; Weis, he of the Series-leading .455 average, at second; Harrelson at short; Ed Charles at third; Jones in left; Agee in center; Swoboda around in right; and Koosman on the mound. Dave Johnson represented the tying run for the Orioles, but what were the odds of that representation morphing into reality?

For a split second, as Johnson ripped into Koosman's final pitch, a worst-case scenario couldn't help but cross 57,397 minds. He hit it deep. He sent Jones back to the track. But that was as far as Cleon needed to drift.

The ball landed in the left fielder's glove. It was the third out...the final out...the coronation of the New York Mets as champions of the baseball world.

The New York Mets were world champions.

You could add to the conclusion from there.

You could follow Jones through the ever-lovin' madness that enveloped Flushing as the so-called miracle became uncontestable fact at 3:17 PM, and he'd attribute the Mets' new status to "togetherness...25 guys who stayed in there all year and picked each other up time and again."

You could check in with World Series Most Valuable Player Clendenon who, in the spirit of Mets unity, declared, "There are no superstars on this club."

You could seek out the exception to Clendenon's rule, superstar Seaver, who explained calmly that the Mets were simply "a team that does what it has to do."

You could track down Casey Stengel, the man who invented the Amazin' Mets back when it was painfully obvious they needed all the embellishment he could conjure, as he summed up his old charges' progress succinctly, observing, "This is a team which has come along slowly fast."

You could listen to the throngs who made the Shea Stadium surface their playground for the third time in just over three weeks as they cried, "We're Number One!" and meant it in every accurate way possible.

You could take in the echoes of the on-field celebration in the champagne-soaked Met clubhouse — Mayor Lindsay, front and center once more — and throughout the spontaneously ticker-tape coated streets of Manhattan. The *Times* reported a chant of "Gil Hodges for Mayor" went up in Times Square. Luckily for the eventually re-elected incumbent, the manager wasn't on the ballot.

You could ask Gil himself, who could have been chosen by acclamation to any office he wanted in New York, how this compared to when he was the first baseman who caught the final out of the 1955 World Series for Brooklyn. Hodges, however, couldn't tell you definitively. "It's the same and it's different," said everybody's beau ideal of a leader of men. "As a player and as a manager, it's different. It's hard to explain. I'm so proud of them all."

You could even leave room for a taste of the bitter with the onslaught of the sweet if you were interested in what those the Mets vanquished had to say. Lingering Oriole thought, as expressed by Paul Blair: "I still don't believe they beat us." And that's how he put it approximately three decades after Koosman's complete game victory went in the books. Earl Weaver, however, was grudgingly gracious in the present tense: "They're not lucky. They're a good ballclub."

Yeah, good enough to be world champions.

There were millions of words spoken in the aftermath of the 1969 Mets becoming world champions, and probably tens of millions written since. But perhaps the first words transmitted following Jones's catch of Johnson's fly ball, as hand-lettered on Shea Stadium sign man Karl Ehrhardt's last placard of the year, preserved what had just happened — across this Series, across this season, across the incomprehensible trajectory of this inimitable franchise — most perfectly of all:

THERE ARE NO WORDS

1972-1971-1970-1969

SMILING
FACES
SOMETIMES

M an walked on the moon before the Mets won the World Series, but only by three months. It took almost another six months before the Mets accomplished something that once seemed as impossible as either of those 1969 dream scenarios.

They won on Opening Day. It took a whole new year and a whole new decade, to say nothing of a whole new identity, but the world champions finally did what mere standard-issue squads did as a matter of occasional course. They started their season 1-0.

Somehow it had never happened before. Every other National League team won at least once on Opening Day between 1962 and 1969 — but not the Mets. The franchise that began its life on a nine-game losing streak seemed determined to pay tribute to its birth at the outset of every baseball calendar by losing at least one game before it could garner a win. Even 1969 began as homage to 1962 when the Mets dropped an 11-10 decision to the expansion Expos. The Expos went on to lose 110 games while the Mets were on their way to a miracle, so it was clearly not where everybody involved started but where they finished.

Still, it would be nice to win one and take it from there. Finally, the defending champions did just that. It took extra innings this particular Tuesday in early April — Donn Clendenon singling home a pair in the eleventh at soon-to-be-vacated Forbes Field and Tug McGraw sealing the deal with a scoreless frame — but the Mets finally got off on the right foot in 1970, beating the Bucs, 5-3.

It was a sweet beginning, all right, but the season ahead couldn't help but loom as something of a 162-game morning after. Leonard Shecter articulated the internal sense of the longtime Mets fan in *Once Upon The Polo Grounds* when he wrote, "It is different now." The results of 1969 were wholly magnificent and would remain inscribed in the book of great doings for all time, "yet it is somehow sad [...] We have tasted victory and we shall root not for survival, but for more victory." The comical Mets of 1962 and 1963 were long over before 1969, but there was always a reserve of patience on which to be drawn for when the Mets stumbled, whether out of the gate or for extended periods of a given season. The Mets were still a growing team until 1969.

They were entering only their ninth season in 1970, but as the titular rulers of baseball, it wasn't unreasonable to ask whether the Mets' wonder years had prematurely expired...and to wonder what life would hold in store for a team that had already failed and succeeded in unprecedented proportions. Going after a second consecutive world championship would certainly be a worthwhile Met endeavor (worthwhile enough to draw record crowds to Shea Stadium), but if the success — if not the surprise — of 1969 wasn't to be repeated, the Mets wouldn't be wondrous winners and they couldn't be lovable losers. They would be, essentially, just another ballclub.

The morning after was at hand.

I t was Earth Day, the very first one. Yet it was otherworldly. The stuff Tom Seaver had as he faced the San Diego Padres at Shea Stadium this extraordinary

Wednesday had to have come from another planet. Seaver had already given Mets fans every reason to believe he was not of this realm, in no way to be compared to mere mortals let alone other pitchers. He hadn't lost a regular-season decision since the previous August 5. Though he did absorb a defeat to open the 1969 World Series, so what? He was still Tom Seaver: Cy Young, near-MVP, *Sports Illustrated* Sportsman of the Year and Hickcock Belt winner, signifying his status as Professional Athlete of the Year.

Year? Tom Seaver had lifted the Mets from laughingstocks to contenders to champions in three years' time. In the eyes of those idolized him, he was Athlete of the Decade and in early 1970 was en route to making it two in a row.

Before Earth Day was out, Seaver would be doing a lot in a row.

Tom Terrific, who was presented with his National League Cy Young award before the game, didn't flirt with perfection as he had the previous summer versus the Cubs. Staked to a 1-0 lead by a first-inning Ken Boswell double, he gave it right back when Padre left fielder Al Ferrara homered to tie the score leading off the second. A Bud Harrelson triple regained the lead for the Mets at 2-1 in the bottom of the third. By then, Seaver had punched out five Padres on strikes, an impressive partial total, but nothing noticeably out of the ordinary for the Met ace.

Earth Day began to spin in historic proportions soon enough. Two more San Diego K's in the fourth; another pair in the fifth; and then, Ferrara was out looking to end the sixth. That was 11 strikeouts in six innings, with only two hits allowed. Very Seaveresque, but such mastery was not unprecedented for the man the team's beat writers referred to as The Franchise.

Precedent, however, was about to be shattered. In the seventh inning, Nate Colbert swung and missed at strike three. Dave Campbell took strike three. So did Jerry Morales. Now it was 13 strikeouts over seven innings and, for what it was worth, four consecutive.

Notice was gathering. Gil Hodges could tell Seaver was firing on all cylinders, but needed pitching coach Rube Walker to bring him up to speed on just how many K's were in Seaver's corner. Johnny Podres, who won the Dodgers' only World Series clincher when the Bums were in Brooklyn, was now working for San Diego as a pitching guru and watched from the stands. He once struck out a record eight in a row, so he knew a great performance when it was unfurling before him. "Fantastic," he said to a companion. "As hard as he's throwing, he's still hitting the spots. If you don't swing at it, it's still a strike."

The last Padre to do Seaver damage, Ferrara, could see it as well. "He can't wait to throw the ball," this ex-Dodger told a teammate. Seaver would confirm later that "I was working fast, I guess, but I had my rhythm and my momentum. I didn't want to lose it."

He didn't. In the top of the eighth, Bob Barton took called strike three. Ramon Webster, pinch-hitting for opposing pitcher Mike Corkins (who'd had a pretty good day himself, limiting the Mets to two runs in seven innings), struck out swinging.

Another pinch-hitter, Ivan Murrell, did the same. The total was now 16 strikeouts, the most any Met had ever accumulated in a single game.

Seaver said he didn't know he was that high until he saw it on the scoreboard. Realizing, with two out in the eighth, that he was one K away from the club record (set days earlier by Nolan Ryan), he made a conscious decision to go for it.

And so he went. Seaver's sweet sixteenth left him in position to tie the record for most strikeouts in a single nine-inning game, set by Steve Carlton against the Mets in September 1969. It was already legend that Carlton, pitching into the teeth of an onrushing miracle, lost that game when Ron Swoboda reached him for two two-run homers. Seaver similarly had reason to be concerned that all the strikeouts he was notching didn't guarantee victory. It was still only 2-1 and waiting for him as the third batter of the ninth inning was Al Ferrara.

But first, Van Kelly struck out swinging. Then Cito Gaston struck out looking. That made it 18 strikeouts total, one shy of Carlton, and nine in a row — more than Podres, more than any pitcher had ever struck out consecutively. All that was left was Ferrara and the bat that homered off Tom in the second.

That was in the second. This was in the ninth. This was a time for more history: strike three, swinging. Al Ferrara went down on a low fastball on a one-two count. The Mets won 2-1, with Seaver striking out 19 batters. It was the most any pitcher had fanned in a day game. And the consecutive strikeout feat of 10 straight...never before touched, never again — not for forty years, at any rate — nudged. That Earth Day afternoon made a prophet out of coach Walker, who declared after the game, "I'll stake a lot on this prediction: I don't think anyone's going to come along for a long, long time and match those ten strikeouts in a row."

MAY 9, 1970

88

METS 14 GIANTS 5

SHEA STADIUM

If the New York sports scene was a mountain range, it contained three memorable peaks carved into the Metropolitan Area's consciousness over an unprecedented sixteen-month span. In January 1969, there were the Jets upsetting the Baltimore Colts to capture Super Bowl III. That October, the Mets made Maryland miserable once more, defeating the Orioles to take the 1969 World Series. Finally, on May 8, 1970, the New York Knickerbockers sent the so-called 51st State into yet another state of euphoria, slaying the Los Angeles Lakers in the seventh game of the NBA finals.

The center of the action was Madison Square Garden, where an injured Willis Reed strode determinedly onto the court, sunk two quick baskets and set the tone for one more historic evening. Out at Shea that Friday night, the Mets graciously ceded the spotlight, losing, 7-1, to the Giants, even providing a mid-game rain delay that allowed the 43,000 in attendance a chance to listen to Marv Albert call the Knicks' first championship on their transistor radios. When things went final in Manhattan, the familiar chant of "We're Number One!" returned to Queens despite the 13-14 Mets' doldrums.

Saturday, the baseball team would rebound in style.

While Reed and his teammates let their freshly minted status sink in, the Mets soared to a 14-5 victory over San Francisco, propelled by an eight-run bottom of the fifth that tied the franchise record for most productive inning. It was a mark originally set against the Milwaukee Braves in 1964. The Mets banged out nine hits, with two apiece from Art Shamsky and Donn Clendenon and one that was particularly noteworthy off the bat of Tommie Agee. When Agee singled home third baseman Joe Foy to make it 8-4, Mets, it made him the first Met to ever hit in 20 consecutive games. Tommie had broken Frank Thomas's club hitting streak record of 18 the night before.

Agee's streak, which would end the next day, was a statistical anomaly in the context of the Mets' post-championship season thus far. The romp put the Mets back to .500; they hadn't won more than two in a row or lost more than two in a row yet. Tom Seaver was 6-0, which was Terrific, but it also meant the rest of the staff was 8-14. Foy, acquired in the offseason for outfield prospect Amos Otis, was batting around .200, and even Agee's twenty straight games with a hit hadn't raised his overall average above .250. It had been nearly three weeks since the Mets had last scored more than five runs in a win. Still, it was early and the Mets were by no means doomed. Because the N.L. East was mired in something of a malaise, the Mets' 14-14 record had them only 2 1/2 out, in second place.

Yet as the Knicks reminded the Mets the night before, New York had grown accustomed to coming in first.

MAY 13, 1970

METS 4 CUBS 0

WRIGLEY FIELD

How close can you come? How close can a one-hitter get to being a no-hitter? Besides one hit away, that is?

Gary Gentry found out for himself relatively early along the trail of tears better known as Mets Pitcher Near-Miss Gulch. You could pitch brilliantly, you could vanquish your opponent and, of course, you could earn a Happy Recap for your efforts, but you still missed the brassiest of rings.

In 1970, it hadn't even been a decade that the Mets had gone without pitching a no-hitter. It didn't yet stand out like an official scorer's thumb. Things were happening for the Mets. They'd won a World Series a mere seven months earlier, and nobody saw that coming. The no-hitter...it was bound to happen eventually.

As for Gentry, he was as good a possibility to throw it as any Met. He'd put up plenty of zeroes on plenty of scoreboards, judging by what he accomplished in just over a year in the big leagues. He won 13 games as a rookie in 1969, tossing the four-hitter that clinched the National League East title. Though he wasn't around at its end, he started the game that gave the Mets their first N.L. pennant. And he won the first World Series game ever played at Shea Stadium — with lots of help from his friends Nolan Ryan in relief and Tommie Agee in the field, but it was Gentry's W.

First, Tom Seaver came up in 1967. Then, Jerry Koosman in 1968. Gentry was the next arm in that logical progression. In a way, it was no wonder Gary Gentry and Tom

Seaver were able to fool out-of-town writers covering the 1969 World Series by trading uniform tops during a Memorial Stadium workout and dispensing disparaging quotes about "each other" for laughs. Nos. 41 and 39 were different pitchers, yet it seemed the Mets were cutting a string of hard-throwing righthanders from the same talented cloth. And now, in May of 1970, Gentry was attempting to one-up Seaver, who had thrown an intensely memorable one-hitter ten months earlier.

Like Tom the previous July, Gary was taking aim at a dangerous Chicago Cubs lineup, this time at Wrigley Field. It was the first meeting of the year between the two rivals whose fortunes passed in the midsummer night in '69. Once again, the Cubs and Mets were one-two in the N.L. East, Chicago up by 2 1/2 games in the early going. They had a hard-throwing righthander of their own, Bill Hands, going for them this Wednesday afternoon, and Hands would give his manager, Leo Durocher, nine innings and twelve strikeouts.

But Art Shamsky homered with no one on in the fourth and Gentry nicked Hands for his first hit of the year in the fifth, singling home Wayne Garrett. With a 2-0 lead, Gary became the story of the day, for he was pitching a perfect game at Wrigley Field.

Perfection lasted only until Ron Santo walked to lead off the home fifth, but Gentry erased that flaw from his ledger immediately, when he got right fielder Johnny Callison to ground into a double play. When Ernie Banks grounded to Garrett at third, the no-hitter was still intact. And when the Cubs could generate no more than two grounders and a strikeout in the sixth, Gentry was nine outs away from untrod Met territory.

Gentry received an enhanced cushion in the seventh when Garrett tripled home rookie Mike Jorgensen and Jerry Grote singled in Garrett to up the Met lead to 4-0. Perhaps Wayne's presence in the middle of these Met rallies was an indicator that destiny was unfolding. The redhead wasn't even in the starting lineup. He had come on to replace Joe Foy after Foy was hit by a Hands pitch (on, of course, the hand). Maybe that was the sort of sign Mets fans could take as gospel that Gary Gentry was really going to outdo what Tom Terrific accomplished on July 9, 1969, when he one-hit Chicago at Shea.

When he got through the bottom of the seventh by retiring Don Kessinger, Glenn Beckert and Billy Williams, Gary was only six outs away from making the Mets the fourth expansion team in the modern era to claim a no-hitter. Bill Stoneman of the Montreal Expos recorded one in 1969, his team's first year. Bo Belinsky of the then-Los Angeles Angels chalked up a no-no in 1962, that franchise's second season. And the Houston Colt .45s/Astros had been a veritable no-hit machine since entering the National League alongside the Mets in '62, with Don Nottebart, Ken Johnson and Don Wilson (twice) turning the trick.

As the bottom of the eighth commenced, Gary Gentry and the Mets stood poised to join their ranks.

First up, perennial All-Star Santo. He flied to Agee in center for the first out.

Next, Callison, the former Phillie who won the 1964 All-Star Game at Shea with a three-run homer. He flied to Shamsky's defensive replacement Ron Swoboda in right for the second out.

Four outs to go. The next batter would be Ernie Banks, another Cub with All-Star credentials (impeccable ones) and a 6-for-12 track record versus Gentry in 1969. The two faced off in five games the year before and the pitcher never completely shut down the slugger in any of them.

Gentry worked Banks to a 2-2 count. On the fifth pitch of the at-bat, he threw a chest-high fastball that the pitcher wanted to come in with. "But," as Gary would recount later, "I didn't get it in enough."

The goal was to get Banks to hit the ball in the air. The wind was blowing in off Lake Michigan and Gentry figured he had a good chance to pop up Mr. Cub. But Mr. Cub had other ideas. He lined a looping fly ball to left. The left fielder, Dave Marshall, came running in and stuck out his glove in hopes of making a shoestring catch. The ball tipped off Marshall's glove and fell in fair.

All eyes on official scorer Jim Enright...

Base hit all the way.

Marshall had no beef with the decision: "There's no question but that it was a hit. I slid a little just when I got to the ball. At first, I didn't think I had a chance for it, but the ball seemed to stay up and I went for it."

Gentry couldn't quibble either: "I'm glad it wasn't a cheap hit." But don't think Gary wasn't aware of what was going on. "I started thinking about a no-hitter in the fourth inning," he admitted after finishing off what became a 4-0 one-hitter, "and kept thinking about it until Banks broke it up in the eighth."

A 4-0 one-hitter over the Cubs...just like Seaver had done, though nobody was going to mistake Ernie Banks for 1969's spoiler Jimmy Qualls. But as with Seaver's gargantuan effort, a shutout victory was a shutout victory and a win that pulled the second-place Mets that much closer to the Cubs was what — in the standings, anyway — counted the most.

Gentry's masterpiece went down as the fifth one-hitter in Mets history, filed alongside one apiece from Al Jackson, Jack Hamilton, Seaver and, earlier in 1970, Ryan. Five one-hitters in less than nine seasons, but no no-hitters...and with so many talented arms of late. Definitely a curiosity of sorts, though not a franchise trademark yet for a team still so relatively young. The Mets had achieved a miracle in their eighth year. Everything next to that world championship had to be considered a small wonder. Certainly they were capable of effecting small wonders after 1969.

The wonders of magnificent pitching were not to be underestimated, as Gentry unleashed a three-game stretch that encompassed the best burst of mound work in Met history. In the club's next contest, Friday night at Philadelphia, Seaver tossed another one-hitter (Mike Compton spoiling the party with a third-inning single) while striking out fifteen. On Saturday, it was Jerry Koosman putting an emphatic period at the end of the sentence, "*Boy do the Mets have good pitching.*" Kooz's performance against the Phils was relatively pedestrian compared to what had just transpired: merely a ten-strikeout four-hitter. The sum total of Gentry's, Seaver's and Koosman's consecutive days at the office was microscopic. In unfurling three straight complete-game shutouts, the trio allowed all of six hits — five singles and a double — in 27 innings while striking out 32 would-be hitters.

There are statement games and there are statement series. This one was surely the former and confirmed that it would be the punctuation of the latter.

The Mets and Cubs, bitter rivals in 1969, were at it again in 1970 — at it for an extended stay at Wrigley, too. Thanks to a May rainout, the Mets would be playing a five-game set on the North Side of Chicago. It would be, by definition, long on innings and, as the divisional race was developing, fraught with implications. When the series began, Gil Hodges's second-place Mets trailed Leo Durocher's Cubs by 3 1/2 games, while sitting just a game ahead of the Cardinals and Pirates. The quintet of contests presented the Mets with a rare opportunity to gain massive amounts of ground in the standings. Or it could backfire and send them reeling in the other direction. Anything in between could happen, too.

How would this five-part midsummer sequel to the soap opera that made 1969 famous unfold? Very favorably, it turned out.

First Game: A back-and-forth affair sees the Mets go forth and claim victory after Donn Clendenon clouts a three-run pinch-homer in the eighth to break a 5-5 tie. Tommie Agee's fifth-inning home run helps the club overcome Gary Gentry's shaky start.

Mets win, 9-5; move within 2 1/2 of first place.

Second Game: A seven-run fourth inning, featuring consecutive run-scoring singles from Jerry Grote, Ray Sadecki and Agee, puts the Mets up, 8-5. But it's not enough. Cubs storm back to lead, 10-8, after five. A Ken Boswell two-run single ties it in the ninth. Duffy Dyer, the personification of "light-hitting backup catcher," gets ahold of a Phil Regan pitch and sends it out of Wrigley for the decisive tally.

Mets win, 12-10; move within 1 1/2 of first place.

Third Game: A four-run eighth in this doubleheader opener blows open a game firmly in Tom Seaver's control. Perhaps Seaver loses a bit of control thereafter, as his 8-1 lead is reduced to 9-5 in the bottom of the ninth when Ernie Banks socks a three-run pinch-dinger, the 505th tater of his career. *Well, they are playing two.* Seaver holds on to beat Bill Hands, striking out eleven in the process.

Mets win, 9-5; move within a half-game of first place.

Fourth Game: It's actually kind of quiet batwise in the nightcap. Nolan Ryan gives up one hit in seven innings. Tug McGraw gives up one hit in the next two. Mets collect all the runs they need off prototypical second-game-of-a-doubleheader starter Archie Reynolds.

Mets win 6-1; move into first place with a half-game lead.

That would be enough of a high to leave Chicago on, but the Mets can't go until they play some more. Nobody would rightfully complain about a 4-1 series versus the dangerous Cubs, but a loss in the finale would undo some serious Met momentum and elbow them out of first place almost as soon as they arrived there. The Mets had thus far in 1970 made only a token appearance at the top of the division, in the middle of May. All the struggling the erstwhile Miracle workers had done might be for naught if they couldn't get out of Wrigley in first.

So the struggle continued this Thursday afternoon. And if it had been a struggle for the Mets, imagine the state the Cubs were in: they had given up an instantly legendary large lead in 1969 and now, in 1970, they were fumbling another sizable margin. As recently as a week earlier they led the pack by 4 1/2. Now they were behind. But a win would flip the order and give Durocher's darlings something to cackle about.

No such luck, Leo.

The Mets dug a hole for Cub starter Ken Holtzman in the top of the second, kicked the lefty in and proceeded to methodically shovel dirt all over him. Clendenon led off with a single. Ron Swoboda doubled him to third. Joe Foy's infield hit scored Clink, while Rocky raced to third when All-Star shortstop Don Kessinger made a poor throw to first. A Wayne Garrett single brought home Swoboda and put Foy on second. Red and Joe put themselves a base ahead on a double steal, with Foy scampering home as catcher Jack Hiatt's throw landed in the outfield.

Mets led, 3-0, by now and were positioned to do a little more damage as Holtzman walked Grote. Jerry Koosman struck out on a bunt attempt, but that was just a temporary reprieve for Holtzman and the Cubs. Agee singled in Garrett and Bud Harrelson doubled home Grote, with Agee taking third. Now it was 5-0 and Durocher was removing Holtzman. Roberto Rodriguez came on in relief and got Ken Singleton to ground to Glenn Beckert at second base, another All-Star infielder.

And another All-Star infield error for the Cubs. Beckert booted the ball for Chicago's third miscue of the inning. Agee raced home and the Mets led, 6-0.

From there, it was mostly Koosman. He'd give up an RBI single and a two-run homer to Jim Hickman but would keep the Cubs ice cold otherwise. And for insurance purposes, Foy singled Clendenon home in the seventh inning for the Mets seventh run and scored the Mets' eighth run when he stole home on the back end of yet another double steal (notorious speedster Grote taking second).

Ahead, 8-3, in the ninth, Kooz closed the deal: Hickman flied to right, Ron Santo popped to first and Banks — who was not known to suggest, "Let's play five in four days!" — grounded to short. The Mets held on and swept the five-game series to go up a game-and-a-half on the Cubs, two on the surging Pirates and five on the fading Cardinals.

The Mets had never before taken every game of a five-game series.

But they had won a division title and were suddenly positioning themselves to possibly win their second straight.

If "Let's win two!" wasn't their rallying cry, they were sure playing like it was.

91 JULY 24, 1970
METS 2 DODGERS 1 (10)
SHEA STADIUM

For every runner who ever danced off third to distract a pitcher with a game on the line, Tommie Agee has a question:

Why are you just dancing? Why aren't you running?

Tommie Agee ran this particular Friday evening in a game against the Dodgers when the score was tied at one in the bottom of the tenth. Apparently, Tommie wasn't in the mood to hang around all night.

Jerry Koosman and Bill Singer pitched as if hardly anybody was going to score for a very long time, each of them going nine, each of them giving up just a run apiece. Extra innings were handed over to the screwballers, Tug McGraw for the Mets, Jim Brewer for L.A. Tug pitched a swift 1-2-3 top of the tenth. Brewer's bottom of the frame, however, loomed as more complicated.

Gil Hodges liked what he saw out of Tug's arm and he left him in to bat to lead off the tenth. McGraw must have known a screwball when he saw one, because he singled off Brewer. Now the order would turn over and traditional leadoff hitter Agee found himself in the unusual position of being asked to bunt a pitcher to second. Agee bunted, but not all that effectively. Six-time Gold Glove first baseman Wes Parker snared Tommie's bunt and fired it to second, where Dodger shortstop Billy Grabarkewitz attempted to force McGraw. But the plan became *Mission: Impossible* when the first four letters of Billy's last name proved something of a misnomer. Grabarkewitz could not grab the ball, and his drop of Parker's relay meant McGraw was safe at second and Agee was on first.

At this point, Gil, smelling a win, removed McGraw for Al Weis. And Brewer, smelling redemption, picked off the pinch-runner.

And Agee? He stole second.

So now the Mets have a runner on second — one who's stolen 22 bases on the season — with one out. Buddy Harrelson is at the plate (and has been the whole time Weis and Agee were doing their respective things). And Buddy will continue to stand there as Brewer uncorks a wild pitch. It doesn't get very far from catcher Tom Haller, but it has enough distance to allow Agee to zip to third.

After all that activity, Buddy strikes out. But Ken Singleton walks. And Donn Clendenon, pinch-hitting for Mike Jorgensen, also walks. Now the bases are loaded, and Cleon Jones is at bat. He works the count to one-and-one when he hears his Alabama *amigo* Agee shouting, "LOOK OUT! LOOK OUT!"

Tommie Agee has decided to steal home. He's watched Brewer's long windup, seen the pitcher was paying him no mind and figured he could make it. He had tried something similar in the playoffs against Atlanta the October before. At that time, Jones didn't see him coming and fouled a liner that nearly took off Agee's head.

Not this time, though. Cleon faked a swing and Agee slid home ahead of Haller's tag, inciting "the capacity crowd at Shea Stadium" to a fine froth of "standing and roaring," per Bob Murphy. The Mets won, 2-1, on Tommie Agee's club record-tying 23rd steal of the season (matching Jones's 1968 mark), his second steal of the inning, his second steal of home of the season, the first and only time a Met has ended a game by stealing home.

"I was almost 80 percent sure I could make it," Agee estimated. "If [Brewer] had just looked over at me, I couldn't have gone."

Hodges had another take on playing the percentages: "Ninety-nine and nine-tenths of the time, you always steal home on your own. And I've never given the sign for the other one-tenth. It was a very nice time to be safe."

For a slugger obtained in 1969 to make lefthanded pitchers nervous, Donn Clendenon turned out to be not all that particular whose ERAs he damaged. By 1970, his bat was a source of power against all comers. On a Tuesday night, with the Giants in town, he showed just how evenhanded he could be.

Donn started innocently enough, against San Francisco righty Rich Robertson. The Mets were up, 1-0, in the bottom of a first after a Bud Harrelson triple scored Tommie Agee. Clendenon's fly ball to Willie Mays was deep enough to bring home Buddy and give Jim McAndrew a two-run lead.

Two innings later, Clendenon's intentions grew bolder. Robertson allowed Harrelson a double and walked Ken Singleton ahead of the Mets' first baseman. The righty-on-righty matchup favored the hitter in a big way. Clendenon blasted a Robertson delivery clear into Shea's left field Mezzanine, boosting the Mets' third-inning margin to 5-0.

And for an encore? With the Mets ahead 6-0 in the fourth and two more runners on base, Donn stepped to the plate against a Giant lefty, Mike Davison. The southpaw felt pretty small once Clendenon did his now-customary damage to him. It was another three-run homer to left, not only putting the Mets out of reach for the night — they'd win, 12-2 — but giving Clink the club's single-game RBI record, with seven. Two three-run bombs plus that innocent sacrifice fly placed his total one over the mark established by Frank Thomas in 1962 and tied by Jerry Buchek in 1967.

Clendenon crashed the Met record books again by the end of 1970 by notching 97 runs batted in for the year, the most by any Met to date...and he did it on a team that scored the fourth-fewest runs in the twelve-team National League. He also became the first Met to post a slugging percentage of better than .500 (.515) in at least 400 plate appearances. The previous RBI high belonged to Thomas, who totaled 94 in '62. Frank benefited from the Polo Grounds' friendly dimensions and playing almost every day. Donn, though, was deployed by Gil Hodges in only 121 games in 1970, in accordance with his manager's predilection for platooning, and wound up coming to the plate 190 fewer times than Thomas had eight years earlier. His 1969 lefty-swinging counterpart, Ed Kranepool, had slumped badly enough to be sent to Triple-A Tidewater for the bulk of the summer, but Hodges spelled Clendenon (who was prone to striking out when not driving in runs) with lefty outfielder Art Shamsky quite a bit in midseason.

After his seven-RBI performance against the Giants, however, the 35-year-old Clendenon was the starting first baseman in all but ten of the Mets' remaining 63 games. The end result was, pound-for-pound, the best power season any Met produced across the franchise's first decade.

In coming to grips with the humble Mets' "inevitable" rise having come "so soon, so swiftly," author Leonard Shecter comforted himself and his readers in 1970's *Once Upon The Polo Grounds* by reasoning, "Still, the Mets are still there (at slightly higher prices)

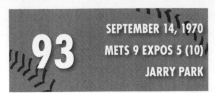

and there is still much joy to take from them."

That was true enough for the 2,679,479 who anted to enter Shea Stadium in the Mets' post-championship year. Collectively, those folks represented the highest paid attendance any New York baseball team had ever drawn, and that was in the days when tickets sold but not used weren't included in the totals. The defending champion Mets gave their fans their money's worth in terms of making most every game count. There was a second consecutive pennant race in Queens in 1970 and the Mets attempted to finish it with another flourish.

On the second Monday in September, in Montreal, they pulled a tenth-inning rally out of their recent past, scoring four runs in the top of the tenth to take a 9-5 lead over the Expos. Nolan Ryan pitched the final inning to seal the win and assure the 78-69 Mets a share of first place with Pittsburgh, one length ahead of the Cubs. With fifteen games remaining — and Cleon Jones riding a new team-record 22-game hitting streak (he would stretch it to 23) — the Mets appeared to be taking a page from their 1969 manual by getting hot at exactly the right time. They were 11-5 in their previous sixteen outings and had Jerry Koosman and Tom Seaver poised to take the ball the next two nights against the cellar-dwelling 'Spos.

Imminently, however, 1970 proved itself something less than 1969, for September 14 marked the last day the '70 Mets ended atop their division.

The age of miracles was fading too soon to black. No way the Mets would have lost back-to-back September starts to a last-place club a year earlier with their pair of aces on the mound, but their studs seemed close to spent this mid-September. Koosman battled elbow miseries all year and Seaver, in the midst of throwing a personal-high 290.2 regular-season innings, was struggling for the first time in his brilliant career. Tom had started 1970 at 17-6; he would end it at 18-12. His 2.82 ERA would lead the league (as would his 283 strikeouts) but it had risen steadily from the 2.28 he carried to the mound in mid-July when Gil Hodges started him in the All-Star Game.

After leaving Montreal disappointed, the second-place Mets came home a game-and-a-half out to host a four-game series against the front-running Pirates. They dropped one-run heartbreakers Friday and Saturday before taking on the Bucs in a Sunday doubleheader they pretty much had to sweep. The twinbill drew a season-high 54,806 fans who hoped 1969 would come out to play one more time.

If there was going to be a sequel, it would have to happen with a noticeably revised cast, since several Mets who were darlings of New York the previous October were now receiving their mail in distant precincts. The first to go was elder statesman Ed Charles, released barely a week after a ticker-tape parade in his and his teammates' honor cloaked lower Broadway. If you could efficiently delete your poet laureate from your roster, you could forego sentimentality altogether. Thus, the 1970 Mets would compete without the Glider; without Jack DiLauro (lost in the Rule 5 draft to Houston); and without J.C. Martin (traded to the enemy Cubs late in spring).

Top prospect Amos Otis was given up on and traded for third baseman Joe Foy in December of '69; Otis made the A.L. All-Stars as a Royal, while Foy floundered in Flushing. Supersub Bobby Pfeil would be dealt mid-season '70. Rod Gaspar, who scored the winning run in Game Four of the World Series, would get no more than a callup cameo and then would go to the Padres as payment for just-passing-through Ron Herbel a year after he was one of 25 heroes. Don Cardwell became a Brave in July 1970, a month after reliever Cal Koonce was sold to the Red Sox. And foreshadowing the unfolding upheaval of on-field personnel, Johnny Murphy, the GM who shepherded the Mets to their 1969 destiny, suffered a fatal heart attack in January and never saw the championship flag raised. He was succeeded by Bob Scheffing.

Despite so many pieces of the '69 puzzle having gone askew, Koosman sparked genuine hope in the opener when he twirled a vintage two-hitter to pull the Mets to within 2 1/2 of first. But those good vibes dissipated in the nightcap when Pittsburgh knocked Seaver out of the box in the sixth en route to a 9-5 thrashing that pushed the Mets 3 1/2 behind with nine to play.

The club left Shea Stadium on September 20 as defending champs. When they returned eight days later, they were still entitled to hoist their 1969 flag, but their title defense was over. The Mets' last road trip of 1970 finished off their aspirations of a repeat. The Pirates eliminated them at brand new Three Rivers Stadium on September 27, clinching their *first* division championship in the process. The Mets would play out the string as also-rans (third place, 83-79, six games out) and head into the playoffless winter not as perennial bumblers, nor as workers of miracles, but as just another baseball team... one that would enter 1971 by shedding signature '69er Ron Swoboda.

Swoboda no longer a Met? It was as if the club, having failed to repeat at doing the impossible, had consciously decided being Amazin' could only get them so far.

They hadn't been bad in 1970, mind you. Slightly subpar Seaver was still Seaver; the pitching in general was relatively solid — surely off from '69, yet the class of the league in earned run average, hits allowed and strikeouts; and the fielding had been a strong suit, particularly up the middle. Jerry Grote continued to enhance his defensive reputation behind the plate, Ken Boswell set a league record for consecutive errorless games at second (85), Bud Harrelson tied one at short (54) and Tommie Agee earned a Gold Glove in center.

But clearly they hadn't been great in 1970, especially when it came to hitting. As *Sports Illustrated*'s Alfred Wright winced with a month left in the season, "their bats usually seem to be made of Styrofoam and rolled up copies of the *Daily News*." Impressive stats from Agee (24 homers, 31 steals) and Donn Clendenon (22 homers, 97 ribbies) were the exceptions on a team that batted .249 as a unit. Even Jones's 23-game hitting streak provided mostly window dressing for a batting average (.277) that plunged 63 points from a year earlier. The club finished second in the N.L. in walks, yet ninth in runs scored. All things considered, the Mets and their .512 winning percentage were crammed right where they deserved to be: squarely in the middle of the pack.

While there would still be much joy to take from these mid-level Mets in the seasons ahead, most of it would have to be mined precisely, precariously and painstakingly. As nearly 3 million paying customers had just learned, once-in-a-lifetime years hardly ever happen twice.

Twenty-four years old, with the stuff to have struck out as many ten batters a in game eleven times already. That describes the pitcher the Mets sent to the hill for the nightcap of a doubleheader at San Diego Stadium this Saturday.

That's quite a weapon to have at your disposal. Why you'd want to give up on it is anybody's guess. But the Mets weren't giving up on Nolan Ryan at this stage of the 1971 season. They were giving him the ball and he was giving opposing lineups like the Padres nothing to swing at but a blur.

To be fair to those early Friar batters, the blur started its journey toward their bats as a ball at some point, but it was hard for any individual San Diegan to tell. That's how fast young Ryan was as a rule...and make no mistake: in this game, Nolan Ryan ruled.

Every inning that Ryan pitched — and he went the distance — included at least one Padre strikeout. Seven frames ended on a strikeout. The bottom of the sixth gave the home team some hope, as Nolan lived down to his reputation for wildness and walked the first two batters. The Padres' three best hitters were up next. They were also down next.

Cito Gaston...K

Nate Colbert...K

Ollie Brown...K

This was what Nolan Ryan did. It was his *modus operandi* to blow balls by hitters. Sometimes other things happened. Sometime he missed. In the first inning, a walk to second baseman Don Mason led to a run via a fielder's choice, an error and a wild pitch, but that was all the damage Ryan sustained this Saturday. He struck early, he struck often.

He struck out Gaston and Ivan Murrell three times apiece. He struck out every starter at least once, except for shortstop Enzo Hernandez, but he made up for it by striking out pinch-hitter Angel Bravo. And, as if to mix things up, he got third baseman Ed Spiezio to fly out to Tim Foli at short for the final out of a 2-1 win (Art Shamsky drove in both New York runs).

Nolan Ryan had just struck out 16 batters, the most he had ever struck out as a Met, the second-most any Met pitcher had ever fanned. Only Tom Seaver's National League record-tying performance against the Padres a year earlier yielded more K's (19); only Dwight Gooden and Sid Fernandez would ever match 16 as Met pitchers in the ensuing four decades. What's more, Ryan turned in his twelfth double-digit strikeout showing as a Met that Saturday in San Diego. They weren't all as neat as this four-hitter. Sometimes he walked more than four. Sometimes he could throw as hard as he wanted and he wasn't effective enough to win.

But he was 24, and no one could deny his talent. Six starts into 1971, his record was 6-1 and his ERA was 1.08. Ryan couldn't keep up that pace for the rest of the season. There'd be a game in June when he'd walk seven and give up six runs in less than six innings. In July, he'd go five and walk nine. But there was also to be an outing at Montreal when he scattered eleven hits en route to a 4-1 complete game victory, striking out 10. And later, he'd K 12 in six innings, walking only one for his 14th double-digit strikeout game with the Mets.

Surely the flamethrowing young man from Alvin, Tex., was a mixed bag. Surely there were some clunkers buried deep in that sack. His final start of the season saw him face five St. Louis Cardinals. He'd walk the first four he faced and then surrender a two-run single to Ted Simmons. Gil Hodges removed him then and there, leaving Nolan Ryan with a 1971 mark of 10-14, an ERA that had ballooned to 3.97 and a walk total that topped a hundred: 116 BB in 152 IP, against 137 SO.

Ryan was what would later be known in the industry as a project, though by the time that kind of nomenclature was catching on, Nolan would deliver on his promise. He'd strike out 10 or more 201 times from 1972 to 1993, matching or exceeding the 16 he fanned against San Diego 15 times. After recording 29 victories in 67 decisions for the Mets through 1971, he'd compile a record of 295-254 for the rest of his career, becoming baseball's twentieth 300-game winner before he was done pitching. Seven of those wins would be no-hitters.

But Nolan Ryan wouldn't do any of that in a New York Mets uniform.

JUNE 19, 1971
95 METS 6 PHILLIES 5 (15)
SHEA STADIUM

Good thing this Saturday at Shea was Helmet Day. The fans needed protection from all the balls flying off all the bats. The Mets and Phillies sent their respective aces to the hill: Tom Seaver versus Rick Wise. Didn't matter. Seaver was socked. Wise was wasted. They gave up a combined 19 hits and neither man got past the sixth. When the dust cleared on their ledgers, the score was tied, 4-4.

And then, suddenly...no scoring. The Met and Phillie bullpens went into lockdown mode. The Mets had one mammoth chance to untie matters in the seventh when Woodie Fryman loaded the bases, but Tim Foli struck out to end the threat. Fryman gave way to Joe Hoerner and he gave up next to nothing in five innings of work — two hits, two walks and no runs. Hoerner was matched zero for zero by Tug McGraw. The Tugger allowed only a walk and a single over his five innings. It stayed 4-4 from the sixth through the thirteenth, by which time Hoerner and McGraw had handed their scoreless strings to Billy Wilson and Danny Frisella.

But just in case any of the youngsters in what remained of the crowd of 52,171 thought about using their helmets as pillows, the game was about to return to offensively minded. In the top of the fourteenth, with Larry Bowa on second and Oscar Gamble on first, the Phillies tried to make something happen with two out. They put on a double steal that gave them a little more than they hoped for. Thanks to some fancy rundown footwork on Gamble's part, Bowa scored to give the Phils a 5-4 lead (Larry was credited with a pair of stolen bases). Gamble landed on second and eventually third as two walks followed. Frisella, however, extricated himself from total disaster — potentially Hell Met Day— by flying John Vukovich to center for the final out.

The Mets' response against Wilson was much simpler. With one out, Ken Singleton homered to retie the game at five in the bottom of the fourteenth. Frisella, still out there in the fifteenth, gave up two more Phillie singles (their seventeenth and eighteenth hits of the day), but stranded the runners by striking out Willie Montañez. The final blow of the day belonged to Donn Clendenon, whose two-out home run off Wilson brought the curtain down on a 6-5 affair. It was Clendenon's third extra-base hit of the game, and he entered as a pinch-hitter in the ninth. The Mets rapped out fifteen hits altogether and were treated to three Phillie errors and six Phillie walks yet left sixteen runners on. Philadelphia, however, outdid them in the LOB column, with seventeen men who never found their way home.

They called Atlanta Stadium — later Atlanta-Fulton County Stadium — the Launching Pad. On this Saturday night in Dixie, there was an obvious reason for the nickname: it was the ballpark that launched the 1971 Mets into the record books.

AUGUST 7, 1971
METS 20 BRAVES 6
ATLANTA STADIUM

In an era when NASA still counted down to moon launches at Cape Kennedy (née Canaveral), the Mets took the reverse tack in the first inning: not so much 3-2-1...but lifting off with 1...2...3 runs to get their exploration of line score space going against Braves righty Ron Reed. An error by Brave shortstop Marty Perez on Bud Harrelson's leadoff grounder was just the nudge the Mets needed to start soaring. Agee singled, sending Harrelson to third. Agee stole second. And then the Mets orbited their average 1971 per-game run total of 3.6 via a Cleon Jones single, an Ed Kranepool sac fly and a Ken Boswell double that right fielder Mike Lum leapt and batted down at the fence before it could shed its booster rocket and become a two-run homer.

Nice effort, though one is tempted to say Mike needn't have bothered.

Because of the right fielder's effort, the Mets were limited to three runs — not an inauspicious start, but not necessarily ostentatious. And once Lum nicked Nolan Ryan for an RBI single in the bottom of the first, you would have guessed both teams would avail themselves of the offensive amenability of the Launching Pad.

You would have guessed wrong. The top of the second proved the only glare rockets would give off at Atlanta Stadium would be of the blue and orange variety.

This is how the Mets blasted off toward double-digits:

Jerry Grote singled.

Nolan Ryan bunted him to second and was safe at first.

Harrelson bunted them over and was also safe at first.

Wayne Garrett lifted a fly ball to Sonny Jackson in center to make it Mets 4 Braves 1, as Grote scored and the other baserunners moved up.

Jones was intentionally walked to set up a double play. Except it set up an RBI single for Cleon, increasing the Mets' lead to 5-1.

Ron Reed handed the ball to manager Lum Harris who handed it to lefty reliever Mike McQueen who threw it four times out of the strike zone past the righthanded Donn Clendenon, inserted by a run-ravenous Gil Hodges to pinch-hit (or, technically, pinch-walk) for lefty Kranepool.

That made it 6-1, Mets. And that was as close as the Braves would be until Sunday, because McQueen didn't miss the strike zone with the next batter, Boswell. Didn't miss his bat, either. The only thing McQueen's pitch of greatest consequence missed was a landing spot within the chummy confines of Atlanta Stadium. Ken struck it but good, blasting it off the right field foul pole for a grand slam that brought the moon, the stars and the heavens down on the Atlanta Braves.

Mets 10 Braves 1 in the top of the second. A long night was at hand for at least one of those teams.

Sometimes somebody gets that big a lead and things settle down. Sure enough, a combination of Ryan, McQueen and complacency conspired to keep the score unchanged through the fourth. But come the fifth, the Mets' bats grew restless once more. After two outs, Grote singled, Ryan singled, Harrelson walked and Garrett singled to drive in two. 12-1, Mets. Mike McQueen's evening ended and Steve Barber's began...but not happily, as Agee singled home another to make it 13-1, Mets.

Nolan Ryan needed just three outs to qualify for the win, assuming the Mets didn't blow a twelve-run lead. Only the most nervous Mets fan would have considered that a possibility, but Ryan wasn't sharp. Earl Williams singled in Hank Aaron and Zolio Versalles belted a three-run homer to cut the Braves' deficit to 13-5. Under just about any other circumstance imaginable, Hodges would have pulled Ryan, but Nolan had some cushion with which to work. He got the next two outs and would go eight.

Besides, the Mets got back most of what their pitcher gave up when they batted in the top of the sixth. Grote drove in one and Tim Foli, having taken over short for Harrelson, singled in two more. The Mets finished their half of the inning up, 16-5. Ryan allowed another run in the bottom of the sixth, but Clendenon answered with a two-run homer in the top of the seventh to give the Mets a comfortable 18-6 lead.

Comfortable? More like luxurious. But what about historic? A record was at hand if the Mets could grab it. Seven years earlier in Chicago, the Mets famously put 19 runs on the Wrigley Field scoreboard. If it wasn't famous enough for simply being 19 runs or for the notion of the perpetually cellar-dwelling 1964 Mets of all people scoring 19 runs, it took on the stuff of legend when the story got out that somebody called a newspaper somewhere and asked a) if it was true the Mets had scored 19 runs that day and — once that was confirmed as fact — b) did the Mets win?

The Mets were futile enough to be funny back then. By 1971, however, they weren't particularly amusing or terribly exciting. They offered generally superb pitching and reliable defense most nights, but rarely the kind of hitting that would send fans scurrying to their phones to verify their run totals. A 9-20 July knocked the Mets out of contention for the first time in three years, making them, by objective standards as they groped about the .500 mark, a fairly run-of-the-mill operation.

"Everything considered," Leonard Koppett would write just a couple of years later,

"1971 was probably the least satisfying year the Mets had ever experienced. Not only were the mini-rewards of the pre-championship days no longer possible, but also the status of champion was officially gone." By Koppett's reckoning, "The Mets moved into complete ordinariness."

Against this drab backdrop, the Mets aimed for the extraordinary, just as they had done for more than six months two seasons before; just as the U.S. space program had done that very same season. The Mets and man landed on the moon in 1969. For this one night in Atlanta, the Mets were shooting for it again.

In the ninth inning, it was still 18-6 when the Braves' Bob Priddy got two quick outs. But then mission control transmitted word of one final rally to make this Metropolitan score truly astronomical. Clendenon walked. Boswell singled. Ken Singleton singled. The bases were loaded and the stage was set.

Grote grounded to Versalles at third...and the former American League MVP booted it. In came Boswell. In came Clendenon. The Mets had their twentieth run — their most ever. The 20-6 win went into the Mets record book and, like Neil Armstrong's American flag, stayed planted there long after NASA stopped scheduling lunar excursions.

One big night for the New York Mets. One giant leap for Ken Boswell.

AUGUST 10, 1971
METS 6 PADRES 4
SAN DIEGO STADIUM

Decades into the future, when relief pitching would become a more specialized craft, the Mets would seek surefire answers to their periodic ninth-inning insecurities by importing the hardest-throwing relievers on the open market. Yet none of those high-priced closers — nor any of their relievers assigned any other innings — would ever strike out as many in one outing as a humble screwballer did one Tuesday night in San Diego in 1971.

When the Mets fan thinks Tug McGraw, many qualities rush to mind, but strikeout artist isn't necessarily one of them. Yet there wasn't much touching of the Tugger by the Padres in his swingingest and missingest performance.

Gil Hodges called on McGraw in the sixth to hold a 5-3 lead. It didn't begin auspiciously, as Nate Colbert tagged him for a leadoff home run. The occasionally excitable southpaw settled down, teasing two harmless flyballs before striking out Ed Spiezio to end the inning.

Tug apparently decided he liked going this route and kept the K's coming. He struck out the side in the seventh, notched two more strikeouts in a scoreless eighth and, with the Mets up 6-4, made the ninth one for the books. He struck out Spiezio again, then Barton (whom he fanned in the seventh) and, finally, pinch-hitter Fred Kendall, usually a pitcher.

Nine strikeouts for McGraw, the most any Met ever collected coming out of the bullpen. And let's not overlook the endurance factor. Though Tug is recalled as a fireman extraordinaire, closing then and closing now are two radically different concepts. His work at San Diego Stadium accounted for one of nine relief stints of four or more innings in 1971. The load didn't seem to hurt Tug, either. Though he ceded the team lead in saves to righty Danny Frisella, McGraw's ERA of 1.70, WHIP of 1.027 and strikeouts-per-nine-innings average of 8.8 — over a staggering 111 innings (105 in relief) — make a case for this season being his most effective, if not necessarily his most fabled.

The most irresistible force in all of baseball was on the mound at Shea Stadium, seeking his penultimate win...penultimate in the sense that it was the next-to-last step toward his ultimate goal. When Tom Seaver was pitching as he was down the stretch in 1971, could there be any doubt he'd get exactly what he sought?

98

SEPTEMBER 26, 1971
METS 3 PIRATES 1
SHEA STADIUM

As of the first of August, Seaver was having his typically brilliant season, except where the all-important (for forty years ago) won-lost listings were concerned. Despite an ERA of 2.26, Seaver found himself dragging around a pedestrian record of 11-8. "One thing is clear," Jack Lang wrote in the *Sporting News* at that juncture. "It is not Tom Seaver's year."

True to Lang's analysis, Seaver was "pitching well enough to win, but was not winning" consistently across the first four months of the season. He had the same number of losses as his primary pitching rival Ferguson Jenkins — and a demonstrably superior ERA — but the Cub ace had six more wins.

Why? Essentially, the Mets never scored for Seaver. Four of his previous five losses as a starter were absorbed by scores of 3-2, 2-0, 2-1 and 3-2. Tom's 1971 no-decisions included an outing in which he shut out the Reds for nine innings (the Mets won 1-0 in eleven) and held the Braves to two runs in 9 2/3 innings before allowing a tying home to Ralph Garr (the Braves won, 4-3, in thirteen). After being supported lavishly in a 9-1 complete game win on August 6 to boost his record to 12-8, Seaver rediscovered what it was like to be starved for runs when he went ten innings, scattered three hits, struck out fourteen Padres...and had to depart for a pinch-hitter in the eleventh because it was nothing-nothing (the Padres won in twelve).

Much as fictional Lou Brown, manager of the *Major League* version of the Cleveland Indians somehow calculated his club would require 32 wins to capture its division, one can picture Seaver deciding after that August 11 start at San Diego what it was going to take to win 20 games. They can only do that in the movies, maybe, but it sure appeared Seaver scripted himself a purposeful beeline straight to that milestone of excellence.

The Mets were en route to an indifferent 83-79, tied-for-third-place finish, but Seaver never stopped competing. Tom Terrific clearly wanted that round number next to his name. "It takes 20 victories for people to recognize you as a great pitcher," he said as 1971 wound down. "I'd have been satisfied with my season even if I didn't win 20. But this proves something to all those people who may not know baseball as some of us do. All they do is look in the 'W' column."

Seaver was worried about what casual fans thought? Or was he mostly concerned with living up to his own standard? "I feel I'm the best pitcher in baseball," the five-time All-Star and 1969 Cy Young Award winner said. "I really do."

Might as well remind the rest of humanity.

In the six starts that followed his no-decision in San Diego, Seaver went 6-0, with each win a route-going effort and only one of them yielding as many as two earned runs allowed. The Mets gave him six or more runs to work with in five of those starts, but before he could feel comfortable about making a mistake, his supporting cast went back to its previous offensive stupor. Seaver lost a 1-0 complete game heartbreaker to the Cubs at Shea when opposing pitcher Juan Pizarro homered in the eighth. "I pitched very well," he said of his effort. "I didn't win, though, did I? I didn't win. That's all that counts." Tom gave up three hits in seven innings five days later at Wrigley but was bested when rookie Burt Hooton two-hit the Mets to beat him, 3-0.

The back-to-back losses in which the Mets scored nothing for him left Seaver at 18-10. Never mind that his ERA was a mere 1.81. Never mind that he had 266 strikeouts. He wasn't going to get to his goal of 20 wins unless he won his 19th and came back on short rest to go for the big one.

Nineteen, it turned out, was plenty big on its own steam. Taking on the division champion Pirates on a Sunday afternoon at Shea, Seaver could have been working with his groundskeeping pal Pete Flynn — he was mowing down batters like they were blades of grass. Three up, three down in the first; three up, three down in the second; three up, three down in the third.

Seaver was relentless. Given a run in the first on a Donn Clendenon RBI single and two more on hits by Cleon Jones and Tommie Agee in the fifth, the Franchise went about owning the Bucs and this game. Three up, three down in the fourth; three up, three down in the fifth; three up, three down in the sixth.

Tom Seaver was pitching a perfect game against the Pittsburgh Pirates. Roberto Clemente had the day off, but Danny Murtaugh had started several of his dangerous-hitting regulars: Willie Stargell, Al Oliver, Bob Robertson, Dave Cash. Seaver was setting down every Pirate he saw. The strikeouts were piling up. He had fanned ten in the first six innings. Win No. 19 was in sight, and it might come on the wings of the first no-hitter in Mets history...*the first perfect game in Mets history.*

Those particular wings were clipped as soon as the seventh got underway. Cash walked to end the bid for perfection. Then Vic Davalillo, playing in place of Clemente, stroked a clean single to center that chased Cash to third. There went the no-hitter. Oliver's run-scoring fly ball to center spoiled the shutout, too. Now there was the matter of holding on to the lead. A runner was on, only one was out and Stargell, who already had 47 home runs (and had been clobbering the Mets literally since the day Shea opened) was up next.

Tom opted for a sinking fastball. His desire was to get Wilver to pound one into the ground and set up an inning-ending double play. True to the way Seaver planned and executed his pitching over the last two months of 1971, that's precisely what happened:

1-6-3, Seaver to Bud Harrelson to Clendenon.

"That's exactly what I was trying to do," Seaver said. "I know that sounds egocentric, but that's damn good pitching."

Tom and the Mets stayed ahead. And Seaver returned to flawlessness thereafter. He retired the final six batters to win his nineteenth, 3-1. His only blemishes were that walk to Cash and that single to Davalillo. Because of the DP, he wound up facing just one batter over the minimum.

But he was one victory under the minimum for what was universally accepted as part and parcel of the definition of greatness...even though nobody was arguing Seaver wasn't as great a pitcher as could be found.

SEPTMEBER 30, 1971
METS 6 CARDINALS 1
SHEA STADIUM

"The numbers come close to saying, yes, George Thomas Seaver is the best pitcher in baseball," Vic Ziegel wrote in the *Post* as the Mets' 1971 season limped to its conclusion. "There is, Seaver understands, only one more number *he* must add to the list. Seaver will be trying for his 20th victory against St. Louis Thursday in the final game of the season."

That date was only four days removed from the third one-hitter of his career, meaning Tom Seaver would go on three days' rest...which struck some Seaver-watchers as a little too Seaver-centric for a team game. Tom had established he was at his absolute best pitching every five days, something less on his fourth day. He had indicated he'd only go on short rest if it was a really important contest. The Mets were long out of the race by the end of the season. Obviously, the cynics muttered, it's important to *Seaver* that he wins 20.

Single-mindedness, of course, is what lifts a competitor above his peers, and Seaver's drive elevated him to a plane where he had few, maybe no peers. (It also elevated the Mets to a World Championship two years earlier, when nobody outside of Baltimore seemed to mind how badly he wanted to win.) Of course Seaver wanted to pitch the final game of the year. Of course Gil Hodges would let him. And of course he'd win it, attaining No. 20 in a brilliant complete game stifling of the Cardinals, 6-1, striking out 13 Redbirds along the way.

From a deceptively middling 11-8 through two-thirds of the season, Tom Seaver finished 1971 at 20-10. His 289 strikeouts set a record for most K's by a righthanded National League pitcher. His 1.76 ERA was the lowest in the league since Bob Gibson's 1.12 in 1968 and wouldn't be bettered until Dwight Gooden's 1.53 in 1985. Nobody struck out more batters per inning. Nobody gave up fewer walks and hits per inning. It may very well have been the greatest year turned in by someone acknowledged far, wide and forever as one of the greatest pitchers to ever play the game.

But Ferguson Jenkins, who posted an ERA a full run higher, went 24-13 and was voted the Cy Young Award by a pretty wide margin. All those writers voting against Tom must have done was look in the "W" column.

1972

Comebacks in baseball are usually cast in the light of the scoreboard. One team leads, the other team seeks to change that transitory situation. For the 1972 Mets, however, coming back took on a whole other dimension.

100

MAY 7, 1972
METS 8 PADRES 6
SHEA STADIUM

They had to come back from a tragedy.

On April 2, as Spring Training wound down and baseball dealt with its first serious labor stoppage, the Mets' world changed irreversibly. Their manager, their leader and their guiding hand, Gil Hodges, suffered his second heart attack and died immediately. It was a shock to the organization and all of baseball.

One minute he was finishing a round of golf with his coaches.

The next minute, he was dead.

The Mets couldn't be the same after that. Hodges was the singular force behind the world championship achieved by the previously hapless underdogs of 1969. He made men of boys and a fact out of an alleged miracle. He would never be forgotten by Mets fans. Thirty years after his death, an online poll seeking to name an all-time Mets team on the occasion of the franchise's fortieth anniversary indicated how strongly Gil's impact resonated. Gone thirty years, the man was voted the Mets' greatest manager.

In the long term, Hodges's memory would endure. In the short term, once the 1972 players strike was settled and the 1972 season began, the Mets would have to move on.

They would do it with a different face at the helm, albeit one familiar to New Yorkers of multiple generations and dissimilar allegiances. The new manager of the Mets was Yogi Berra, a coach for the club since 1965 and an icon for catching (and, perhaps, not saying those things it was said he said) as a Yankee going back to the late '40s. When Berra had the chance to begin filling in lineup cards — after the first six games on the schedule were cancelled — his team couldn't help but look different from the one Hodges piloted to a third-place tie the year before.

The Mets made a big change in the offseason, giving up on Nolan Ryan's potential and entrusting their pesky third base problem to California Angel shortstop Jim Fregosi. Then, as Hodges's demise was still sinking in — "I don't feel he's gone, in a sense," Bud Harrelson said of the fallen skipper — the front office announced another trade aimed at amping up the Mets' traditionally listless offense. Going to Montreal were three youngsters who had only begun to show promise as Mets: first baseman Mike Jorgensen, shortstop Tim Foli and right fielder Ken Singleton. Coming back from the Expos: legitimate slugger Rusty Staub, an All-Star right fielder each of the five previous seasons.

Berra's lineup was projected to generate more runs than any the Mets had ever regularly sent to the plate, and his pitching was still led by Tom Seaver. With a veteran club boasting enhanced starpower, Yogi figured to have a chance to lead not just a contender but a comeback from uncharted emotional depths.

The Mets coped with their grief by getting off to their best start in franchise history. After donning home uniforms trimmed with black armbands, announcing Hodges's No. 14 would be officially retired — adding it to Casey Stengel's No. 37 — and winning their third consecutive Opening Day (Seaver defeating the defending champion Pirates, 4-0), they steamed to eight victories in their first ten games and were 11-4 after fifteen. Following a couple of weekend losses to the lowly Padres at Shea Stadium, the Mets demonstrated just how resilient they could be.

In the series finale, the Mets spotted Fred Norman and the Padres a 6-0 lead at Shea and then, in the bottom of the eighth, woke up from their Sunday afternoon nap. Three doubles, two singles and a Norman error resulted in five runs to close the gap to one. In the bottom of the ninth, Teddy Martinez led off a second consecutive inning with a single and took second on a Leron Lee error. Tommie Agee, who had doubled behind Martinez in the eighth, drove in the second baseman to tie the game.

The teams went to a tenth inning, when — after Tug McGraw's second inning of spotless relief — Harrelson reached on the Padres' *sixth* error of the day. With two out, Agee delivered his third big hit in as many innings, this one a two-run homer off Ed Acosta to cap a furious comeback for the Mets, 8-6. The improbable win left the Mets six above .500 and tied for first in the young season, a season filled with something that was hard to imagine five weeks earlier when word of Hodges's passing filtered north from Florida:

Hope.

<table>
<tr><td>MAY 14, 1972</td></tr>
<tr><td>METS 5 GIANTS 4</td></tr>
<tr><td>SHEA STADIUM</td></tr>
</table>

If Willie Mays had spent nearly fifteen seasons in California exile as a Los Angeles Dodger rather than a San Francisco Giant, then perhaps a Hollywood ending would have been scripted when Mays came home to New York in 1972 to play his old team. Yes, that's it — Willie would have won the big game by lashing a home run with two out in the bottom of the ninth to beat Dem Bums he used to call his own.

But that would have been too much and too obvious. Willie merely coming home, a decade-and-a-half after being swept up by the westbound Giants, and donning a uniform representing the New York (N.L.) franchise that took their place...that was the drama right there. Anything else would have been *too* Hollywood, and goodness knows sophisticates connected to New York — and San Francisco, for what that's worth — would turn up their noses at such obvious audience pandering.

We had Willie Mays as a New York Met all of a sudden. It was at first a mirage. How could it be real? How could Jack Lang's scoop in the *Long Island Press* be more than a crazy rumor? How could the *Post*'s big block, four-inch type headline —

MAYS A MET

— be airtight accurate? How could the best player in all of baseball for so long, if not so much anymore, have wound up on the Metsies?

It made sense on paper. The Giants' owner needed someone else to pay Mays's freight and the Mets' owner maintained a proprietary interest in doing so. It also clicked in the souls of former New York Giant loyalists like *Village Voice* writer Joe Flaherty, for whom "no matter how Amazin' the Mets were, a part of our hearts was in San Francisco." Restoring Mays to the city where it all started was, Flaherty wrote, "a lover's reprieve from limbo".

Hence, Horace Stoneham and Joan Payson made a deal. The Giants would get a serviceable pitcher named Charlie Williams and a bulging envelope of cash. The Mets would get Willie Mays — the very same Willie Mays who was a New York Giant from 1951 through 1957, back when the very same Mrs. Payson was a minority owner of those very same New York Giants.

Little was very same as it ever was by 1972, but Mays as a Met was no mirage. He was a vision. A very real vision, wearing a New York (N.L.) home uniform again, sporting that trademark 24 on its front and back (courtesy of Jim Beauchamp, who graciously and immediately switched to 5) and, once all was official and relatively comfortable, inked in as the Mets' first baseman and leadoff hitter versus the...oh yes, San Francisco Giants on an overcast Mother's Day afternoon at Shea Stadium.

If any mother ever knew how to land herself the perfect gift, it was Met matriarch Joan Payson.

"We have always wanted Willie Mays ever since the Mets were formed," board chairman M. Donald Grant said in announcing the most instantly celebrated midseason acquisition in Mets history. "We repeatedly have advised Horace Stoneham of our desires. Our offers have been constant and continuous."

Mrs. Payson may have finally gotten her man, but was Mays the perfect fit on those 1972 Mets? Could a 41-year-old part-time center fielder, part-time first baseman and full-time legend possibly be? Mays may have been viewed as a godsend to the nostalgically inclined fans of New York, but new manager Yogi Berra could be forgiven for thinking he'd just come down with Excedrin Headache No. 24. This was no spare part, no mere savvy veteran who might pinch-hit here, fill in there and, as Tom Seaver put it hopefully, "be of tremendous help to us". This was Willie Mays. Yogi Berra was a legend, too, yet his luminescence couldn't hold a candle to the Say Hey Kid's...no matter that said Hey Kid had clearly aged and was batting .184 at the time of the trade.

"On a purely physical basis," a skeptical Joe Gergen wrote in *Newsday*, "the acquisition of Mays should represent an addition. But the entire transaction was conducted in an unreal atmosphere. Emotions surrounding the move were overwhelming."

Whatever conflict might arise from carrying Mays on the roster wasn't the main thing on anybody's mind that meteorologically cloudy but spiritually bright Sunday. All anybody saw was MAYS on the Mets' lineup card and Willie as he appeared in the mind's eye from all those seasons before — before his inevitable decline, before he burnished the Golden Gate, before there were Mets, when there used to be a ballpark right there at Eighth Avenue and 157th Street in Manhattan.

The Polo Grounds was gone, but Willie Mays was here...No. 24 about to play in the Mets' 24th game of the year. It couldn't get a whole lot better.

Yet it did anyway.

Willie leading off the bottom of the first elicited a standing ovation from the paid crowd of 35,505. They were thrilled to see him standing there, they were even happier when Willie worked out a walk against San Francisco starter Sam McDowell. Bases on balls to Buddy Harrelson and Tommie Agee followed, setting the stage for Rusty Staub (no insignificant recent acquisition himself) to slam McDowell for a four-run homer. The smiles in the stands as Mays crossed the plate with his first New York (N.L.) run since September 21, 1957, made the day seem that much less rainy.

Mays had returned. He had scored. What more could be asked of him?

How about carrying his new team to victory against his old team? It didn't appear that would be necessary, never mind physically possible, but the Maysless Giants fought back against Met starter Ray Sadecki in the top of the fifth. A Fran Healy walk, a Bernie Williams triple, a Chris Speier double and a Tito Fuentes home run transpired in uninterrupted fashion. Just like that, Staub's granny had been neutralized, and the Mets and Giants were tied at four going to the bottom of the fifth.

The Mets didn't need what Mays represented. They needed what Mays could do. And leading off against San Fran reliever Don Carrithers, he did it. On a three-two pitch, Mays swung and not so much turned the clock back but set atlases everywhere straight. Willie Mays, New York's favorite ballplaying son, put the New York Mets ahead 5-4 with a home run to left-center. Willie Mays and New York were synonymous once more.

"It's a good thing Shea Stadium is made of steel and concrete," offered Lang in the *Sporting News*, for the wet and wild Mets fans who were rubbing their eyes in joyous disbelief would otherwise "have ripped the place apart with their enthusiasm."

A Willie Mays home run to beat the Giants in his first game as a Met in the bottom of the ninth inning would have indeed been too Hollywood. But the fifth? Just the right climax for Off Broadway.

The denouement was, per Flaherty, "the simple tension of watching Jim McAndrew in relief hold the Giants for four innings," which the righty did. Staub's grand slam and Mays's emotional blast stood up to account for all the runs required for a 5-4 win. It was the third in a row for the first-place Mets, a status they hadn't enjoyed so commandingly since 1969, back when Mays was still stranded in San Francisco.

Not that Mays didn't have that kind of magical year on his mind as he circled the bases after hitting the 647th home run of his storied career. "My first hit as a Giant was a homer," the man of the hour said. "We won the pennant that year, in 1951. My first hit as a Met was a homer. I felt that maybe we'd win the pennant this year. That's what I was thinking."

The Mets win the pennant? The Mets win the pennant? The Mets won Willie Mays. Please — one unbelievable ending at a time.

Tommie Agee homered to put the Mets on the board when they trailed by three in the sixth. Willie Mays homered to give the Mets the lead in the eighth. Each flashed his power against the top lefty in the National League

MAY 21, 1972
METS 4 PHILLIES 3
VETERANS STADIUM

and in support of the top righty, whose record rose another notch as the Mets won yet another game. With Tom Seaver (7 IP, 3 ER) receiving just enough support to overcome Steve Carlton's complete game effort, 4-3, the best team in baseball extended its winning streak to eleven, tying the franchise high from the sainted year of 1969.

The Mets were now 25-7 — Seaver's mark from '69 — six games ahead of the pack in the N.L. East. Tom Terrific himself, who had recently notched his hundredth career win in only his sixth major league season, was 7-1. Agee's average was up to .289. Mays, settling in as a part-time first baseman while Agee remained in center, had been on base in eight of his sixteen plate appearances. Rusty Staub (.287) and Jim Fregosi (.279), a couple of other guys who had come to Queens with impressive credentials, were contributing as well.

The new Met manager was pushing all the right buttons. Seaver had looked mostly sharp this Sunday in Philly, save for giving up a two-run blast to his personal nemesis Tommy Hutton in the fourth (a .248 hitter throughout his mostly unremarkable career, the journeyman bench player batted .320 against Tom Terrific), yet Yogi Berra decided to pinch-hit for his ace pitcher to start the eighth. Jim Beauchamp, another new-for-'72 Met, singled, setting up Mays's homer, which put the Mets up, 4-3. Danny Frisella came on and shut down Philadelphia for the final two innings.

Carlton gave up only six hits in nine innings and struck out nine, but as anyone who remembered September 1969 could tell you, the Mets were old hands at wrecking Steve's most outstanding efforts when he was a Cardinal. Having come to the Phillies for Rick Wise during the offseason, it was more of the same between the talented lefthander and the first-place team he could never count on handling.

First-place Mets. Eleven in a row. Best record in baseball. Biggest lead in baseball. Willie Mays. Rusty Staub. Tom Seaver. If this was a dream, Mets fans didn't want to wake up.

MAY 30, 1972
METS 7 PHILLIES 0
SHEA STADIUM

Despite the Mets getting in his way from time to time, Steve Carlton was on his way to one of the most brilliant seasons any pitcher has ever enjoyed. This Tuesday night at Shea, though, it was another lefthander grabbing the spotlight.

After a brief gap in what had been its steady output, the New York Mets starting pitching factory had produced another certifiably stellar arm, the left one belonging to Jonathan Trumpbour Matlack. Though only 22, the arrival of Matlack onto the Flushing scene had been a long time in coming. Jon was the Mets' No. 1 pick in the 1967 amateur draft (fourth overall) and the apple of many an opposing general manager's eye over the next several years. When the Mets sought hitting, the GMs on the other end of the phone tended to seek Matlack.

But the Mets held him in abeyance, unveiling him to the National League for a peek in 1971, resulting in six mostly rocky starts. They installed him in their rotation for keeps a few weeks into the 1972 season, where he briefly supplanted his fellow lefty, the struggling Jerry Koosman. Kooz came back to starting regularly soon enough, but

Matlack wasn't going anywhere. Against Philadelphia, he was the best he'd been to date, shutting out Carlton (5-6) and his teammates on a three-hit, six-strikeout gem. The 7-0 whitewashing brought Matlack's mark to 6-0, matching Dick Selma's club record for best start to a season. Jon's ERA dropped to 1.95, a full run better than Carlton's.

By year's end, Carlton's numbers would be the more eye-popping (27-10, 1.97 ERA, 310 strikeouts for the 59-97 Phillies), but Matlack would not altogether cede the southpaw spotlight, finishing up at 15-10 and winning the Mets' second National League Rookie of the Year award.

JULY 4, 1972 (1ST)

METS 2 PADRES 0

SHEA STADIUM

So close to lighting up that elusive no-hitter stogie. So close. But no...games with no hits allowed. So who needs a cigar anyway?

You'd think Tom Seaver would have been stocking a humidor by the middle of the 1972 season. Lord knows National League batters (and a few Orioles besides) had gotten smoked by the young flamethrower who was always getting better with age. Here he was, a veteran of 5 1/2 seasons, all of 27 years old, with 105 wins to his credit, going for 106, and something more besides. Tom Seaver was trying to go where no Met, not even him, had gone before.

Tom Seaver was going for the first no-hitter in Mets history.

He'd been as close as anybody. He'd been closer more often than anybody. By Independence Day 1972 — the occasion for a doubleheader at Shea against San Diego — Tom had rolled up a one-hitter per year every year for the previous three years, and the year before that, 1968, he carried a perfect game into the eighth against the Cardinals, an effort that went into the books as a three-hit victory after being broken up by Orlando Cepeda.

Here he was again on this patriotic Tuesday afternoon, pitching his way through familiar territory. First inning, second inning, third inning: nine Padres up, nine Padres down. Perfection for a third of the opening game of the holiday twinbill. The first two batters from the top of the first inning, Derrel Thomas and Dave Roberts, reappeared in the fourth and did more or less what they did before. Eleven up and eleven down.

Then Seaver walked Leron Lee. So much for perfection. He walked the next batter, Nate Colbert, directly after. Didn't seem like a Seaver thing to do, but perhaps Padre starter Clay Kirby had infected the mound. In the bottom of the third, San Diego's ace lost control. With two outs, he allowed a single to Buddy Harrelson, who stole second. In rapid succession, Kirby walked Wayne Garrett and John Milner to load the bases and Jim Fregosi and Ed Kranepool to unload them. The four consecutive walks provided Tom a 2-0 lead, one Seaver made hold up when he shook off the prevailing wildness and struck out Cito Gaston to get out of the fourth with his no-hitter intact.

The Mets would keep walking, collecting ten bases on balls versus the Padre staff, but wouldn't score anymore. Seaver just kept throwing strikes from the fifth through the seventh when he retired all nine San Diego batters, four of them on K's. He had ten on the day thus far. He permitted no more baserunners until two out in the eighth when the wildness bug bit again, with consecutive walks to Larry Stahl and Garry Jestadt. And again, Tom responded, grounding Thomas to second.

Eight innings. Four walks. Eleven strikeouts. No runs. And no hits.

But plenty of awareness. "As that game against the Padres progressed," Tom reflected a couple of offseasons later, "my teammates seemed to get farther and farther away from me. I couldn't find anybody to talk to. No one was around." By the top of the eighth, only the batboy dared to loiter in Tom's dugout airspace.

Come the ninth, everybody would be looking at Seaver. In 1969, Seaver had famously taken a no-hitter into the ninth at Shea. Got one out then. He got one out to start this ninth, on a grounder by Roberts to Garrett at second. The next batter would be Lee, a .311 hitter when the day started, 0-for-2 today, along with that fourth-inning walk.

Seaver threw Lee a sinking fastball. It was golfed by the batter and turned into a looper that eluded the gloves of Garrett and Harrelson as they raced from their respective posts at second and short toward center field trying to preserve what was not to be.

Tom Seaver was now working on a one-hitter. He got it when he threw a double play ball to Colbert to seal the 2-0 victory. For the Mets, it was their ninth one-hitter in eleven seasons of franchise history.

"I wasn't disappointed after the hit because I knew I had to get Colbert," Seaver said afterwards of his eleventh win in twelve lifetime decisions against San Diego. "Now, with the whole thing over, I do feel disappointed."

Close to a no-hitter, but no cigar. A familiar refrain to Mets fans then. A familiar refrain to Mets fans for how much longer nobody could be sure.

Smoke 'em if ya got 'em.

105
AUGUST 1, 1972 (1ST)
METS 3 PHILLIES 2 (18)
SHEA STADIUM

As August came to Queens, the pennant race was long gone. The promise of May dissipated amid a rash of injuries and disappointment, particularly where the offense was concerned.

With Rusty Staub's sizzling start extinguished in June by a fractured bone in his right hand, the Mets lost their most potent bat. Everybody who had joined Le Grand Orange in the Opening Day lineup missed significant time as 1972 progressed, so much so that in the strike-shortened 156-game season, no Met played long (or well) enough to collect 100 hits. Cleon Jones led the team in runs batted in with a paltry 52. While surprisingly productive rookie outfielder John "The Hammer" Milner was a welcome revelation for his club-leading 17 homers, Tommie Agee was the only other Met to reach double-digits in dingers, yet he was slumping through his worst season since 1968 and would be dispatched to Houston in November.

Jim Fregosi's .232 batting average and ill fit at third base immediately certified the deal that sent Nolan Ryan (19 wins, 329 strikeouts) and three others to the Angels as a flop for the ages. Overall, the Mets hit .225, lowest in the league. Their only player to get on base at clip of better than .400 was part-time outfielder-first baseman Willie Mays, 41 and going relatively strong...but probably going a little too often, given the health of the rest of Yogi Berra's troops.

The Mets weren't hitting as a unit, they weren't hitting as individuals and, ultimately, they weren't winning enough to make use of their dependable pitching. No wonder they'd fallen to a distant second place by the end of July en route to another ordinary third-place finish, 83-73, 13 1/2 games behind the Pirates.

It's also no wonder they injected one of their traditional fun days on the calendar with a shot of offensive torpor.

The first Tuesday in August at Shea was penciled in as Banner Night. Maybe "painted in" would be the operative phrase. That's how Mets fans eager to take the field and show their artistic bent would be filling their banners, painting, drawing and otherwise illustrating their fondness for their team so as to march them with pride around the warning track between games of the scheduled Mets-Phillies twinighter.

Technically, that's what they got to do. But "between games" became an elastic concept as this Banner Night wore on. On paper, and even on bedsheet, the implication was nine innings would be played, and then the banners would go on parade.

Not tonight. Not for a while.

Jon Matlack and Wayne Twitchell provided a harbinger of the long night to come when they traded zeroes for the first five innings of the opener. Nobody scored until Cleon Jones's sac fly brought home Dave Schneck in the bottom of the sixth. Bill Robinson evened the score in the top of the seventh with a bases-empty home run, but the Mets retook control of the action when Cleon homered to lead off the eighth.

By now, the better than 3,900 fans who brought banners were summoned to line up for entry through the center field fence. Soon after the final out was recorded, they could look forward to a few moments of Shea glory, their feet touching the same sacred turf on which their heroes had just presumably taken the first game of the doubleheader

Ah, but the best-designed plans of Banner Night were put on hold when Don Money cashiered a Matlack pitch over the same wall that separated the banners from their desired destiny. Money's leadoff home run tied the game at two.

And it stayed tied. Really tied. Tied with no real hope of getting untied. Baserunners occasionally materialized for the Mets or Phillies, but none of them came close to crossing the plate. Nobody got a runner to third base from the bottom of the ninth through the bottom of the seventeenth. The Mets turned three double plays, the Phillies two.

The would-be banner-wavers, deprived of viewing the game, waited patiently...or as patiently as possible. Tug McGraw gave Berra six-and-a-third scoreless innings once Matlack departed with two out in the ninth. Ray Sadecki followed by shutting out the Phillies in the sixteenth, seventeenth and — despite letting pinch-runner Denny Doyle reach third — the eighteenth. Phillie relieving had been just as effective, but at last, in the bottom of the eighteenth, a glint of light reached the Banner Night line. Agee doubled to lead off the frame and Sadecki was safe on a bunt that moved him to third. A Schneck groundout put the pitcher on second, forcing Phils manager Paul Owens to intentionally walk Ed Kranepool in hope of finding a play at any base.

The strategy didn't work. Jones singled to right, scoring Agee, giving the Mets an eighteen-inning, four-hour, twenty-eight minute, 3-2 victory, and swinging wide open, at last, the center field gate. Stadium personnel hustled the swarm of 2,176 banners inside…and got them hustled back into the stands in about 45 minutes.

The ensuing nightcap, a 4-1 loss to Steve Carlton, was — it figures — a nine-inning affair that took only an hour longer than that. A Banner Night that dawned at 5:35 PM finished its baseball procession at 12:45 the next morning.

If there's a statistically verifiable outer limit for not giving up on the Mets in a single game, this Saturday night in the Astrodome proved it was eight runs. If the Mets are down nine, there is no evidence they can come back. But if they're down eight, have faith.

SEPTEMBER 2, 1972
106
METS 11 ASTROS 8
THE ASTRODOME

It worked once.

To best understand the game that encompassed the largest comeback in New York Mets history, it may be best to consider it as two games: less a doubleheader than one game with a split personality.

The first was unappealing, unattractive and unwatchable from a Met perspective. It featured the efforts of two pitchers with little Met past and essentially no Met future. Brent Strom, 24, was making his fourth major league start, attempting to earn his first major league win. The 24-year-old lefty wasn't getting it here. A Lee May two-run homer put him in a hole in the first and a Cesar Cedeño two-run double knocked him out in the third.

Strom was replaced by veteran southpaw Ray Sadecki who gave up only an unearned run to keep the Mets within shouting distance of the 'Stros at 5-0, but their chances were reduced to a whisper when Bob Rauch entered. Rauch was a 23-year-old rookie righty appearing in his eleventh big league game. His previous ten outings came in Met losses, and this one didn't appear destined to be anything different — certainly not once young Robert got his hands on it. Tommy Helms doubled home a run off Rauch in the sixth and Bob Watson singled in two more in the seventh. The Mets trailed, 8-0.

So much for Bob Rauch's chance of pitching in a Met win.

On the flip side, Don Wilson was enjoying an easy night's work for the Astros. He had scattered four hits in seven innings and erased two of those on double plays. The Mets, who had lost to the same team by the same score the night before, were a feeble-hitting bunch as the grind of injury-wracked 1972 took its toll on the back end of their schedule — and it didn't appear they had chosen the notoriously stingy Astrodome as the place to make an offensive stand.

At least not until the eighth they didn't. That's when the first Mets-Astros game ended and the second, more appealing one began.

To say it began innocently enough would be obvious. When you're down 0-8, anything that isn't a nine-run homer is fairly innocent. Thus, Duffy Dyer's leadoff single didn't seem likely to hurt any fly that could survive the Dome's hermetically sealed environs. Buddy Harrelson followed with another single, the first time all night the Mets had put two baserunners on in the same inning. Still very innocent.

Rauch was due to bat next, but that wasn't happening. Yogi Berra tabbed Dave Marshall as his pinch-hitter, and Marshall walked to load the bases with nobody out. It was technically a jam for Wilson, but how tight could it be if he was pitching with an eight-run lead?

Tommie Agee came up and lifted a fly to right, caught by Jimmy Wynn but traveling deep enough for Dyer to tag up and score and for Harrelson to move to third. Astro skipper Leo Durocher (in his post-Cubs managerial twilight) would gladly trade an out for a run at that point.

But he probably wasn't too gladdened when the next Met, Ken Boswell, whacked Wilson's next — and last — pitch over the fence for a three-run homer. That pulled the Mets to within 8-4 with one out. Out went Wilson and in for the ungladdened Durocher came Fred Gladding. Gladding's mission wasn't all that complicated: Control the Mets' burgeoning ambitions by getting five outs without giving up another four runs.

But now the Mets had a taste for scoring and they seemed to like it enough to want more. John Milner singled. Ed Kranepool singled. Cleon Jones doubled in Milner to make it 8-5, as lead-footed Eddie hoofed it to third.

Durocher: Not at all gladdened. Out went Gladding, in came Jim Ray to face Wayne Garrett, the ninth batter of the top of the eighth. Garrett singled in the two baserunners and the Mets, behind 8-0 a few minutes earlier, were trailing, 8-7.

This second game was pretty darn good.

Dyer batted for the second time in the inning and singled for the second time. Ray, however, straightened out at last, retiring Harrelson on a foul pop and Marshall — still technically pinch-hitting for Rauch — on a foul to right.

While the Mets take the field to try and hold the Astros at eight runs, ponder Dave Marshall's role for a moment. He pinch-hit for the pitcher and batted once more in the same inning. It was as if the Mets right then and there invented the designated hitter rule and some American League scout saw it, liked it and reported it back to the home office. One year later, the DH was junior circuit law.

Yet before you take out your purist-loving hostilities on Mr. Marshall, a Met bench staple with the rotten timing to have arrived just after 1969 and depart just before 1973, know that what he did in the eighth wasn't unprecedented in Met annals — though it was and remains pretty rare.

According to Baseball-Reference's Play Index tool, Marshall was one of seven Met pinch-hitters to bat for the pitcher and come up twice in the same inning without remaining in the game thereafter for defense. The first time it happened was exactly one week earlier when the pinch-hitter was Jim Fregosi and the pitcher was human strange-luck charm Bob Rauch. The Mets scored five against Atlanta in that inning to take the lead but lost when Sadecki gave up a three-run homer to Mike Lum.

After it happened twice in a one-week span, it wouldn't happen again for another nine years. On May 5, 1981, Mike Cubbage joined a hopeless mission already in progress: the bottom of the ninth at Shea with the Mets trailing the Giants, 9-0. Future interim manager Mike walked as the offensive replacement for Jeff Reardon with one on and one out, and nine batters later found himself up again as the potential winning run, the Mets having narrowed the gap to 9-7. Cubbage, however, flied out to end the inning and the game.

Others who were de facto designated hitters for the Mets in National League competition: Howard Johnson versus the Astros in 1985, Gregg Jefferies against the Pirates in 1991, Vance Wilson in a game with the Cardinals in 2003 and Daniel Murphy in 2011 at Philadelphia. HoJo and Jefferies were the only DF DHs in this bunch to help their team to victory. None of them reached base twice. Wilson made two outs but reached once on a strikeout that got away. Fregosi made two outs and didn't reach at all. Everybody else walked once, except for Murph, whose single accounted for the only hit (and RBI) in the fourteen plate appearances in question.

Some DHs.

Special mention is merited for Boswell in this context. He batted for Dyer leading off the ninth inning at Candlestick on May 29, 1973, and walked. Harrelson followed him with a single. Since the Mets trailed only 2-1, Berra stuck with his pitcher, Tom Seaver, to bunt. Being Tom Seaver, he not only successfully sacrificed the runners but beat out the play at first. The Mets went on to score four runs, with Ken batting in Duffy's place a second time in the same inning. Then Seaver went out and retired the Giants 1-2-3 to win the game, 5-2. So the pitcher didn't have a designated hitter but the catcher did.

Now back to Houston, where the Mets just scored seven runs to turn an 8-0 Astro laugher into a potential Durocherian nightmare — a 1969 Cubs in miniature, you might say.

Yogi went with Jerry Koosman to keep the Mets close in the bottom of the eighth. Kooz yielded mixed results. He hit Helms to lead off the inning, got two outs but then allowed an infield single to Roger Metzger. With two on and so steep a mountain already scaled, Yogi didn't want to tumble back down, so he replaced Koosman with relief ace Tug McGraw (his fourth lefty of the game). The switch worked as Tug struck out the dynamo Cedeño, a .340 batter. The Mets reached the ninth still just one run down.

Their last chance began with Agee facing Jim Ray. Tommie prevailed by walking. Boswell singled, signaling the end of Ray's night. Tom Griffin was Durocher's choice to take on Milner. The Hammer bunted to the third baseman Doug Rader, soon to be awarded the third of an eventual five Gold Gloves for fielding prowess. But because it was just one of those evenings, Rader turned a sacrifice into an E-5. When the Dome dust settled, Agee scampered home with the tying run as Boswell raced for third and Milner for second.

Yes, tie game. 8-8.

Not long ago it was 8-0.

Funny game — or games — this baseball.

While Durocher's legendary good humor was tested, he saw fit to order Griffin to walk Kranepool to load the bases. It was a desperation move that didn't work all too well. Jones singled in Boswell and Milner and the Mets led, 10-8. The only Astro solace was provided by Kranepool's attempt to lumber into third. Eddie's ambition backfired when Cedeño threw him out. But Jones took second, and Griffin's wild pitch sent him to third. From there it was an easy ninety feet to trot when Garrett singled.

The Mets led, 11-8. They hurdled an eight-run eighth-inning lead by scoring eleven unanswered runs. There'd be nothing else of note to put on the board from there — the Mets would leave the bases loaded after one more Durocher pitching change and Tug would mow down the Astros in the bottom of the ninth.

But what else did there have to be?

Brent Strom and Bob Rauch never appeared in another Mets game as sensational as this one...unless you count the last Mets game in which both men appeared. They, like all the Mets, showed up on the wrong end of Expo Bill Stoneman's 7-0 no-hitter at Jarry Park on October 2. Soon enough, Strom would be shipped to Cleveland for reliever Phil Hennigan. Brent enjoyed a couple of decent seasons in San Diego down the line before an elbow injury curtailed his major league status for good in 1977. He'd hang on in the minors until 1981, quitting pitching when he was 33. He'd transition into coaching at the minor league level, still instructing kid Cardinals some four decades after excavating the first layer of the biggest one-game hole from which the Mets would ever emerge.

Rauch? Sent to Cleveland in the same deal. Never saw "The Show" again. Never even got a baseball card: not as a Met, not as an Indian, not as a Tucson Toro, whose uniform was the last he wore as a player, in 1975. His professional career was over at 26.

The Mets were a 3-8 club in games Brent Strom pitched for them in 1972. When Bob Rauch took the mound, they went 3-16. Yet each man was, perversely, part of the largest comeback in Mets history...an integral part, really. As their manager might have said, it was their pitching that made that night when they overcame an eight-run deficit necessary.

KNOCKIN' ON HEAVEN'S DOOR

1973

How much coffee was brewed in the name of staying awake to catch every last pitch of a West Coast start that became the Mets' longest win to date? An extra three hours on top of an extra ten innings...Postum wasn't gonna getcha to the postgame.

Someday Mets fans would rise with five o'clock in the morning approaching to take in a pair of season-opening games from Japan. But that was 27 years into the future. For now, it was enough to hang in there until 4:47 AM to watch the end of a Mets-Dodgers game that didn't have its first pitch thrown until after 11 PM New York time Thursday and showed few signs of finishing before sunrise Friday.

It was not a game made for Sanka drinkers.

Tom Seaver faced off against Tommy John, though neither would last past the seventh inning, which is when the Mets, down 3-1, began ensuring a long night would ensue for everybody. Buddy Harrelson doubled home George Theodore to pull the Mets to within 3-2. An inning later, with Pete Richert pitching, the Stork singled home Cleon Jones to tie it.

That was in the top of the eighth. The score would stay rigid for quite a while, though the basepaths would get a workout, starting with the bottom of the eighth. Tug McGraw replaced Phil Hennigan and found himself pitching with the bases loaded and one out. L.A. could go ahead and put the Mets to sleep early, but instead, Bill Russell grounded to Harrelson, who threw home to Duffy Dyer, cutting down the Dodgers' elusive fourth run. Tug would get out of the jam.

The theme would be revisited in the tenth. Two Dodger singles and an intentional walk started the home half of the inning, a tangle from which it would be tough for Tug to emerge unscathed. But emerge he did: twice! First, he drew Ron Cey into a 5-2-3 DP that snuffed out Willie Davis at the plate. Yogi Berra ordered a second intentional walk, and it worked again, with pinch-hitter Chris Cannizzaro grounding to Wayne Garrett.

One more chance arose for the magical McGraw to make a Dodger rally disappear, in the twelfth. Hits by Joe Ferguson and Willie Crawford were followed by an unintentional walk to Cey. There was one out. A golden opportunity awaited... and was wasted when Russell touched off yet another play at the plate, another 5-2-3 double play that nailed Ferguson coming in from third.

Thus ended the long evening for the Tugger. He pitched five innings, the eighth through twelfth, gave up four hits, walked five men (two intentionally) and had to overcome a Willie Davis steal of second — with Davis taking third on Dyer's throw into the outfield — but somehow he went unscored upon. Three plays at the plate all went in favor of the New York defense.

Tug also singled in the tenth and landed on second on a poor throw by Russell, but was left stranded there.

McGraw did all he could for five, and now the Mets' portion of the affair was handed over to George Stone for the next six innings. Seven Dodgers reached base between the fourteenth and seventeenth — including two who made it to third — but nobody scored. Stone, acquired in the offseason from Atlanta with second baseman Felix Millan for Gary Gentry and Danny Frisella, had pitched only seven innings in 1973 to that point; it took a marathon to put him squarely on his skipper's radar.

"You have to give their pitchers credit for the way they got out of all those jams," said admiring Dodger manager Walt Alston. Meanwhile, Charlie Hough and Doug Rau both kept the Mets at bay as night became day on both coasts and all the players were noticing just how late it was getting.

"I wore out two gloves," Harrelson reported. "My regular glove and the golf glove under it."

Rosters were stretched thin, too. Berra used every Met except for a handful of pitchers. Jon Matlack was called on to pinch-run for John Milner at one point, but Matlack, like every other Met, proved allergic to advancement home. On the Dodger side, Davis racked up six base hits in nine at-bats to equal a franchise record that dated back to Cookie Lavagetto in Brooklyn. Manny Mota, on the other hand, might have preferred a rainout. Starting in left field, the pinch-hitting specialist took a size 0-for-9 collar. For the Mets, Garrett was 1-for-2 by the third inning, 0-for-8 thereafter, striking out four times.

The tipping point came in the top of the nineteenth when the Mets' offense finally loosened up. Jones led off with a single. Rusty Staub doubled him home with his fifth hit of the evening/morning. Pinch-hitter Ken Boswell (batting for Stone) picked up Rusty and suddenly, after all these hours, runs were coming cheap. The Mets were up, 5-3; then 7-3, when Ed Kranepool doubled in a pair.

Jim McAndrew came on for the bottom of the nineteenth, recorded two quick groundouts, gave up a single to pinch-hitter Von Joshua but then induced a grounder from Davey Lopes to Millan. Felix was a 1-for-9 batter on the night, but blissfully surehanded here, feeding Harrelson for the 114th out of the game, five hours and forty-two minutes after it began. The Mets, with 7 runs, 22 hits and 3 errors, defeated the Dodgers, who totaled 3 runs, 19 hits and 3 errors. An estimated 1,000 Angelenos — or 26,000 fewer than showed up in the 8 o'clock hour — were on hand to witness the conclusion of what became Stone's first Met victory.

At 1:47 AM Pacific Daylight Time and 4:47 AM Eastern Daylight Time, the Mets had secured their longest win. They had been on the wrong end of a 23-inning score in 1964 and were shut out, 1-0, over 24 tedious innings in 1968. For Mets fans who pried their eyes open clear to the end as Friday dawned, that morning's last or perhaps first cup of coffee tasted anything but bitter.

For a franchise barely into its second decade, the Mets were uncommonly skilled at laying on the nostalgia. Having been formed spiritually from the ashes of the departed Dodgers and Giants, it made perfect sense that the first-year expansion club held

108

JUNE 9, 1973
METS 4 DODGERS 2
SHEA STADIUM

an Old Timers Day as soon it could. There wasn't yet a present let alone a future in 1962, but a tradition was born and Old Timers Day became one of the Mets' signature events.

The 1973 version was particularly ripe to be portrayed in sepia tones. The highlight of the pregame festivities this Saturday at Shea was the presentation of Gil Hodges's No. 14 to his widow, Joan. The number had been taken out of circulation at the beginning of the 1972 season when the organization was still in shock from the manager's passing. Here, in advance of a game between Gil's two old teams, there was an opportunity for a hearty round of applause for what the man meant to the Mets, the Dodgers (in Brooklyn and L.A.) and baseball as a whole.

When the scheduled game came around, the fellow who was the closest thing the sport had to an active old-timer stole the show. Willie Mays, 42 years young and senior to many of the retired players celebrated in the pregame ceremonies, was the starting centerfielder and third-place hitter, just as if it was 22 years before, when he first assumed those roles for the New York Giants. Willie wasn't quite the specimen he'd been in 1951 by 1973, plagued as he was by an aching right shoulder, two balky knees and a body that had given its all across nearly 3,000 big league games.

Willie's muscle memory was mammoth, but his contemporary output lagged. He had just come off the disabled list (a career first) and wasn't close to getting untracked. Coming into Old Timers Day, Mays was batting a sacrilegious .095 with exactly one run batted in for the season. He hadn't homered since the previous summer. His insertion in the lineup was less about nostalgia than something approximating desperation. Yogi Berra was without three regulars — Jerry Grote, Bud Harrelson and Cleon Jones — and needed all the relatively healthy help he could get, even if he had to reach back into the past to find it.

He found it. With the Mets trailing, 1-0, in the bottom of the first, Willie reached on a walk and scored the go-ahead run from first on Rusty Staub's two-run double. With the Dodgers having tied the score on Bill Buckner's sacrifice fly in the visitors' third, the Say Hey Kid spoke up again, robbing his opposite number, L.A. center fielder Willie Davis, of a sure extra-base hit when he effected a sensational grab. As described by Joe Durso in the *New York Times*, Mays initially misjudged the deep fly, righted himself, backpedaled and reached over his head for the putout. "It became even more remarkable, though," Durso wrote, "when he fell backward and rolled twice across the dirt track at the base of the wall."

And for an encore? Willie whacked an Al Downing pitch well into the left field bullpen to give the Mets a 3-2 lead. Willie's long ball was his first home run of 1973, the 655th of his career, third-most by anybody in major league history (he had been passed for second place lifetime by Hank Aaron almost exactly one year before). Staub later provided insurance via an eighth-inning double to bring home Felix Millan, and Jon Matlack — who took a line drive to the forehead in May, yet missed only one start — completed the seven-hitter to win it for the Mets, 4-2.

The nostalgia was intoxicating, especially at a moment when Mets fans could be forgiven for growing wistful for the good, not-so-old days. The injury-riddled Mets were 23-27, in fourth place, 7 1/2 games out, placing them in their least competitive position after 50 games of a season since Hodges's first year at the helm in 1968.

JULY 17, 1973
METS 8 BRAVES 7
ATLANTA STADIUM

Yogi Berra doesn't require any extra quoting, but here goes, nonetheless. When he was managing the Mets, Ken Boswell allegedly went to him for help in kicking a bad batting habit, namely that "I keep swinging up at the ball."

To which, Yogi replied, "Well, swing down."

Not quite up there with other Yogi gems, but if we can craft a Yogi-ism from that exchange (and the man does claim, "I never said most of the things I said"), it might be that you have to stop doing what's not working if you want to stop doing what's not working. That perfectly sound Berraesque logic was put into play this Tuesday night in Atlanta when the most important element of the Met bullpen was offering his team virtually no relief.

Tug McGraw was a National League All-Star in 1972, when giving relievers such honors was a relative rarity. American League manager Earl Weaver thumbed his nose at bullpens everywhere by taking nine pitchers — all starters — while his counterpart, Danny Murtaugh, made McGraw one of his staff's two lefties (Steve Carlton, in the midst of his 27-10 season for the 59-win Phillies, was the other).

"Earl certainly doesn't recognize us," McGraw lamented.

Tug turned out to be the winning pitcher in the '72 All-Star Game at Atlanta Stadium, throwing the ninth and tenth and keeping the score tied at four until Joe Morgan singled in Nate Colbert with the winning run. His several years as one of baseball's best relievers should have been evidence enough that McGraw belonged, but the Mets' fireman didn't necessarily feel completely at ease.

"I started getting nervous when they introduced Mays and Aaron before the game," Tug admitted. To alleviate the butterflies, the lefty decided to, in the vernacular of the day, take "myself on a confidence trip."

He had no problem making that sort of psychic sojourn in 1972. His confidence was born of his success: Tug posted his second consecutive ERA of 1.70 and his 27 saves were second-most in the N.L., behind fellow All-Star Clay Carroll of Cincinnati. Confidence trip...smooth sailing...whatever you wanted to call it, Yogi knew if he called on Tug in the late innings, he'd probably have no regrets when the game was over.

Fast-forward a year, and the only trip Tug was on when the Mets came to Atlanta was a bad one. McGraw was in the midst of "my famous slump of 1973," times when he was so wild batters didn't even bother swinging. As he recalled it in his book, *Screwball*, it was a mystery to him:

"I couldn't figure out what had happened to me. I couldn't even say to myself, forget about it, you're human. Tug, you're human. I wanted to figure it out, hassle it out."

Tug had no answers. Yogi had no answers. All anybody could divine was Tug's bottom line by mid-July. He was 0-4, he had blown seven saves (while recording only eleven) and his ERA was just a smidge below six. He was having an awful season and, not surprisingly, so were the Mets. They were in last place, twelve under .500 and eleven games out of first. It was a year straight out of the early portion of Tug's Met career, except prior to 1969, there were no expectations for him or them. These 1973 Mets were supposed to be contenders. They appeared to be dead.

"Don't know what to do," Tug wrote in his soul-baring style. *"Cannot hack it anymore."*

So for a night, Berra decided McGraw didn't have to, not as a reliever, at any rate. After being skipped in a Monday night 8-6 loss when the Mets clearly needed relief help, Tug showed up at Atlanta Stadium on Tuesday to discover a baseball sitting in a shoe in his locker. It was the manager's way of telling Tug he was going to be that night's starter.

It wasn't unprecedented in McGraw's career. He made 25 starts from 1965-67 and four more in early 1969 before Gil Hodges decided Tug would better serve the team (and his career) as the lefty complement to Ron Taylor in the Mets' bullpen. Except for a token start in the second game of a doubleheader late in 1971, Tug transformed exclusively into a reliever for the next four years, making 229 appearances out of the pen. There was no reason to think he'd ever return to the Mets' rotation. But nothing was working for Tug and little was working for the Mets, so, in essence, why not start him?

Tug was surprised by this assignment, but tried to play it cool, even kidding Yogi that he'd been on a bender the night before. Whether Berra got the joke or not, he had a message for McGraw: "You're starting tonight and you better do a good job."

There had been no bender, but there wasn't much clarity. Tug did not take comfort in taking the mound in the bottom of the first. "But then," he wrote, "I gave myself the old pep talk: Got to fight your way out of it. Can't feel any different just because you're starting the game instead of finishing it. Get hold of yourself, beginning right now."

The uplifting conclusion to the story would be that McGraw fought the good fight, figured out what he was doing wrong and pitched the game of his life that night. But baseball is no fairy-tale world. What really happened was Ralph Garr hit his first pitch over the center field fence. Yet Tug did take some solace in falling behind, 1-0. "At least it can't get any worse," he decided, opting to view his start as "an experiment: one pitch, one run. Maybe I can get the next guy out."

He did. Marty Perez flied to John Milner at first for the first out. McGraw escaped the inning without further damage. But it wasn't really happening for him out there on the Atlanta mound, at least not as discerned from the scoreboard. A wild pitch scored Paul Casanova in the second; Dusty Baker and Davey Johnson drove in runs in the third; and with the Braves ahead, 4-1, in the sixth, Tug gave up a two-run homer to Perez and a solo shot to Henry Aaron, the 698th of Hammerin' Hank's career.

Most of America was zeroing in on Aaron's chase of Babe Ruth's lifetime home run mark that summer, and Tug's gopher had allowed 39-year-old Bad Henry to move within sixteen long balls of the Bambino. To Aaron, the important thing was he put his team up, 7-1: "I felt like when I hit it, it was just another run, like icing on the cake."

As for McGraw, you might say he was wearing a hit-eating grin. Yes, he'd given up the three homers, the seven runs, had plunked Darrell Evans and unleashed that wild pitch — and yes, he had his team in a six-run hole — but Tug could feel himself hacking it again: "I was just beginning to relax. I thought what the hell, I'll just have a ball tonight, whatever they do." Despite the ugly pitching line, he judged himself having had "a fair night" and left after six.

That appeared to be that for Tug, enjoying a small, intangible private victory amid yet another dispiriting Met defeat in a season crammed with them.

Except for this: John Strohmayer pitched a perfect seventh for the Mets; Buzz Capra pitched a perfect eighth for the Mets; and the Mets offense still had to bat in the top of the ninth.

Braves manager Eddie Mathews didn't see trouble ahead. He pulled Aaron and his 698 home runs (25 of them hit thus far in '73) from left field and sent Carl Morton out to bid for a complete game. Wayne Garrett singled to lead off the ninth, but ex-Brave Felix Millan lined out. Rusty Staub homered, but that only made it 7-3. Morton stayed in the game to face Cleon Jones, who singled. He stayed in to face Milner. Milner homered.

The Mets trailed, 7-5.

Mathews had seen enough of Morton and brought in Adrian Devine, who got Ron Hodges to ground to Johnson at second. Two out, nobody on...the Braves appeared to be in Devine shape.

But Don Hahn singled to keep the game going. Pinch-hitter Ed Kranepool walked, and was pinch-run for by Teddy Martinez. Jim Beauchamp was Berra's next pinch-hitter and he singled. Hahn raced home, Martinez went to third. Now the Mets were down, 7-6, with runners at the corners. They had batted around and knocked out Devine. Matthews chose Tom House to pitch.

And Yogi Berra chose Willie Mays to hit for Garrett.

Unlike his longtime superstar contemporary Aaron, Mays was no longer producing like his young self. Willie was 42 and batting .214 as a part-timer. It was clear Aaron had outlasted him. But two other things were just as clear as Mays stepped in to take on House:

1. Willie Mays was batting, while Hank Aaron was out of the game.

2. Willie Mays was batting.

That's an aspect of a baseball game that can never be underestimated, as Tom House discovered. Mays worked House for a three-two count, which meant the Mets' runners were in motion when Willie swung and lined a single into deep right field. Martinez scored easily to tie the game at seven. Beauchamp, nobody's idea of pinch-runner, had a more difficult challenge as he took off from first.

"It was lucky it was a three-two count on Willie," Jim said, "because I got a big jump. Halfway between third and the plate, I ran out of gas." It wasn't a fortuitous moment for an energy crisis, but Beauchamp had a little more in the tank than he suspected. Garr's throw from right was high and Jim slid in safely with the Mets' seventh run of the ninth inning. In the final game in which Willie Mays and Hank Aaron both appeared, the Mets went ahead, 8-7.

This would have been an ideal time to bring in an accomplished closer like Tug McGraw, but McGraw was obviously not available. So Berra went with his third reliever of the night, rookie Harry Parker. Due up first was Evans, and Parker struck him out. Due up next should have been Aaron, except Mathews's routine substitution in the top of the ninth meant Harry would face not Henry, but Sonny Jackson. Sonny struck out. Finally, Baker fouled to Milner and Parker joined Strohmayer and Capra in having pitched perfect innings, ensuring the Mets' 8-7 win.

Blowing a six-run lead in the ninth couldn't have gone over well in the Braves' clubhouse, where the volatile Mathews was known to "hurl a tray of Church's Chicken" at the wall when frustrated, according to Tom Stanton, author of *Hank Aaron and the Home Run That Changed America*. Aaron himself, however, was more philosophical than furious.

"That's baseball for you," he said.

McGraw, meanwhile, was in the midst of a much happier scene, one in which the poultry was treated much better.

"The clubhouse man," he wrote in *Screwball*, "had fried chicken on the table in the locker room and we gobbled up all the beer he had, too, and went out and had a big time. We felt we had to do something crazy to get back into contention, and that night we did."

Contention was still a ways away, actually. The Mets were still in last place and McGraw's ERA was up to 6.17. But Tug was thinking positively, anxious to learn where that confidence trip might take him.

You might even say he was beginning to believe.

AUGUST 1, 1973 (1ST)
METS 3 PIRATES 0
SHEA STADIUM

One pitcher was having a season so surreal you could practically feel the sand running out of its Salvador Dali-imagined hourglass. The other pitcher was throwing as if he never heard of being paid by the hour. The first pitcher didn't last in the opener of this Wednesday twinight doubleheader nor very long after it. The second pitcher — second to none, really — was all about endurance.

Steve Blass of the Pirates and Tom Seaver of the Mets were having very different 1973s, yet when they crossed paths to open this doubleheader, they wound up as what you might call fast acquaintances.

Blass, who pitched the Pirates to their Game Seven win in the 1971 World Series and followed up with 19 more victories in 1972, was living a pitcher's worst nightmare. His control abandoned him, and as his walks piled up, his ERA rose to dizzying heights. It was even worse than what had been plaguing Tug McGraw. By the time Buc manager Bill Virdon dropped him from the rotation in early July, he was giving up approximately ten earned runs for every nine innings he pitched. Steve spent the ensuing month all but inactive, relegated to the back end of the Pittsburgh bullpen. Needing a starter for the doubleheader, Virdon gave Blass another shot against the Mets.

It didn't work. A walk and a wild pitch led to a Met run in the first. Four walks and a hit batter in the second marked the end of Steve's evening. The Mets were up by three and Blass was bounced from Virdon's rotation for the next six weeks. Forevermore, a pitcher completely and mysteriously losing the strike zone would become known as suffering from Steve Blass Disease. As the pitcher told Roger Angell in 1975, when he was out of baseball at age 33, "Maybe your control is something that can just go."

Such misfortune was in no danger of befalling Seaver, yet again the brightest spot in an otherwise dreary early-'70s Met summer. While Blass was walking Mets, Seaver was striking out Pirates: three in the first and two in the second. There was a Pittsburgh double in each inning, but no damage. Relievers Bob Johnson and John Lamb righted the Pirate ship, allowing only one walk and three hits to the Mets in six-and-a-third innings, but by then it was too late...at least for the Bucs.

Really, "too late" was the last thing it was in this game. Despite Blass missing the plate, the action zipped along at what would become record speed. Seaver (13-5, 1.87 ERA) struck out eleven altogether, walked nobody, hit one batter and gave up only two hits over the final seven innings. Tom's 3-0 complete game victory was a done deal in exactly one hour and forty-four minutes. Ten weeks after setting a record for their longest win by innings (19), the Mets established a standard for their swiftest nine-inning triumph. The 1:44 remains the least time it's ever taken the club to win a regulation game.

The Mets were still mired in sixth place and presumed to be out of the running in the National League East, but for one night it was accurate and not necessarily uncomplimentary to claim they were going nowhere fast.

O n a Friday night in St. Louis, Ray Sadecki and the sixth-place Mets fell behind, 3-0, in the first on consecutive Cardinal hits from Joe Torre (double), Ted Simmons (single) and old friend Tommie Agee (triple). Sadecki stiffened for the next five innings, giving up no

more runs to the Redbirds, while the Mets chipped away on a Buddy Harrelson RBI single in the second and a Cleon Jones sacrifice fly in the third — though aggressive baserunning ran them out of each inning before they could get anything else. Ed Krancpool singled in the tying run off Mike Nagy in the sixth, with yet another Met (Rusty Staub) going out on a throw from the outfield.

After pinch-hitting for Sadecki in the top of the seventh, Yogi Berra — who not too many weeks earlier was the subject of dismissal talk — turned to Tug McGraw, who had only recently begun to turn his season around, however subtly. He won his first decision all year on August 22 and had lowered his ERA from 5.45 on August 20 to 5.18 entering this game five appearances later. McGraw had been a puzzle through the summer of 1973, but now summer was ending, so maybe his mysterious miseries were wearing off as well.

Tug held the Cardinals scoreless in the seventh, eighth and ninth, long enough for the Mets to arrive in the tenth inning still tied at three. After Diego Segui struck out Harrelson and McGraw to begin the festivities, the Mets sprung into action with five consecutive singles: Wayne Garrett, Felix Millan and Jones off Segui, and Staub and Kranepool off ex-Met Rich Folkers. Three runs resulted and gave McGraw a 6-3 lead to take to the bottom of the tenth. He'd give up a run, but nothing more and the Mets would win, 6-4.

A nice win, to be sure, but much nicer was that the Mets, unwilling basement tenants for so much of July and August, vacated last place in the N.L. East on the last night of August and would enter September in fifth place. That may not sound like a great position to start the traditional final month of the schedule, but it was not a traditional year in the division. Upon leapfrogging the Phillies, the Mets sat only 5 1/2 games from first place at the dawn of September 1973.

None other than Berra had reasoned that a season that was not yet over was, well, not yet over. His players obviously understood the perfect sense he was making.

SEPTEMBER 7, 1973 (2ND)
METS 4 EXPOS 2 (15)
JARRY PARK

The long, hard slog from a frustrating last straight into an improbable pennant race gained traction in two languages. The Mets traveled to Montreal for a Friday night doubleheader, and if you had to ask anyone to choose which team was the surprise contender at *Parc Jarry*, the standings would suggest you take a close look at *Les Expos*, who entered play in second place, three games out of first. It was the first time the 'Spos — now in their fifth season — were in anything resembling a pennant race. The Mets, on the other hand, had only, in the space of the previous week, tiptoed from sixth to fifth and then fifth to fourth. But if the calendar and Customs didn't stop them at their respective borders (September and Canada), why should the Expos?

After Jon Matlack, aided by a one-out save from resurgent Tug McGraw, made Wayne Garrett's leadoff homer hold up for a 1-0 win in the opener, the two teams settled in for a very long Quebec night. Jerry Koosman extended his then club-record scoreless innings streak to 31 2/3, before Bob Bailey drove home Felipe Alou in the third to give the Expos a 1-0 lead. It held up until the seventh, when a Pepe Frias error and a Mike Torrez fit of wildness (three consecutive walks) allowed the Mets to tie the score.

It stayed tied for a very long time, as relief aces Mike Marshall and McGraw (following Harry Parker's three scoreless frames) steered the game deep into extra innings. Tug wriggled out of a bases-loaded jam in the tenth by striking out pinch-hitter Clyde Mashore. Marshall, who would go eight-and-a-third, danced through figurative raindrops as well, grounding out Rusty Staub with Mets on second and third to escape the fourteenth.

The big breakthrough came in the fifteenth: John Milner singled, Ed Kranepool doubled and, one out later, Don Hahn lifted a fly ball to push the Mets' second run across. McGraw would be allowed to bat for himself and he'd single home two runs later in the inning, though he'd be thrown out trying to take second.

Yogi Berra, tuned into McGraw's hot-handedness (going for his sixth win or save in his last six appearances), left him in to pitch a sixth inning, but after one Expo run scored, he finally removed him in favor of Ray Sadecki. The veteran lefty retired Pepe Mangual and Alou, and the Mets came away 4-2 winners. They had swept the Expos and climbed to within four games of first-place St. Louis and a half-game of now third-place Montreal in one of the most fluid pennant races anybody had ever seen. Five teams were within five games of first, yet none of them was more than three games above .500. If you were scoring at home, the Mets, at 68-73, were smack dab in the thick of things.

And if you were translating at home, *vous devez croire* was French for the phrase that was about to become this franchise's calling card for the rest of the year and, really, for the rest of all time.

A rallying cry was working its way into the Met vernacular, probably because there w a s no reason to shout it down. The Mets hadn't shown the slightest inclination toward getting involved in a pennant race through most of the season, but in September, as exemplified

113

SEPTEMBER 18, 1973
METS 6 PIRATES 5
THREE RIVERS STADIUM

by Tug McGraw's power of positive thinking, they were making their move.

Now came the time for them to turn it into a great leap forward.

The night before, belief could have taken a hit. Tom Seaver pitched at Pittsburgh and was battered, with the Mets losing, 10-3, sticking the team 3 1/2 back, leaving them in fourth place. But the key phrase there is "3 1/2 back". It was anybody's division with a dozen games to go. It could conceivably belong to the Mets, as it was the Pirates who sat in first place and the Mets were about to play four more games against them: another at Three Rivers Stadium, three directly thereafter at Shea.

Seeing their ace get spanked and watching their momentum frozen could have seemed like a bad sign to Metsdom, but that's where that positive thinking came in. That's what Tug's mantra was all about. Tug hadn't been going well in the middle of summer, either, but he had been convinced by no ordinary Joe that he could turn his season around.

The Joe was Joe Badamo. As Tug put it in *Screwball*, "He sells insurance. Insurance and motivation." Tug knew Joe through Duffy Dyer, who, along with some other Mets, was introduced to him by the late Gil Hodges. He may not have been a guru, but Tug was willing to follow what he had to say.

"*We rapped a while,*" Tug wrote (with co-author Joe Durso), eventually coming around to the twinned subjects of confidence and concentration, and the only way the motivator said the pitcher could ensure having both was *"to believe in yourself. Realize that you haven't lost your ability. Start thinking positively. Damn the torpedoes, and all that jazz."*

Tug took it to heart. *"I said, 'You gotta believe. That's it, I guess, you gotta believe.'"*

From one conversation with one person, a movement was born. Tug threw "You Gotta Believe" to a few fans at Shea and they threw it back to him as if in a game of catch. He brought it into the clubhouse and it caught on. Without thinking, he blurted it in the middle of a pep talk delivered by chairman of the board M. Donald Grant (and later had to convince the stodgy executive he wasn't mocking him). "You Gotta Believe" took root in July, when the injury-riddled Mets were still in last place, when Tug was still in his epic 1973 slump.

Yet it was ready to bloom come September when the Mets and their fans were brimming with belief that a team in last place on the next-to-last day of August could roar from behind to win the division. Before the Pirates beat Seaver, the Mets had taken 12 of 17. In a year when nobody could gather a head of steam and take definitive control of the N.L. East, the Mets could still be the ones to do it. They just had to, per Joe Badamo and Tug McGraw, believe.

And start beating the Pirates head-to-head immediately.

Game two of their five-game series loomed as a turning point either way. For eight innings this Tuesday night, it appeared to be turning clearly in the direction of where the Allegheny and the Monongahela meet to form the mighty Ohio. Pittsburgh took a 4-1 lead off Jon Matlack in the third inning, knocking out the talented lefty one night after having their way with Seaver, and the score remained unchanged through the eighth. Ray Sadecki and McGraw had pitched well to keep the Mets in the game, but New York hadn't done anything with Pirate starter Bob Moose or his successor Ramon Hernandez, who stood two outs from saving a victory when he fouled out Bud Harrelson to start the Met ninth.

Ed Kranepool was due up next, but Yogi Berra pinch-hit with Jim Beauchamp, a righty batter versus lefty pitcher decision. It worked, as Jim singled. Then Wayne Garrett, in the midst of a career month (OPS 1.015) doubled. Felix Millan, who would establish a new franchise record for hits in 1973 with 185, got his most important hit to date: a two-run triple that cut the Mets' deficit to 4-3. After Hernandez walked Rusty Staub, Danny Murtaugh pulled Hernandez in favor of his fireman, Dave Giusti.

But Giusti only inflamed the Mets' rally, giving up a pinch-single to Ron Hodges to tie the game at four. Teddy Martinez ran for Hodges. Cleon Jones followed with a walk. And Don Hahn, who played more center field than any Met in 1973 despite never being fully entrusted with the full-time job by Berra, singled in Martinez and Jones.

The Mets led the Pirates, 6-4, heading to the bottom of the ninth. Clearly, the tide had turned away from the Three Rivers and toward Flushing Bay. But first, a little business would have to be taken care of. Three outs had to be nailed down, and this was where Tug and his Belief would normally come into play.

Except Berra had to pinch-hit for Tug in the eighth. So he went to as untested an arm as he had: 23-year-old Bob Apodaca, a righty being asked to make his major league debut in the makest-or-breakest situation imaginable.

Apodaca nearly broke the Mets. He threw eight pitches: four to Gene Clines, four to Milt May. Each was a ball. The Pirates had two on and none out. Dack's trial by fire had burned Berra, so he took out the kid and brought in a slightly more seasoned hand, 25-year-old Buzz Capra.

Would there be a feelgood, Capraesque ending from all this maneuvering? Well, Dave Cash bunted the runners over. Al Oliver grounded to the right side to score one of them. Willie Stargell was intentionally walked, then pinch-run for by rookie Dave Parker. Richie Zisk walked.

The bases were loaded. There were two out. The Mets led by one. The dangerous Manny Sanguillen stepped to the plate. It was all on Capra to give the Mets a wonderful life. Could he?

You had to believe it was so. Buzz, whose strategy was "go with my fastball and make sure he hit it," flied Sanguillen to Jones in left and the Mets held on, 6-5. They were now 2 1/2 behind the first-place Pirates, but they had three more shots at them, and all of them would come at Shea.

Cue the power of positive thinking.

If you're going to have momentum, there's no sense in waiting around for the optimal moment to use it. The Mets came out of Three Rivers after winning a thrilling come-from-behind victory the night before, so who better to bring with them to Shea but the same Pirates they had just beaten?

Strange schedulemaking, but there it was and here they were, the Mets and Bucs, now locked with the Cardinals and Expos in a four-way battle to determine who, if anybody, was going to emerge as National League East champion for 1973.

These two contenders go back and forth in the early innings. The Pirates strike first on a leadoff home run by Rennie Stennett off George Stone. Cleon Jones one-ups Stennett by smacking a two-run homer off Nelson Briles in the second.

Advantage Mets. Stennett returns with a vengeance in the third by tripling and scoring on Dave Cash's single to left.

Advantage Pirates? Felix Millan grabs back the momentum on behalf of the Mets when he singles home the .271-batting Stone, who had led off the inning by helping his own cause (something decent-hitting Mets pitchers were known to do for much of the first half-century of Mets baseball).

The Mets' 3-2 lead grew by a run in the fifth when Jerry Grote doubled, Bud Harrelson singled and Stone grounded to second. That insurance policy became a smart buy when Stone was befallen by an act of Pops: Willie Stargell, who hit more home runs against the Mets than any opponent in the team's history, delivered per usual. Luckily, Stargell's sixth-inning blast was a solo job, so the Mets still held a 4-3 lead when George left after six.

Stone's successor was Tug McGraw, Yogi Berra's favorite reliever in September — *everybody's* favorite reliever in September, but it was Berra who wouldn't or couldn't wait to use him. Firemen, as closers were known then, weren't kept on ice for the ninth. McGraw came bounding onto the mound in the seventh and wasn't particularly sharp. He walked pinch-hitter Gene Clines and surrendered a pinch-single to Fernando Gonzalez. The runners wound up on second and third with one out, but Tug stiffened as he almost always did in September 1973, popping up Stennett and grounding out Cash.

Tug encountered a bit more trouble in the eighth, allowing a leadoff single to Al Oliver, but two ground balls — the second of them a 5-4-3 double play — resulted in three outs and kept the Mets ahead by a run. Finally, some breathing room emerged in the eighth when, against Dave Giusti, Rusty Staub singled, John Milner walked and Jones homered for the second time on the evening. With his third, fourth and fifth RBIs of this Wednesday night, Cleon had put the Mets up, 7-3. Tug mowed down the final three Buc batters in the ninth and the Mets moved into a third-place tie with St. Louis, a half-game behind Montreal for second and a game-and-half from first-place Pittsburgh, with two more games coming up against those Pirates at Shea.

It all made for very exciting bookkeeping...and it was about to make for so much more.

It was time to carefully remove the m-word from the ark in which it had been kept undisturbed for nearly four years, for the Mets were about to perform the most sacred act the faith of their fans permitted.

115

SEPTEMBER 20, 1973
METS 4 PIRATES 3 (13)
SHEA STADIUM

It was time for a miracle.

But first, the relatively mundane from this about-to-be extraordinary Thursday night at Shea Stadium:

- Jerry Koosman pitched eight innings, struck out eight Pirates and allowed only one unearned run, which unfortunately put him behind, 1-0, because Jim Rooker had held the Mets scoreless through seven.
- Jim Beauchamp, making the final regular-season appearance of his ten-year career, pinch-hit for Koosman to lead off the bottom of the eighth and singled.
- After he was pinch-run for by Teddy Martinez, and Martinez was bunted to second by Wayne Garrett, Felix Millan singled home the tying run.
- Harry Parker, usually a rookie revelation in Yogi Berra's bullpen, came on to preserve the tie in the top of the ninth but couldn't quite do the job. Two runners were on when Dave Cash doubled one of them in to return the Pirates to their lead, 2-1.
- Bob Johnson, who pitched two games for the 1969 Mets, was tabbed by Danny Murtaugh to finish off his old team. A win here would erase the Mets'

recent momentum, leaving them 2 1/2 back with a scheduled nine to play. It wouldn't clinch anything for the Pirates, because others were still alive and contending, but it would put a crimp in the Mets' plans, no matter how much they Believed. But Johnson allowed a leadoff pinch-single to Ken Boswell and a sacrifice bunt to Don Hahn before exiting for Ramon Hernandez.

- Hernandez struck out pinch-hitter George Theodore for the second out of the ninth, but another pinch-hitter, Duffy Dyer, delivered a double, scoring Boswell to tie the game at two.
- The two teams went to extra innings, as Yogi Berra went to veteran swingman Ray Sadecki. Sadecki gave Yogi three perfect innings. The Mets, meanwhile, failed to score against Jim McKee and Luke Walker. The game would go to a thirteenth inning, when Sadecki, with one out, would allow his first hit, a single to Richie Zisk. After he retired Manny Sanguillen for the second out of the inning, he faced September callup Dave Augustine.

This is where The Miracle occurs.
This is where it's best left to Bob Murphy to deliver The Word:

> *"The two-one pitch…*
> *"Hit in the air to left field, it's deep…*
> *"Back goes Jones, BY THE FENCE…*
> *"It hits the TOP of the fence, comes back in play…*
> *"Jones grabs it!*
> *"The relay throw to the plate, they may get him…*
> *"…HE'S OUT!*
> *"He's out at the plate!*
> *"An INCREDIBLE play!"*

If you're scoring at home, the interpretation would be 7-6-2, Cleon Jones to Wayne Garrett to Ron Hodges, the rookie catcher who ascended to the Mets' starting lineup for much of the summer from Double-A Memphis because of injuries. Zisk, the runner from first, tied a piano to his back when he took off around the bases. The man was slow. But The Man Upstairs was quick-thinking. He (or Something) prevented what looked like, on Channel 9, a certain goner for Augustine from landing in the left field bullpen for what would have been his first — and only — major league home run. Had the ball made it past the wall, the Mets would have been down, 5-3.

But it didn't go quite far enough, at least from a Pirate perspective. It bounced off the very top of the fence and caromed right back into Cleon's glove. He made a strong throw to Garrett, who made a strong throw to Hodges, who made a strong stand in front of the plate, bringing down an emphatic tag on Zisk.

"The ball hit the corner and it just popped up to me," Jones recounted. "I didn't think he hit it high enough to go over. I knew the ball was gonna hit the fence, but it could've gone anywhere."

Garrett, who had moved to shortstop from his usual third base in the tenth after Bud Harrelson had been pinch-hit for, aimed low when he made his relay throw to Hodges. "I wanted it to hit the ground," Wayne said, and he got his wish. The ball arrived in Hodges's mitt the same time Zisk was charging into Hodges's body. The kid catcher held the ball, and home plate ump John McSherry held his right arm upwards, signaling the lumbering Pirate runner out.

"It has to be one of the most remarkable plays I ever saw," Garrett swore.

The Mets weren't done being remarkable. The aptly named Walker walked his first two batters in the bottom of the thirteenth. Luke walked off the mound. Dave Giusti walked on. He got one out, but that was all. Hodges, having the night of his career, singled, scoring John Milner from second. The Mets had won, 4-3, in a game that would be forever remembered for the Ball Off the Top of the Wall and how it bounced in the only direction it could.

Up...the same direction the Mets were going in.

SEPTEMBER 21, 1973
METS 10 PIRATES 2
SHEA STADIUM

It's worth backtracking over the season to date so as to note there was a time when the 1973 edition of the National League East behaved like all the other divisions in baseball. On July 1, the N.L. East's first-place team was the Cubs, sporting a perfectly normal first-place record of 48-33 and holding a lead of eight games, the largest of any frontrunner at that moment. The Mets were in last place, eleven games back — the closest any basement denizen was to first in any division, but nobody dared connect any dots on behalf of 33-40 New York.

The Cubs were actually further ahead of the pack at the midpoint of their 1973 schedule than they were when they were a summertime juggernaut in 1969. Yet just as it wasn't to be for the '69 Cubs, their successors four years later fell far from grace. By July 26, they had lost 14 of 18 and stumbled out of first.

The new N.L. East leaders were the Cardinals, on a 16-7 tear, which certainly indicates first-place capabilities, though the bigger picture was a bit murkier. Because the Cubs had fallen so fast, the Cardinals didn't need much of a platform from which to stage their assault on first. They had been a sub-.500 club before getting hot, which meant that even as they opened up a five-game lead on August 5, their record was a fairly pedestrian 61-50, a pace translatable to an 89-win season. Most years that wasn't enough to take a division title, but the five-game bulge was still the most substantial in any division. For what it was worth, the last-place Mets sat 11 1/2 games out of first, remaining in pretty dire straits, yet compared to other sixth-place clubs, not completely buried.

St. Louis, however, had peaked. The Cards didn't know it, though they might have had a hunch once they lost Bob Gibson to injury (against the Mets, no less). They clung gamely to first in their ace's absence, but after dropping 23 of 34, the Redbirds gave way at the top of the division to the three-time defending East champion Pirates. By the time they rose to prominence on September 12, though, it was apparent something was very askew in the subset they'd ruled from 1970 through 1972.

Unlike the Cubs, who started scalding, or the Cardinals, who heated up, the Bucs took control by playing a shade better than ordinary, 17-16 since St. Louis began to crumble. In the other three divisions, no first-place club owned a lead of fewer than five games and all of them were at least sixteen games above .500. The N.L. East had become a statistical anomaly, to put it kindly. They were led by a team that was *exactly* at .500. The Pirates were 71-71, a half-game ahead of the Cards. The last-place Phillies, were only 7 1/2 out. The next-to-last-place team, the Cubs, were a mere three behind. Montreal was in third, one game removed from first.

And those Mets, who had been so disregardable for so long, were 2 1/2 behind on the night the Pirates floated past the Cardinals. They were in fourth, yes, but they were perfectly positioned in this tightly packed madhouse of mediocrity. As they couldn't help but notice as they shook off the injuries and the cobwebs that had held them back for five-sixths of the season, they had as much of a chance as anybody to take a turn at the top and perhaps parlay that toehold into a title.

Never mind that they were in fourth place. Never mind that their record of 70-75 was the *seventeenth-best* in all of baseball and that fewer than three weeks remained before the playoff participants had to be determined. This wasn't a tournament seeking a Sweet Sixteen. This was a division that was up for grabs in every sense of the phrase.

The Mets commenced to grabbing. As of September 12, they had won nine of thirteen. They'd take an additional three of four as they headed into Pittsburgh to begin their two-city, five-game showdown against the Bucs. They'd lose one, then win the next three. And finally, on the evening of September 21, they ascended to a place nobody in his right mind would have predicted the morning of August 31.

Tom Seaver threw a Friday night five-hitter while his teammates pounded luckless Steve Blass and five Pirate relievers to beat the Bucs at Shea, 10-2. In a four-day span in September, an unprecedented Metamorphosis occurred. The Mets not only picked up one game per day in the standings, they picked up one place per day. From fourth and 3 1/2 out after Monday, they climbed to first and a half-game up on Friday. It had been barely three weeks since they were in last place. Now they were in first place. And for good measure, they brought their record to 77-77, .500 for the first time since they were 21-21 on May 29.

Everybody else was under .500, but only the Phillies could be written off as out of it. The Pirates trailed by that half-game, the Cards by one, the Expos by one-and-a-half and the lately undead Cubs by two-and-a-half. The National League East was still up for grabs, but there was no mistaking that it was the first-place Mets — on a four-game winning streak and a 16-6 roll — who had chosen the ideal moment to make their play.

They'd grabbed hold of a lead. With eight games left, the challenge would now turn to holding on to it.

A ny thoughts the Cardinals had of doing to the Mets what the Mets did to the Pirates — using a head-to-head matchup to craft a quick climb up the standings — suffered an immediate setback at the hands of two men who exemplified the concept of peaking at the right time.

SEPTEMBER 22, 1973
METS 2 CARDINALS 0
SHEA STADIUM

Hitting like he was born to play in pennant races was Wayne Garrett, so often the Mets' starting third baseman through the early '70s more by default than choice. Acquisitions of veterans Joe Foy, Bob Aspromonte and Jim Fregosi all fizzled and, eventually, the dugout turned its exasperated eyes to Ed Charles's hot corner platoon partner from 1969. When the Mets officially gave up on Fregosi and sold him to Texas in July, the third base job became Garrett's for good.

Garrett proved himself worthy of regular's status as September intensified. He was practically a star by the time the Cardinals came to Shea this Saturday, doing his best Brooks Robinson impression on both sides of the ball. While taking care of the defense just fine, the redhead's bat caught fire. He would hit .422 over the season's final dozen games and produced the biggest blow of his biggest month in the third inning when he homered with Bud Harrelson on second to give Jon Matlack a 2-0 lead.

Matlack was so appreciative, that he never let it go, tossing a four-hit, nine-strikeout complete game gem to solidify the Mets' grasp of first place. The 1972 National League Rookie of the Year experienced some sophomore rough patches but hadn't lost a decision since August 13. He won this one, 2-0, extending the Mets' winning streak to five and their lead in the East to a full game over the rained-out Pirates.

118

SEPTEMBER 23, 1973
METS 5 CARDINALS 2
SHEA STADIUM

T ommie Agee was in the house, but there was nothing ceremonial in his role. Sure, he was a Miracle Met, but the franchise he helped make famous wasn't honoring the 1969 club's feats this Sunday at Shea.

But they did seem set on replicating them.

It may be heresy to suggest what the 1973 Mets were in the midst of attempting to do was tougher, more unlikely and every bit as thrilling as what their Amazin' predecessors pulled off a quadrennium earlier, but consider that Agee's Mets, for all their underdog status, had lit their fuse by mid-August and weren't too bad in the months before that. When the 1969 Mets reached the end of the penultimate week of their schedule, the magic number count was in full effect and a division-clinching was inevitable.

Nothing was inevitable for the 1973 Mets as they prepared to play the second of their two-game set against Agee's Cardinals. Tommie's post-Flushing campaign had been anything but miraculous. He didn't thrive in Houston (where the Mets sent him for instant washout Rich Chiles and minor leaguer Buddy Harris) and he didn't exactly ignite for St. Louis when the then first-place Redbirds picked him up for the stretch drive in August. But he was still Tommie Agee and this was still Shea Stadium in a pennant race, so it was little wonder that the center fielder who almost single-handedly won a World Series game on this same field in 1969 would come through for his team when they desperately needed a lift. With one out and Ted Sizemore on second in the top of the first, Agee belted a George Stone pitch over the familiar Shea wall to stake starter Mike Thompson to an instant 2-0 lead.

It was a fitting locale for what became the final home run of Tommie Agee's big league career. The rest of the day, however, would be devoted to a blend of new and old Met heroes coming through for a new Met miracle.

Stone, one of the Mets' opponents in the 1969 NLCS as a Brave, had provided an unexpected boost to New York fortunes all year long, but the lefty didn't have it against the Cards. Yet as things continued to click for Yogi Berra's bunch, a pitcher from whom even less was anticipated in 1973 emerged to dash St. Louis's hopes. Harry Parker, given up on by the Cardinals a couple of years earlier, became a bullpen stalwart for Berra in his first full season on a major league roster. The righthander took the ball from Yogi in the third and stayed on the mound through the sixth, allowing only two Redbird baserunners.

While Parker pitched, the Mets did a bit of walking at the expense of another former teammate. Rich Folkers, who was part of the eight-player trade that brought Parker to New York, was on for the Cardinals in the third and went wild. He walked Wayne Garrett, Felix Millan and Rusty Staub to start the inning. Folkers wouldn't be around by its end when a Cleon Jones sacrifice fly cut the Cardinal lead to 2-1. Staub (a .387 batter over the Mets' final fifteen games) tied the score in the fifth on an RBI single off Folkers's immediate successor, Orlando Peña.

In the sixth, Mr. September — Garrett — tripled to bring home Harrelson and Ken Boswell, making it Mets 4 Cardinals 2. In the seventh, Jones, having his own magnificent month, homered. Before his finishing kick would be over, Cleon would notch six homers and 14 RBIs in the Mets' final ten games.

All that was left was for someone to close out the Cardinals in style, and in September 1973, that could only be one person. To the glee of the 51,926 You Gotta Believers on hand, Tug McGraw emerged from the bullpen buggy to pitch the final three innings. Because it was September 1973 and Tug was now the mirror image of what he'd been in the five months prior, he could do no wrong. There was a little turbulence in the eighth via two walks, but a 6-4-3 double play bailed him out. There was a little more in the ninth when he gave up two singles and allowed the tying run to come to bat with two out, but the Cards' last hope, light-hitting shortstop Mike Tyson, had no more than a puncher's chance against the sport's most untouchable reliever. McGraw flied Tyson to left and, in an instant, Tug was slapping his glove against his thigh in trademark ebullience at having done his job so well when it counted so much.

The 5-2 win he nailed down was the Mets' sixth in a row, their longest such streak all season. Because the Pirates swept a doubleheader in Montreal, Pittsburgh actually trimmed the Mets' divisional lead to a half-game. But the Mets had done nothing to surrender that lead, giving McGraw, Jones, Garrett and three of the other four 1969 Mets on the field this Sunday at Shea in September 1973 cause to feel that maybe they were experiencing the *second* ride of a lifetime.

The presence of the seventh '69 Met — Agee — in a different uniform on such an otherwise uplifting afternoon perhaps served as a small reminder of just how fleeting a lifetime can be and just how precious those rides are.

What mattered most, per the parameters of any pennant race, was how the game ended, and on this Tuesday night, it ended spectacularly well, with Tug McGraw coming on to throw two-and-a-third innings of shutout ball to seal Jerry Koosman's 2-1 victory over the

119

SEPTEMBER 25, 1973

METS 2 EXPOS 1

SHEA STADIUM

fast-fading Expos. Sparked by yet another Cleon Jones home run, the Mets won their seventh in a row, stretching their lead over second-place Pittsburgh to a game-and-a-half with five to play. McGraw was doing everything in his power to back up his You Gotta Believe credo. From September 5 to September 25, as the Mets took 15 of 19, McGraw made a dozen appearances. Every one of them was a personal and team success: he saved nine games and won three more. Eight of the outings were at least two innings long.

Tug's pitching put the usual exclamation point on the Shea festivities, but nothing could have made more of a statement about the magical properties of this Met month than the way the evening began. Hours before Tug bid *au revoir* to the team from Canada, his most revered teammate was issuing a memorable signoff to a whole other nation.

It was Willie Mays Night, marking the end of a career surpassed by nobody for utter brilliance. Mays began it in 1951 in the same place where the Mets learned to crawl, at the Polo Grounds in Upper Manhattan. Six years and a slew of indelible images later, Willie and his team, the New York Giants, were whisked away to San Francisco. Their departure, along with the Brooklyn Dodgers', facilitated the birth of the Mets, which was a good thing for the millions wrapped up in total Belief by September of 1973, but old-timers would tell you there was always a little something missing from the New York National League baseball scene as long as the quintessential New York National League baseball superstar was plying his trade on the West Coast.

Mrs. Joan Payson attempted to turn back time and make all right with the world in 1972 when she plied a trade of her own: Charlie Williams and cash to the Giants in exchange for Willie's homecoming. It was a dramatic success from the Say Hey get-go... though after the euphoria of Willie Mays in a New York uniform settled down, it couldn't help but be noticed that a season later, the Mets were left with a 42-year-old legend who had never been anything but a legend — but had never been 42 before.

Willie contributed a few timely hits in 1973, but after going 0-for-2 in Montreal on September 9, his batting average sank to a most unMayslike .211, accompanied by six homers, 25 RBIs and a mere 24 runs scored in 66 games played (Willie had scored more than a hundred runs annually from 1954 through 1965). He was hurting physically after cracking two ribs on a metal rail at Jarry Park in pursuit of a foul ball, and mentally, not being the Willie Mays whom fans from coast-to-coast idolized and idealized finally caught up with him. Thus, he announced his retirement at a press conference at Shea's Diamond Club on September 20.

Phil Pepe covered the SRO event for the *Daily News*, reminding any readers who were perhaps momentarily dismayed by Mays's descent into cranky mortality — a couple of times as a Met, he hadn't shown up when and where expected, making Yogi Berra's managerial tenure no easier — what Willie represented beyond his 660 home runs, 1,903 runs batted in, 2,062 runs scored, 3,283 base hits and .302 lifetime average. "[It] is not the records or the statistics or the awards that distinguish him," Pepe wrote. "It is the memory of the way the man played the game, with a zest and a daring, with an excitement that is unmatched."

"I've had a love affair with baseball," Mays told the media, but acknowledged, "you just can't play at 42 the way you did at 20."

The Mets had already scheduled Willie Mays Night before his retirement went official. When they announced their intention to honor him, it was before there was any inkling that it would serve as a sidebar in a sizzling-hot pennant race...or that a pennant race might provide the backdrop to Willie Mays Night. Where No. 24 was concerned, it was unfathomable that he wouldn't be the main attraction.

Sure enough, a full house of more than 53,000 showed up at Shea to bestow its appreciation on Mays. After a 45-minute tribute in which Willie was showered with all manner of gifts and applauded by a veritable Hall of Fame cast of his Giant, Dodger and Yankee contemporaries from the golden age of New York baseball, it was the man of the hour's turn to speak.

Those who heard what the Say Hey Kid had to say in his baseball twilight will never forget it. He thanked the crowd for remembering him for the player he had been rather than the player time forced him to become: "If you knew how I felt in my heart to hear you cheer and know I can't do anything about it..." He thanked the visiting Expos for enduring the delay, apologetically explaining to the Mets' rivals *du nuit*, "This is my farewell. I thought I'd never quit." He thanked the Mets for waiting patiently on such a big night in the course of their own journey: "I hope you go on to win the flag for the New York people. This is your night as well as mine."

Actually, for as long as Willie spoke and for as long as Willie's words resonated, it would always belong to him, especially given the sendoff he gave his own sendoff:

"I see these kids over here, and I see how these kids are fighting for a pennant, and to me it says one thing: Willie, say goodbye to America."

Was there any doubt after that that those kids — his Mets — would go out and win their seventh in a row? Was there any doubt, either, that Willie's New York departure was every bit as fortuitous as his introduction? That came 22 years earlier, when the Giants were struggling, far removed from first place until August. Yet with

rookie Willie Mays on board, those Giants caught fire, passed the Dodgers and —
after Bobby Thomson (in attendance at Shea this night) went deep off Ralph Branca
(also there) — won the pennant.

"Look at it," another Willie Mays Night guest, Brooklyn Dodger icon Joe Black,
suggested. "It was Willie largely who brought the Giants out of the doldrums and now
it's Willie's inspiration — in another way — that I think will carry the New York Mets
to the National League championship and maybe to their second World Series title."

SEPTEMBER 30, 1973 (2ND)

120   METS 9 CUBS 2

WRIGLEY FIELD

For a pennant race that came along all at once,
the lunge for the 1973 N.L. East flag sure
got stubborn about getting over with. But by
the time this unfathomable season was reaching
its inevitable conclusion, only recalcitrance
threatened to stop the New York Mets.

First, the weather over Chicago, where the Mets were slated to play their final
series, wouldn't budge. After a scheduled off day Thursday, it poured Friday,
knocking out one game. It poured Saturday, too, taking out a planned doubleheader.
As of Sunday, they hadn't played since Wednesday, when their seven-game winning
streak was snapped by the Expos. The Mets left their last homestand with a record
of 80-78 and a lead of a half-game over second-place Pittsburgh. Sitting inactive for
three days hadn't exactly damaged them. They were still 80-78, but their divisional
lead had increased to a game-and-a-half, though it was now the Cardinals who were
their closest competitor.

That's indicative of the other element that wouldn't get a move on in the Mets'
world: the race. Like the rain, it wouldn't go away. Everybody who was ever a
contender in 1973 remained a contender as the final scheduled day of the season
commenced. Five teams — five! — were still mathematically alive that Sunday.
Taking into account makeup dates that still loomed as playable for Monday, the
following scenario was, at the very least, conceivable on September 30:

- The Mets could drop two doubleheaders to the Cubs and fall from 80-78
  to 80-82; the Cubs, in turn, would correspondingly rise from 76-82 to 80-82.

- The Cardinals could lose to the Phillies and drop from 80-81 to 80-82.

- The Pirates (79-81) could lose to the Expos — who would complete their
  schedule at 80-82 — but then beat the Padres in a makeup game and move up to
  80-82.

That would create the first five-way tie for first place in the history of baseball,
and the Federal Reserve couldn't authorize enough coins to toss to determine how
a quintuple-tiebreaker might work. It wasn't very likely the National League East
would come down to that daffy a conclusion, but the fact that the possibility existed

spoke to the unhinged nature of the 1973 stretch drive.

Which, in turn, spoke to how spectacularly the Mets had to play to drive the division into such glorious disarray. It's fair to say that no 80-78 team has ever sat in first place on the final scheduled day of the season more deservedly.

At the heart of the operation, just as in 1969, were three eminently trustworthy starters. That's what had to give Yogi Berra the core of his confidence when the clouds finally parted enough to play two in sodden Chicago that final Sunday, September 30. He tabbed Jon Matlack for the opener, and the second-year lefty did not disappoint, firing a complete-game five-hitter, with nine strikeouts. The only problem was the Mets' bats sat idle, perhaps not being notified that the rain, rain had gone away. The Mets scored nothing for Matlack. The Cubs scratched out a solitary run. It was enough to beat the Mets, 1-0. Paired with the last game the Mets had played, a loss to Montreal four days earlier, the hottest team in baseball was suddenly in the midst of its first losing streak of any length since August 26.

Not exactly the juncture a Mets fan would choose for his team to cool off, but another game remained that Sunday, and another stellar lefty, Jerry Koosman, was taking the mound. In the nightcap, Jerry was just about as good as Jon: nine innings, six hits, seven strikeouts, two runs allowed...and this time, the Mets' bats got the memo that the game was on. Led by Cleon Jones's two-run homer and Rusty Staub's three RBIs, Kooz cruised to a 9-2 win. With the Cubs defeated, the five-team tie scenario disappeared. And with Pittsburgh topping Montreal, the Expos were eliminated. The Cardinals, however, won their game and stayed in the race, as did the Bucs.

So here's where the recalcitrant 1973 pennant race stood at the end of the day when it was, on paper, supposed to end: three teams were still alive. The Cardinals, at 81-81, would sit back and monitor what would happen in Pittsburgh, where the Padres' presence was kindly requested to make up a previously postponed game, and in Chicago, where the Mets and Cubs owed the senior circuit one more twinbill. If the Pirates, at 80-81, won, and the Mets, at 81-79, were swept, a three-way tie would occur. A Pirate loss would make Pittsburgh superfluous, but no Mets win in two games would pit New York and St. Louis in a tiebreaker.

A Mets win would make all the statistical potentialities blissfully academic. And if anybody was capable of erasing the National League East's overcrowded blackboard once and for all, it was Lawrence Peter Berra's starting pitcher for Monday's opener, George Thomas Seaver.

There were worse options for a manager. There was none better.

N ever mind that as the Monday after the "final" Sunday dawned in Chicago, Tom Seaver was a tired ace pitcher, coming to the end of a season in which he surpassed 250 innings for the seventh time in his seven-year career. Never mind that two of his most recent outings

121

OCTOBER 1, 1973
METS 6 CUBS 4
WRIGLEY FIELD

went only three innings and two innings. Never mind that, at 18-10, his standard of 20 wins was out of reach. Tom Seaver, 19-Game Winner, might not quite roll gracefully off the tongue after he'd won 25, 20 and 21 in three of his previous four seasons, but this was no ordinary nineteenth win sitting on the Wrigley Field table.

"When you get to where Tom Seaver is," Larry Merchant wrote in the *Post*, "it doesn't only matter how many you win, but which ones you win."

He was Tom Seaver. He was the Franchise. He was going to lead the National League in strikeouts with 251, in ERA at 2.08, and in the as yet uncalculated category of walks and hits per innings pitched (0.976). He had the bona fides to match his reputation. And he was ready. "I'm not going to put intangible pressure to bear on myself," Tom promised. He was just going to try to put his team in the postseason any way he could and then look forward to having "more work to do" five days hence at Riverfront Stadium.

After Seaver and Burt Hooton swapped zeroes in the first inning, Cleon Jones got the first big swing of the day in, belting one of the Cub starter's knuckle-curves into the mostly deserted right-center field bleachers (paid attendance in Wrigleyville, where the Mets' fortunes didn't elicit much interest: 1,913). The score stayed 1-0 through three, with Seaver's first brush with adversity — two on, one out in the third — cleared away by a Harrelson-Millan-Milner DP.

Hooton loaded the bases in the fourth on a single to Rusty Staub and walks to John Milner and Jones. Perfectly set up, Jerry Grote lined a single to center to increase the Mets' lead to 3-0. Seaver gave up two more hits in the fourth, bringing the Cubs' total to five, but again emerged undamaged.

The top of the fifth appeared to bury the Cubs once and for all. Wayne Garrett led off with a double. Felix Millan singled him to third. Cub skipper Whitey Lockman (a teammate of Willie Mays's on the Giants' championship clubs of '51 and '54) pulled Hooton and inserted Mike Paul. Paul was greeted by a run-scoring single from Rusty and a sac fly off the bat of the Hammer. The Mets led, 5-0, and the division title was so close the Mets could taste it...a fact the Pirates no doubt wanted to spit out. At Three Rivers Stadium, the score from Chicago flashed as the national anthem was performed. Pittsburgh assumed its fate was sealed.

The only actor not reading from the script was Seaver. Instead of being buoyed by the relative surfeit of Met runs, he struggled. Four Cubs recorded base hits in the fourth, with the last two producing runs. It was 5-2 heading to the sixth. It stayed 5-2 until the seventh when a Ron Santo error allowed a sixth Met run to plate. Tom Seaver and a four-run lead were all anybody who bled orange and blue could wish for three innings shy of a divisional dream coming true.

Nevertheless, at the end of a season that had been so nightmarish for so long, sweet dreams were elusive. The home seventh began with Dave Rosello dunking a single into center. It was the Cubs' tenth single of the day. Then Rick Monday, Seaver's teammate almost a decade earlier on the semi-pro Alaska Goldpanners, mined Seaver's exhaustion for a two-run homer. It was now 6-4. It was now getting dicey.

It was now time to take out one ace and call on another.

If Tom Seaver had to be the pitcher to start the game that could put a cap on the

1973 regular season, Tug McGraw had to be the pitcher to end it. Like Seaver, he was ready to take the ball.

"I was pretty hot by now," Tug wrote in *Screwball*, "all jacked up and believing like hell."

Sure enough, Tug set down the Cubs 1-2-3 in the seventh...and 1-2-3 in the eighth. His streak was snapped when Ken Rudolph opened the ninth with a single, but he then struck out Rosello. Still leading, 6-4, Tug faced pinch-hitter Glenn Beckert with Rudolph on first.

Which brings us, as all Happiest Recaps should, to Bob Murphy:

> *"Now the stretch by McGraw, the three-two delivery...the runner goes, and a little popup! Milner grabs it — he'll run to first...double play! The Mets win the pennant! The Mets have just won the pennant in the Eastern Division! It's all over, the Mets have won it with a magnificent stretch drive. They won nineteen and lost only eight in September, they've won their first October ballgame, and with it, they have won the pennant in the Eastern Division."*

The Mets were a 21-8 club dating back to the final day of August, the day they moved out of the cellar. They were an 82-79 team overall, which in every other season to that point in major league history would have meant a ticket home. Instead, in the wild and wacky year of 1973 — when "eternal optimist" Tom Seaver admitted the odds facing the Mets in summer "strained even my eternal optimism" — it was a ticket to the National League Championship Series against the Western Division-winning Reds. They were division champs for the second time in five years, creating a miracle every bit as incomprehensible as the one from 1969.

Stranger, probably.

In '69, the Mets materialized as if from thin air, but they did it sooner and grabbed first place earlier. This team took it to the wire and then needed one more day besides. They had four teams on their tail on the supposed last day, two still hanging around the day after. But now the Cards were done, the Pirates (losing to San Diego) were done and even they could finally take a breath. The makeup doubleheader's second half was no longer needed, and the umpires didn't need much of an excuse to defer to the endlessly gray skies that enveloped Chicago's north side and call it off.

Geez, these Mets had, like McGraw, gotten so hot, that they didn't even need an entire season to zoom from last on August 30 to a clinch of first on October 1. They wrapped things up in 161 games. The stubbornness of this fractured fairy tale of a season may have been taking a nine-inning break, but now it insisted on continuing deep into October. Per Yogi's summertime pronouncement, it really wasn't going to be over until it was over...which was fine with all concerned, one Met maybe more than any other.

In September, when Willie Mays was announcing his retirement, he was already on the sidelines. He never played in another regular-season game after September 9. But he promised that if the Mets were successful in extending their fight for a pennant, he, like all the teammates he called "these kids," Mays told, would be prepared to take part.

"If we get into the World Series," Mays told reporters, "I'll be there."

As it turned out, Willie became one of the reasons the 1973 Mets would get to the World Series, as the NLCS demonstrated he wasn't done playing. But before that showdown versus Cincinnati could take on its own legend, there was the matter of getting the Say Hey Kid on the plane out of Chicago.

"Where's Willie?" Seaver asked amid the raucous clubhouse celebration at Wrigley.

"He took two sips of champagne," Tom was told, "and he's passed out on the training table."

Which is pretty much how every Mets fan at the end of a month like no other felt at that moment.

POSTSEASON

OCTOBER 7, 1973
METS 5 REDS 0
RIVERFRONT STADIUM

The Lilliputians of the National League East — where every team that finished behind them wound up with a losing record — were a thing of the very recent past for the division champion Mets. They had something much bigger facing them five days after clinching their demi-title.

Much bigger.

It required little exaggeration to refer to Cincinnati's ballclub as the Big Red Machine. The nickname took on currency in 1970 when the erstwhile Redlegs churned out an easy N.L. West romp and resonated that much more when they did it again in '72. On both occasions, the Reds won the pennant and took their mechanical marvel of an offense to the World Series. Each time, though, their gears ground to a halt, with the Machine producing only disappointment, losing in to the Orioles in 1970 and the A's in 1972.

The Reds' return engagement for October baseball was in serious doubt at the end of June when they trailed the white-hot Dodgers by eleven games. The tide turned with the calendar, and from July 1 until they clinched on September 24, Cincinnati won at a staggering .716 pace. What the Mets did for about a month, the Reds did for close to three.

Except Cincy conducted their winning business very differently. As in its pennant-winning years, the Machine was fueled by a high-octane offense that scored 741 runs, second-most in the league. By comparison, the Mets crossed the plate 608 times, or second-least in the league. These were the Reds whose first five batters generally included three eventual Hall of Famers in Joe Morgan, Johnny Bench and Tony Perez and another, Pete Rose, whose on-field accomplishments certainly qualified him for Cooperstown. All were in their prime, each had been to the postseason, none was an easy out.

Rose, leading off and playing left, won the batting crown (his third) with a .338 average. Morgan, the second-place hitter and Gold Glove second baseman, posted numbers that would later be revealed as accounting for the best Wins Above Replacement figure (9.9) in the N.L. First baseman Perez, batting fifth, had his usual excellent season, whether expressed in the statistics of the day (27 HR, 101 RBI, .314 BA) or translated sabermetrcially (.919 OPS). And in the middle of everything, cleanup hitter and all-world catcher Johnny Bench continued to be Johnny Bench. His power numbers were a bit off his MVP peaks of '70 and '72, but were still superb (25 homers, 104 ribbies) for a backstop or anybody. And in a league where Jerry Grote was an acknowledged defensive wizard, it was Bench who won Gold Glove after Gold Glove.

Bench handled a pitching staff whose credentials didn't quite rate with the Mets, yet was by no means a bad bunch. New York would see Jack Billingham (19-10), Don Gullett (18-8), Ross Grimsley (13-10) and, if the best-of-five series exceeded the minimum, Fred Norman (12-6). Manager Sparky Anderson wasn't shy about going to his bullpen, mixing and matching righties Pedro Borbon and Clay Carroll with lefty Tom Hall.

The Reds weren't necessarily impregnable. Their talented young shortstop Davey Concepcion had been lost to injury since July, third base was left to the inexperienced Dan Driessen and the segments of the outfield that weren't Rose's garden required some improvisation on Anderson's part. But there was no getting around the core of this 99-win team, at least not when the 82-win Mets traveled to Cincinnati on Saturday afternoon, October 6, to begin their second National League Championship Series.

Yogi Berra threw Tom Seaver, working on his usual four days' rest, thanks to baseball's built-in lag between the regular season and the playoffs. Seaver faced Billingham and both men were utter anathema to the players paid to hit against them. For seven-and-a-half innings, only one batter had a significant impact on the course of events, and it was one of the pitchers. In the top of the second of a scoreless game, Buddy Harrelson walked with two out. Seaver, the ninth hitter in Berra's lineup, epitomized the phrase "helped his own cause" when he lined a double that brought his roommate Buddy all the way around.

With a 1-0 lead, Seaver turned ferocious. Entering the eighth, he had held the Reds to four hits, one hit batter and no walks while striking out eleven. In this autumn when "Believe" was every Mets fan's mantra, one might have had a little more faith had Tom had been blessed with more run support. But on this particular Saturday, there were weightier matters far from Riverfront Stadium, namely the outbreak of the Yom Kippur War, which began when Egypt and Syria chose the holiest day on the Jewish calendar to launch a surprise attack on Israel. Assuming a Higher Power was distracted by the goings-on in the Middle East, Seaver — who suggested in 1969 that God was a Mets fan, or at least rented an apartment in New York — was on his own.

Come the eighth, with the score still 1-0 (Billingham giving up essentially nothing after Seaver's double), the afternoon morphed into a day of Red atonement. After Tom fanned pinch-hitter Hal King for his twelfth strikeout, Rose nailed him for the tying home run. And with one out in the ninth, Seaver, whose K count had reached thirteen, surrendered the game-winner to Bench. The Mets lost, 2-1, behind their best pitcher.

Which made winning Game Two, on Sunday, a necessity. Fortunately, their second-best pitcher was pretty darn good, too.

Jon Matlack took on and took out the core of the Reds lineup. Batting first through fourth, Rose, Morgan, Perez and Bench went a collective 0-for-16 against the lefty. The only hitter to do anything — anything — versus Matlack was journeyman outfielder Andy Kosco, who started in right and collected a pair of singles. Jon's ledger was nearly spotless, resulting in a line of two hits, three walks and nine strikeouts. Only in the fifth did the Reds mount a semblance of a threat, when shortstop Darrel Chaney drew a base on balls to push Kosco, who had also walked, to second. Anderson, true to his Captain Hook reputation, pinch-hit for his starting pitcher, Gullett, but Phil Gagliano struck out.

Gullett had given up only a fourth-inning homer to one of the redder Mets, Le Grand Orange Rusty Staub. He and Carroll, who took over in the sixth, combined to keep the game at 1-0 until the top of the ninth when Cleon Jones, Grote and Harrelson all delivered run-scoring singles, giving Matlack ample breathing room to complete his gem. When he flied out Morgan and Perez and struck out Bench, the Mets put a deceptively easy 5-0 win in the books and tied the series at one.

The Ohio portion of the NLCS was over. The teams headed east, to Shea. There the alleged machine that won 99 games and the hot hands whose 82 victories landed them a flukish division flag would start all over, best-of-three, to determine the identity of the 1973 league champion.

I n an era when comedians could get a cheap laugh at the expense of the violence-riddled NHL — *"I went to a fight and a hockey game broke out"* — a touch of Broad Street Bullying came to the intersection of 126th Street and Roosevelt Avenue. Except unlike the Stanley

OCTOBER 8, 1973
METS 9 REDS 2
SHEA STADIUM

123

Cup-bound Philadelphia Flyers of 1973-74, whose brawl-encompassing season was about to begin, the Cincinnati Reds saw their attempt to win with their fists what they couldn't win with their skills amount to naught.

That's because by the time they decided to come out swinging this sunny Monday at Shea Stadium, they had already had the hell beaten out of them where it counted.

The Mets and their perennial offensive blues were reflected in the first seventeen innings of this NLCS when they provided Tom Seaver and Jon Matlack with all of two runs for their brilliant efforts. Finally, in the ninth inning of the second game, the Met bats woke up. The four runs that secured the Game Two win must have served as a shot of caffeine because those bats stayed wide awake as the series set down in New York.

For the first time since the last time Jerry Koosman started, eight days earlier in Chicago, the Mets scored in the first inning. The trigger man was again Rusty Staub, providing his second solo home run of the series. The early lead grew quickly. In the bottom of the second, Wayne Garrett's bases-loaded sacrifice fly and Felix Millan's RBI single extended the Met lead to 3-0 and ended Cincy starter Ross Grimsley's day. With two on and two out, Sparky Anderson opted for his lefty reliever, Tom Hall, to face the sizzling lefty Staub.

Rusty was not to be faced down. He took Hall on a tour of downtown Flushing via his second home run of the game and third of the series. The Mets presented Koosman with a 6-0 lead. It got trimmed in the third when Denis Menke homered and three singles strung together a second run. But Kooz got half of that back on his own, driving in Jerry Grote in the bottom of the third to make it 7-2. And in the bottom of the fourth, Cleon Jones and John Milner each knocked in runs.

It was 9-2, Mets. They had scored in every inning dating back to the ninth the day before. Despite their starter's earlier hiccup, their pitching now appeared on Kooz control. Jerry struck out Roger Nelson (Anderson's fourth pitcher of the day) to begin the fifth. Pete Rose touched him for a single, but then Joe Morgan grounded to Milner at first to start a 3-6-3 double play to end the inning.

Except in the middle of that otherwise routine twin-killing, Rose got it into his head to reach out and do more than touch Buddy Harrelson. That's how Buddy saw it from his vantage point at the business end of the onrushing Rose. "He came into me after I threw the ball," the skinny shortstop swore. "I'm not a punching bag." The much larger Rose resented the implication that he played dirty, testifying he slid hard but clean.

Buddy might have added he wasn't a sliding pit, either.

"And a fight breaks out! A fight breaks out!" was Bob Murphy's call of the scene once the DP was turned. "Pete Rose and Buddy Harrelson! Both clubs spill out of the dugouts, and a wild fight is going on! Jerry Koosman's in the middle of the fight! Everybody is out there!"

Yes, everybody. The Mets' starting pitcher was too much the competitor to keep his left arm from danger. The Mets' relief pitchers weren't going to stand idly by from their safe haven in the right field bullpen, either. Tug McGraw figured that by the time he and his colleagues joined the fray, the fray would be dying down. No such luck. Tug grabbed Rose; the Reds' third base coach, Alex Grammas, grabbed Harrelson; Ray Sadecki pitched in to quell the rabid Rose. "But finally," McGraw recounted in *Screwball*, "we ripped them apart and the hassle seemed over."

But it wasn't, because the Met relievers weren't the only recent arrivals at the scrap. The Reds' pen men showed up, and one had a taste for...well, something.

Murphy: "And now, Buzzy Capra is in a fight. Out in center field, another fight breaks out."

McGraw: "Pedro Borbon came tearing in and broadsided Buzz Capra with a shot out of left field that you wouldn't believe."

Mind you, this is Tug McGraw who'd just spent six weeks telling everybody who'd listen that You Gotta Believe. Yet it was pretty unbelievable. Borbon went after Capra, so Duffy Dyer went after Borbon and "cold-cocked" him by McGraw's account, "then everybody started to hassle all over again."

As if the scene needed a coda, it was provided by Borbon, who grabbed what he thought was his Reds cap and placed it on his head when all the hassling was losing its zip. Alas, Borbon picked up somebody's Mets cap, and when he realized he was sporting the gear of the enemy, "he went into a real rage," according to Tug, stuffing the cap "in his mouth, with his eyes all like fire, and started to tear it apart with his teeth" before flinging it to the ground and stomping off the field.

That would have been that, a pugilistic interlude (or two) to liven up a seven-run rout, except one more corner had yet to be heard from. There were 53,967 on hand at Shea, and as proud as they were of Harrelson for standing up for himself — and, by proxy, for them — a minority of the spectators didn't think Charlie Hustle had quite gotten what was coming to him. So they were going to take care of that themselves.

When Rose took his position for the bottom of the fifth, he learned left field had been rezoned for sanitation disposal by popular referendum. Garbage came flying out of the stands, all meant for him. Rose liked to cast himself as a tough guy, but taking on the malcontents in a sellout crowd was far above his pay grade. The fruit and paper cups didn't bother him, he said later, but glass receptacles were another matter: "They just missed me with a bottle of J&B."

When the critical mass of debris ramped from nuisance to danger, Sparky Anderson scotched the idea of the Reds just standing there and taking it. He pulled his players from the field for their own safety. National League president Chub Feeney and the umpiring crew could hardly blame him and were forced to confront the Mets with a very unpleasant fact: get this barrage stopped or forfeit this game.

It took a diplomatic mission more suited to solving the crisis enveloping the Middle East — Yogi Berra, Willie Mays, Seaver, Jones and Staub — to head to left field and negotiate some sense into the slice of the crowd that wanted the grass to run red with the blood of Rose. Cut it out, they urged the cranks, or our 9-2 lead becomes a 9-0 loss.

They cut it out and the game proceeded without interruption for the final four innings. Amazingly, no one was ejected. Borbon even pitched the eighth and ninth (in his Reds cap). Koosman just kept on keeping on despite hanging around for the donnybrook. When he retired Phil Gagliano to end the most memorable Columbus Day in Shea Stadium history, the Mets discovered themselves 9-2 winners in Game Three and 2-1 leaders in the series overall.

With one more win, they'd sail into the World Series. But the waters grew choppy on Tuesday. Met pitching continued to baffle Red hitting, but the Met bats went into a coma right around the time Borbon got his hats straight. The Mets didn't need to hit in the third game once they had their 9-2 lead, so it was no big deal that they didn't. But in Game Four, all they could muster was a Millan RBI single to score Don Hahn in the third. George Stone kept the 1-0 lead aloft until the seventh when Tony Perez homered to tie the game. Tug replaced George and held the fort good and tight, pitching four-and-a-third shutout innings, though not without an element of tightrope-walking. He left the bases loaded in the ninth and tenth and stranded two more in the eleventh, bailed out when Staub slammed into the right field wall to take a go-ahead hit away from Dan Driessen.

Rusty's heroics came at a cost. He hurt his right shoulder, which would need serious time to heal, time the Mets wouldn't have if they needed to play a Game Five of this NLCS — or, worse, time nobody would track if the Mets lost a Game Five. Getting to the Red bullpen here in Game Four was paramount, but just as they didn't do enough against starter Fred Norman, they did absolutely nothing against Don Gullett for four innings or Clay Carroll for two. Altogether, the Mets were being three-hit. Thus, when Harry Parker came on for McGraw in the twelfth and gave up a solo homer to, yup, Pete Rose (who didn't exactly curb his enthusiasm as he rounded the Shea bases), it was worrisome. Borbon pitched the bottom of the inning, protecting a slender 2-1 lead by retiring a courageous Staub, then Jones and Milner to make sure there'd be a Game Five.

There wouldn't be a Rusty, who'd hit all three of the Met homers thus far in this alternately tense and rollicking NLCS. He was out for sure for Wednesday. But there were still 24 other Mets, every one of them having proven willing to fight for what they Believed in, literally and figuratively. They'd be fighting in Game Five for a flag and, in the best tradition they'd established all the way back in September, simply to keep their 1973 going beyond all reasonable expectations.

OCTOBER 10, 1973

METS 7 REDS 2

SHEA STADIUM

It was a good day to quit, to give up, to throw in the towel...but that applied only to those who played their games in Washington. In the nation's capital, this Wednesday would be marked by a historic resignation. Spiro Agnew, the Vice President of the United States, under grand jury investigation for tax evasion, cut a deal and vacated the post to which he'd been re-elected in a landslide less than a year earlier.

In New York, however, the thought of quitting never crossed anybody's mind, certainly not in Flushing, where the Mets, unlike Agnew, had been toughened by autumn's adversity. Why shouldn't they have been? They were losing the National League East by the kind of landslide that had buried George McGovern the previous November, yet turned a midsummer 12 1/2 game deficit into a 1 1/2 game mandate to govern their division. It was the kind of stuff kids were taught about in social studies class...Mets-in-first destiny, if you will.

But that was just the primary. In the playoff series projected by DEWEY DEFEATS TRUMAN-style gun-jumping pundits to exist exclusively in a Red state, the party of blue and orange was locked in a race that was too close to call. Four of five precincts had reported. The Mets had won two, their opponents two. The time had come to cast the deciding vote.

Yogi Berra's choice for Game Five was perfectly clear: Seaver Now, More Than Ever. That one was obvious enough. Of course Tom Terrific was going to start the

Mets' first-ever postseason win-or-go-home game. But the manager had another decision to make. After writing in the same eight position players in the same eight spots in the batting order for four games, Yogi was deprived of his cleanup hitter. The injury Rusty Staub absorbed in his right shoulder prevented him from swinging a bat or throwing a ball (Staub batted left but threw right). Without one of the rocks of his lineup, the skipper had to scramble.

The answer he came up with was the one that had been available to Met managers longer than any other in the history of the franchise.

Ed Kranepool hadn't started a game since September 15, when he spelled John Milner at first base. He hadn't started a game in the outfield since taking a turn in right on July 16. But Berra wasn't asking him to play right. He instead moved Cleon Jones, the better outfielder, from left to right in deference to Sparky Anderson deploying a left-leaning lineup against righthanded Seaver. Krane was thus stationed in left, terrain with which he wasn't completely unfamiliar, having started there thirty times when Yogi was clustering whatever healthy Mets he could find when he was strapped for his usual starters before September.

There wasn't any terrain at Shea Kranepool couldn't have known by 1973 seeing as how he had been a part of the team longer than the stadium had stood. He was the one Met who could claim to have been a part of every Met squad since the first one, in 1962. He was just a kid then, 17 and getting his first taste of the bigs under Casey Stengel that September in the Polo Grounds. Krane persisted across the '60s, never achieving the stardom the Mets wished for him, but remaining relatively young and relatively useful. His investment of time as a Met — and the Mets' investment in him — paid off when he contributed significant base hits as half of Gil Hodges's first base platoon in 1969.

By the middle of 1970, Kranepool was a Tidewater Tide, not hitting and not happy to be Met property. He was presumed gone when he was put on waivers, but no other team scooped up his services and he returned to the major league club before long. Having experienced the near-death of his professional career, Ed underwent a renaissance in 1971, putting up the best numbers of his life and getting back into Hodges's good graces. He was less effective in 1972 and less effective, still, in 1973, but he was on the roster, he knew how to play the outfield and nobody had ever been more of a Met than Ed Kranepool.

"I'll be out in Pete Rose's Rose Garden," the crafty Bronx-born veteran promised upon learning of his assignment. "I just hope I bloom."

After Seaver avoided a patch of proverbial crabgrass in the top of the first and escaped a bases-loaded jam, Ed Kranepool's hope came true quickly. Against Jack Billingham, the Mets filled the sacks on singles from Jones and Felix Millan and a walk to Milner. The Krane was up next and he delivered a two-run single to left. The Met who'd been around longest put the Mets on the board first.

Down in Washington, the buzz over Agnew was overriden in at least one branch of government. Found among papers released five years after the 1999 death of former Supreme Court justice Harry Blackmun was a note handed to Blackmun by fellow justice Potter Stewart, dated October 10, 1973. The note was jotted down by Stewart's clerk and delivered to him while the highest court in the land was in session:

V.P. Agnew just resigned!!
Mets 2 Reds 0

Back in Flushing, the honorable George Thomas Seaver presided over the 2-0 lead with liberty and justice for all...or guts and guile, at any rate. This wasn't quite the Seaver of the preceding Saturday when he blew away most of the Reds in a losing cause. Going on three days' rest, he had to rely on his offspeed arsenal and the guidance of his catcher, Jerry Grote. The combination got Tom through the third with a 2-1 lead after Dan Driessen's sacrifice fly halved the Mets' advantage, and it functioned effectively through the fifth despite Tony Perez singling Pete Rose home from second to knot the score. Billingham was doing his share of presiding as well, as the Mets' offensive drought reached arid proportions. From the fifth inning in Game Three through the fourth inning of Game Five, encompassing twenty innings in all, the Mets had scored only three runs.

Change, however, was at hand. It started with Garrett — so hot in September yet ice cold in the playoffs — doubling to lead off the bottom of the fifth. Millan bunted to Billingham, who had a play on Garrett at third. He threw to Driessen who stepped on the bag for the force...which was a rookie mistake at the worst possible moment for Cincinnati because the force wasn't on. It meant Garrett was safe at third while Millan took first. Wayne dashed home and Felix ran to third when Jones doubled to put the Mets back in front, 3-2. Anderson pulled the righty Billingham and went to a lefty, Don Gullett, seeking to gain an edge on lefty-swinging John Milner. But Milner didn't have to swing; he walked to load the bases.

The next batter scheduled was another lefty, Kranepool. If the longest-serving Met could deliver one more blow, it would give 50,323 fans an emotional jolt. But what if the *oldest* Met were to come through here? Not just the oldest Met, but the most highly decorated player in all of baseball in the dimming twilight of his storied career?

Willie Mays hadn't played since September 9. He'd announced his retirement, received an outpouring of affection on a night dedicated in his honor on September 25 and was in every way but official done as a player. Except he was on the active roster and he was still Willie Mays. So Yogi told the Say Hey vet — a righty, in case anybody'd forgotten during his lengthy period of inactivity — to grab a bat and hit for Kranepool.

The crowd loved it. How could it not? As Anderson's next reliever, Clay Carroll, came on for the righty-righty ritual, anticipation built. Could the man who'd hit 660 homers since 1951 add to his bulging portfolio of legendary moments? Might the last of the New York Giants perform once more in a larger-than-life capacity?

Let's just say that unlike Spiro Agnew, Mays wasn't ready to quit. He attacked Carroll's first pitch and sent it...oh, inches when measured on a line, but as high as it needed to be. It was a Baltimore chop practically straight up off the plate. By the time it came down, everybody was safe. Millan scored from third, Jones moved up from second, Milner replaced him there and, with the final hit he'd record in National League competition, Willie Mays made it to first base.

Twenty-two years and one week after standing in the on-deck circle as a nervous rookie while Bobby Thomson won the pennant for the Giants, Willie Mays extended the Mets' lead in a potential pennant-clinching contest, 4-2...the same sequence of numbers that nowadays constituted his age.

Two more runs would score in the fifth to give Seaver a 6-2 lead. Jones moved from right to left. Don Hahn moved from center to right. And Mays stayed in to play center, where he'd catch the final out of a 1-2-3 sixth. In the bottom of the inning, Seaver led off with a double and scored on a Jones single. His lead was 7-2 when he started the seventh. He kept it as such then, and again in the eighth.

Finally, it came down to Tom Seaver and three outs for the pennant. It was an ideal setup, especially after Cesar Geronimo led off by lining out to Millan to start the ninth. But it wasn't an ideal environment to complete such an Amazin' story. Unsavory elements of the restless crowd began trickling onto the field. Play had to be halted a couple of times, impeding Seaver's rhythm. While Tom attempted to cope, pinch-hitter Larry Stahl (a Met teammate of Seaver's in 1967 and '68) singled. Another pinch-hitter, Hal King, walked. Then Rose did the same to fill the bases with Reds. The lead was still five runs and the pitcher was still Tom Terrific, but now was the time for neither arithmetic nor reputation. Yogi knew he'd gotten plenty out of Seaver. He also knew how to pick up the phone and ring the bullpen.

In came McGraw, the signature Met of the improbable drive that had brought this team to this juncture. It wasn't just good strategy to have him go for the last two outs. After Kranepool and Mays set the stage for a pennant-clinching, karma almost demanded Tug's presence on the mound to finish the job.

Joe Morgan, the dangerous second baseman with two MVP awards in his not-too-distant future, popped to Bud Harrelson at short for the second out.

Driessen, the callow third baseman who wore the defensive goat horns from forgetting to make a tag, grounded to Milner, who flipped the ball to McGraw.

Three out.

In a six-week blink, the Mets earned the championship of the National League. In a much more condensed time frame, Shea's playing surface was stormed as if Bastille Day II had been declared. Observers universally agreed this was a far less innocent display of joy than the ballpark had been engulfed by in 1969. The Reds, running for their lives, suggested New York was hardly a part of America and that these people coming after them might have felt more at home in a zoo. The Mets were forced to take quick cover, too, and didn't much indulge the baser instincts that were let loose by their triumph.

"Eerie," Tug described the reaction. "These people," Tom asserted, "don't care anything about baseball, or that we won. It's just an excuse to them to go tear something up."

In the safety of the victorious clubhouse — and wherever millions of true Mets fans celebrated in sincerity — the tenor turned suitably upbeat. All agreed there was something to this power of positive thinking McGraw kept disseminating and to not being resigned to your supposed imminent demise, no matter the assessments set forth by the "nattering nabobs of negativity". Agnew's pet phrase, as coined by speechwriter William Safire, referred to his strawmen in the press, though the now former VP could also have been talking about the poll that ran in the *Post* during the summer. The survey asked readers who should be fired for the disaster the Mets had become: board chairman Don Grant, GM Bob Scheffing or good old Yogi.

At this moment, all were gainfully employed and swimming in champagne.

Beyond bromides about never giving up or giving in, it might have also been worth noting that when you have pitching like the Mets showed in this series, there was no logical reason to think you couldn't hang with and ultimately defeat the best of them.

In five games against the humble 82-79 Mets, the mighty 99-63 Reds of Rose, Morgan, Perez and Bench accumulated a grand total of eight runs. Berra's starting rotation of Seaver, Matlack, Koosman and Stone permitted 26 hits in 41 1/3 innings while McGraw threw five shutout frames of relief, entitling him, as the team's indispensable fireman down the stretch and into the playoffs, to bellow for the record the most famous last words uttered on behalf of the 1973 National League champions:

"You gotta believe!"

OCTOBER 14, 1973
METS 10 A'S 7 (12)
THE OAKLAND COLISEUM

125

Only a cynic would have noticed that the 1973 World Series was about to pit the team with the fourth-best record in baseball against the team with the tenth-best record in baseball. Divisional alignment and postseason preliminaries eliminated the certainty that the team with the top record in the sport would be guaranteed a berth in its championship showcase. So it came to pass in the fifth year of four divisions and five-game league championship series that neither league would be represented in the Fall Classic by the team that had compiled the most wins within its circuit during the regular season.

Nevertheless, you couldn't have asked for a more compelling matchup than what baseball got as a climax to its 1973, for the Mets and their unreal trip to October showed them to be no run-of-the-mill .509 finisher, and certainly the 94-68 Oakland A's, who knocked off the 97-65 Baltimore Orioles in five ALCS games, couldn't be dismissed as anything approximating ordinary.

That the A's — short for Athletics, though nobody was much using the stodgy corporate moniker in those days — were defending champions was only part of their magnetism. The eye was drawn to the A's first by the cutting edge of their cloth, the green or gold or occasionally white softball tops that made them stand out in a crowd of teams just getting the feel of polyester. Next thing you noticed was their faces, almost all of them adorned by mustaches. It was a grooming revolution encouraged by their owner, a self-styled acerbic showman named Charlie Finley, in a sport where the length of a man's hair could still be considered controversial. On aesthetics alone, the A's were attention-grabbers of the first order.

The talent behind the 'staches and inside the unis was not inconsiderable, either. Before they were the consistently fearsome Oakland A's, they were the perennial laughingstock Kansas City Athletics. Yet before they left Missouri due to chronic indifference, Finley was assembling a cast of youngsters that grew together into a powerhouse. Third baseman Sal Bando, shortstop Bert "Campy" Campaneris, second baseman Dick Green, left fielder Joe Rudi and righthanded pitcher John "Blue Moon" Odom all saw time in the majors as those A's were losing 99 games in 1967, the franchise's final year in KC...as did the two players who became the stalwarts of the Oakland edition, ace starter Jim "Catfish" Hunter — his nickname was Finley's creation — and slugging right fielder Reginald Martinez Jackson.

Or just "Reggie," last name almost superfluous.

Sprouting on the farm that same year for Kansas City were two more A's stars-to-be, a clean-shaven would-be starting pitcher named Roland Martin Fingers and a promising southpaw whose name even Finley couldn't have made up, Vida Blue. By 1971, Blue was the most celebrated lefthanded starter the game had seen since Sandy Koufax, and Oakland was a division champion. By 1972, Fingers was known to one and all as Rollie, sporting an anachronistic handlebar mustache and saving the final game of the World Series for the new world champs.

Every one of those KC alumni was still entrenched in Oakland and ready to take on the Mets.

In those last days when the reserve clause allowed an owner to keep a young team together on the cheap, Finley oversaw the coalescing of a magnificent roster that he did his damnedest to not pay a decent wage. Perhaps it was the combination of familiarity and thrift that bred a trademark brand of discontent within the Oakland clubhouse, because the other factor that made the A's so darn compelling by 1973 was they were known to occasionally hiss and spit at one another. That was probably nothing new in the ranks of baseball, but it was rare for the public to know that a team's players didn't necessarily care for each other's company, that the manager — mustachioed (of course) Dick Williams — wasn't necessarily satisfied in his job and that, truly, nobody on his payroll seemed to care for the owner whatsoever.

These Oakland A's were one part traveling circus, one part perfect reflection of the era's cultural zeitgeist and all parts formidable foe to anyone thinking of swiping their two-toned, three-colored crown.

That's what the Mets were encountering as they headed to Oakland for the first two games of the 1973 World Series. And they would do so the way they finished their NLCS versus the Reds, without a healthy Rusty Staub. The Mets' right fielder, his shoulder still recovering from its brush with the Shea Stadium wall in the playoffs, was limited to pinch-hitting for Saturday afternoon's Game One, so Yogi Berra improvised another lineup to take on former Cub Ken Holtzman (like Hunter and Blue, a 20-

game winner) in the opener. Don Hahn, who'd become more or less the regular center fielder during the season, moved over to right. And to the delight of Bay Area fans, Willie Mays — a figure of some renown in nearby San Francisco — would start in center, and register the first hit of the Series on a first-inning single to left.

One constant Berra knew he could count on was his second baseman, Felix Millan. The ex-Brave had proven himself one of the best offseason additions the Mets had ever made. He started 153 games in 1973, every one of them in the middle infield, every one of them batting behind the leadoff hitter. He played second, hit second, produced quietly and consistently, racking up a team record 185 hits (breaking Tommie Agee's mark of 182) and tightening the interior defense. Whereas all Met second basemen helped turn 79 double plays in '72, Felix was in on 99 in '73. Millan also became — unofficially, of course — the most imitated Met in schoolyards around the Metropolitan Area, with kids everywhere choking way up on their bat handles, just like Felix did it on Channel 9.

Yet with all that going for him, Felix Millan wound up the simplistic answer as to why the Mets lost Game One. Jon Matlack was dueling Holtzman in a mutual shutout through the middle of the third. In the bottom of the inning, Jon appeared en route to another zero. He had walked Green, but Grote threw him out trying to steal (the A's liked to run, though they were deprived by injury of the American League's top basestealer, center fielder Bill North). With two out and the bases empty, all Matlack had to do was retire Ken Holtzman in this, the first year of the designated hitter rule. Pitchers had stopped coming to the plate in the A.L. in '73, and Holtzman hadn't been much of a threat with the bat before there was a DH.

But wouldn't you know it, Holtzman doubled off Matlack, bringing up Campaneris. Campy grounded to Millan to end the inning...except the ball skittered under Felix's otherwise dependable glove, the same one that committed only nine errors during the year, and through the second baseman's legs. Holtzman scored the game's first run. Campaneris, who proceeded to steal second, scored its next run on Rudi's single to left.

A 2-0 lead didn't have to be insurmountable, but it was. Cleon Jones's double and John Milner's single got one of the runs back in the fourth, but from there, there was no more scoring. Holtzman, Fingers and Darold Knowles combined to frustrate the Mets, wasting Matlack's and Tug McGraw's joint four-hitter. It was the third consecutive postseason series whose opening game the Mets had lost, dating back to Baltimore and 1969.

That experience turned out well for the Mets, but to effect a similar revival, they would need to generate some offense and some luck in Sunday's Game Two. There'd be plenty of both, if not much of it immediately or necessarily theirs.

There'd be plenty of everything, actually.

It was that kind of Sunday in the Oakland Coliseum.

The most encouraging sign for Berra was his ability to write STAUB onto his lineup card once again. He wasn't completely healed by any means, but one shoulder of Staub, the manager decided, was better than any of his other options. Besides, this was the World Series. Rusty had been excelling in near obscurity as a Colt .45, an Astro and an Expo before coming to the Mets in 1972. He had never been anywhere near a Fall Classic before. Who knew if he'd ever have the opportunity again?

It was also comforting for Yogi to finish off his lineup with KOOSMAN, who gave him such a fine effort in Game Three of the NLCS and was the pitcher who turned around the Mets' last World Series in its second game. Tom Seaver might have been an even more comforting presence, but because of the five-game LCS that ended Wednesday, Yogi's ace (like Williams's main man Catfish, who'd also had to pitch a do-or-die clincher) wasn't yet ready to go. Koosman was no last-ditch alternative, though. He'd made four postseason starts for the Mets in his career, and the Mets won every one of them.

Between Staub and Koosman, you might say the sun was going to shine on the Mets in Game Two. Or you could just look up at the unyielding Oakland sky and reach that conclusion for yourself. Before the day was out, the sun would be impossible to ignore.

Jones was the afternoon's first atmospheric victim, in the bottom of the first when he lost Joe Rudi's deep fly ball in nature's light and it fell in for a double. "It was the worst, the absolute worst" Cleon attested of the view from left field. "I've never played in a major league ballpark where the sun was that bad." Sol was a real SOB and Sal — Bando — was no nicer to Koosman than the sun had been to Cleon. He tripled home Rudi and scored three batters later on Jesus Alou's double. Jones made amends with a leadoff home run in the second off Blue, but though it was 2-1, this was going to be no facsimile to the 2-1 game of the day before.

Kooz had more trouble in the third: another triple (Campaneris's) led to another RBI (Rudi's). Down 3-1, the Mets' attack was reignited by Wayne Garrett's solo blast in the third, making it 3-2. But Jerry couldn't handle a little prosperity. With one out in the home third, he walked Gene Tenace, gave up a single to Alou and made a bad throw to first that let Ray Fosse reach. Now the bases were loaded, so Berra acted. He removed Koosman and brought in Ray Sadecki. The veteran swingman caught a break when Williams put on the squeeze and Green couldn't deliver, making Tenace dead meat at the plate. Green then struck out to keep the A's off the board.

Blue's grip on the Mets loosened in the top of the sixth when he walked Jones, who sped to third on Milner's single. Vida's day ended in favor of Horacio Pina, but it wasn't Horacio's day, either. After hitting Jerry Grote to load the bases, Don Hahn and Bud Harrelson delivered run-scoring singles to give the Mets the lead. Williams replaced Pina with Darold Knowles, who thought he had a force at home when Jim Beauchamp pinch-hit a grounder back to the mound. A bad throw let Grote and Hahn score, and the Mets had a 6-3 cushion to offer Tug McGraw when he came in to pitch the sixth.

Tug pitched the sixth without incident. He pitched the seventh, surrendering an RBI double to Reggie Jackson, which shoulder-strapped Staub could barely fling toward the infield. He pitched the eighth, and took care of the A's in order. After the

Mets threatened in the top of the ninth — Staub singled and Yogi pinch-ran Mays — but didn't score, Berra left Tug in to pitch the ninth as well.

Was it an inning too far for the fireman for whom the manager had been pulling alarms regularly for weeks on end? It didn't appear to be, as McGraw coaxed a fly ball to center field from pinch-hitter Deron Johnson, and Tug had the benefit of possibly the greatest center fielder of all time standing out there. Mays stayed in the game after pinch-running, and in his prime, he was a sure thing to catch a ball like Johnson's. Except Willie wasn't in his prime — Sol was. The sun did the A's dirty work again, blinding Willie, who admitted, "I didn't see Johnson's ball...I'm not alibiing. I just didn't see it."

The Say Hey Kid fell down in centerfield as the ball fell in front of him. In an instant, his stumble became the default example for generations of lazy writers and broadcasters who were eager to usher great athletes out of their sport once they "hung on too long". After all, they tut-tutted, they shouldn't want to wind up like Willie Mays.

In the there and then, Mays's misadventure was less cautionary tale than a genuine trigger for Met crisis. The standard fly ball turned into a sun-splashed double, setting up an inning that crested with RBI singles from Jackson and Tenace. The A's had tied the Mets at six.

The A's tried to give the game right back to the Mets in the tenth. An error — Oakland's third of the day — let the Mets push the go-ahead run to third with one out. From there, Harrelson sprinted ninety feet when Millan flied to Rudi in left. He evaded the tag of Ray Fosse by running to the catcher's right. He crossed the plate with the run to make it Mets 7 A's 6.

But Augie Donatelli didn't see it that way. Donatelli, in one of the worst blunders made by a home plate umpire in World Series history, decided Fosse tagged Buddy. The replays showed otherwise. On-deck hitter Mays pleaded otherwise. Berra argued otherwise. Harrelson absolutely *insisted* otherwise: "I felt I was safe and I didn't know I had been called out until I got near our dugout."

Donatelli was unmoved. The Mets were done in the tenth. The game stayed tied, 6-6. McGraw stayed in to pitch the bottom of the inning, his fifth, which he did flawlessly, and the eleventh, too (after the Mets left two on). Tug had now gone six in relief and the game's score remained stalemated.

It had already been a pretty darn intriguing affair, but it's fair to say the twelfth inning is where things got *really* interesting. There was Buddy, doubling to start things off promisingly. There was Tug — still — left into bunt. He moved Harrelson to third and got on himself when his bunt blooped over the head of the charging Bando. With two outs, up stepped the old man who'd looked so overmatched by the elements in the field. Yes, Willie Mays was batting against Fingers, still dealing with the sun, albeit from a different angle.

But he dealt with it fine, bounding a one-hopper up the middle to score Harrelson. With the very last hit of his Hall of Fame career, Mays put his team up, 7-6, in the twelfth inning of a World Series game.

Willie and Tug each eventually scored when the A's defense continued its daylong deterioration. The culprit in the eleventh, on two consecutive plays, was Mike Andrews, a bit player who committed a pair of errors (one on a grounder, one on a throw) that resulted in three Met runs. It also made him a target for Finley's ire. The owner tried to disown the backup second baseman immediately, attempting to stash him on the DL despite his being perfectly healthy. In the coming days, in a nation where cynicism had ramped up in the wake of Watergate, Finley's ploy would be seen through and Andrews wouldn't be disappeared so easily. But at the moment, the only truth that counted was Mets 10 A's 6, heading to the twelfth.

Tug McGraw continued to pitch. Perhaps Berra forgot he had at least a couple of other options. To begin his seventh inning of work, the southpaw got Jackson to hit a deep fly ball to center field. Willie ran to the wall to track it down. He didn't. Jackson landed on third with a triple. After walking Tenace, Tug was done. George Stone got the call, which appeared a wrong number. Alou tagged him for a single to cut the Mets' lead to three runs. After a forceout and a walk, the bottom line was the bases were loaded, McGraw was finished and Stone had to end a contest headed toward establishing a new record for longest — and nuttiest — World Series game.

Stone turned rock solid, popping up pinch-hitter Vic Davalillo and grounding out Campaneris. The game that wouldn't end was over after four hours and thirteen minutes, and it belonged to the Mets, 10-7. The process was as exhausting as the result was exhilarating. It left the World Series tied at one before it could be packed up and flown to New York.

126 OCTOBER 17, 1973
METS 6 A'S 1
SHEA STADIUM

The sun would present a problem for no one as the midweek portion of the 1973 World Series alighted at Shea Stadium. Television had seen to it that games on weekdays became games on weeknights. The Mets and the A's were prime time players. Very cold prime time players. Flushing By The Bay in October at night was fit for neither man nor beast let alone Franchise nor Catfish. But NBC called the shots and it got Tom Seaver and Jim Hunter in front of a much larger audience than figured to be attracted in daylight.

Tuesday night's Game Three provided more entertainment for the baseball-viewing masses, if an unsatisfying ending for Met partisans. Wayne Garrett led off with a home run, echoing Tommie Agee's swing that started the third game of the Series at Shea four years earlier, and the Mets added another run on a Hunter wild pitch that followed two singles. With a 2-0 lead, Tom Seaver took over the starring role as he did so often at Shea.

Tom was Terrifically strong, going on five days' rest. It showed in the twelve strikeouts to which he subjected the A's over eight innings. In the common refrain of his Met career, he deserved to win. But Hunter shook off his bad first inning and kept the Mets in check through the sixth before handing the game over to Oakland's stifling bullpen. The Mets couldn't manufacture a shred of offense versus Darold Knowles, Paul Lindblad and Rollie Fingers. The A's hitters, meanwhile, worked around Seaver's strikeouts and nicked him for single runs in the sixth and eighth. Two days after playing twelve innings, the Mets and A's arranged for another night of bonus baseball.

The frigid night air took on an additional chill when the reliable and gifted Jerry Grote couldn't hold a strike three from Harry Parker to Angel Mangual. The passed ball sent Mangual to first and baserunner Ted Kubiak to second, and served to set up the go-ahead run when Bert Campaneris singled. Oakland's relief pitching warmed to the task of protecting a one-run lead and the A's won Game Three, 2-1.

It was the first time the Mets trailed a postseason series after three games, putting them in unfamiliar must-win territory for Wednesday's Game Four. It was still cold, but Mets fever was about to rise.

The evening belonged in particular to three men, only two of whom wore Met uniforms.

First and foremost, there was Rusty Staub, shrugging off his shoulder woes and stepping into the October spotlight he'd been waiting to enter since making it to the majors as a 19-year-old in 1963. In bare arms and black batting gloves — which is how Daniel Joseph Staub hit no matter the prevailing winds or fashion — Rusty came to the plate with Wayne Garrett and Felix Millan already on base ahead of him in the bottom of the first. Swinging and connecting, Staub ascended from the agony of the shoulder to the ecstasy of belting a three-run World Series homer that gave his team an immediate 3-0 lead.

His night would only get better in the fourth when he delivered a two-run single after Millan had driven in one. The Mets led, 6-1, having chased starter Ken Holtzman and reliever Blue Moon Odom from the mound and making Dick Williams dig deep into his heavily burdened bullpen (lefty Darold Knowles alone had seen action in each game thus far). Williams would use five pitchers before the night was over, and Rusty succeeded against every one of them, banging out four hits and taking one walk as he recorded five RBIs.

Jon Matlack, meanwhile, cruised across eight innings, scattering three hits and giving up only one error-provoked run in the fourth, a harmless echo of the fate that befell him in Game One. As in his first World Series start, Matlack surrendered no earned runs in Game Four. This time around, though, he had Rusty grilling Oakland pitching on his behalf, leading to a 6-1 victory that tied the Series at two games apiece.

Yet despite the brilliance of the two Met standouts, the Arctic night belonged at least in part to an Oakland A who, by merely walking to the plate, warmed the hearts of the 54,817 Shea denizens.

Mike Andrews experienced an awful Game Two on Sunday, with his extra-inning errors opening the floodgates for Oakland's eventual loss. That was all Charlie Finley had to see to attempt to rig a roster transaction, coercing and dumping the veteran Andrews and replacing him with rookie Manny Trillo. In short, Andrews was railroaded and everybody — including his teammates, who taped his uniform number, 17, to their own jerseys in solidarity before Game Three — knew it. Commissioner Bowie Kuhn put an end to Finley's farce and ordered Andrews reinstated.

Thus, when Williams chose Andrews to pinch-hit for Horacio Pina to start the visitors' eighth, Mets fans temporarily put aside their natural allegiances and rose to give the embattled infielder a monstrous standing ovation. Even if it was an indirect way of thumbing their nose at Finley and all those establishment figures who routinely abused the public's trust by piling deception upon prevarication (the nation was three nights from learning of President Nixon's scheme to fire Watergate special prosecutor Archibald Cox in what became known as the Saturday Night Massacre — kind of a Mike Andrews affair writ large), the applause directed toward an "enemy" batter during a World Series quite possibly represented Shea's classiest moment ever. Mets fans would routinely and respectfully clap for the likes of Koufax, Clemente, Aaron and pre-Met Mays in admiration of their accomplishments, but this was something bigger than just sports.

It was sportsmanship.

Andrews's at-bat went the way Mets fans hoped: he grounded out to third. Happy their team was five runs ahead and that Finley's victim had performed heroically just by persevering to wear his own No. 17, the crowd stood again and clapped again as Mike returned to the Oakland dugout.

Later, the reserve infielder admitted to a different brand of "chills" than everybody else in the bundled-up crowd was feeling that icy night in Queens. "I don't think I've ever had a standing ovation in my life," Andrews said. "To me, that meant everything."

The Shea Stadium scoreboard was hailed as a modern marvel before anybody ever saw it. Billed as "the Stadiarama," it promised to mesmerize every fan who could see it from the 96 percent of seats planted within the foul poles of the new ballpark. One of its highlights
would be the large field given over to electrically transmitted messages, enabled by "approximately 28,000 lamps, arranged in clusters capable of forming letters and numerals [...] [T]hrough one of the message display groupings, it is even possible to show 'Sing Along' messages when it's time to break into song!"

That's how Met management put it in the Shea preview pages of the team's 1963 yearbook sold at the Polo Grounds. Ten years later, the reality of the Shea Stadium scoreboard wasn't quite as breathtaking, and not just because the Mets never seemed to put enough runs on it. As Shea's first decade wore on, the scoreboard made mistakes. Those letters and numerals didn't necessarily flash as planned. Lamps that burned out weren't immediately replaced. From the stands, it looked like a segment of the "approximately 80 miles of wiring" was prone to shorting out.

Yet for as gaffe-prone as the Shea scoreboard could be as it matured, there was no telling that it got a basic fact of the 1973 World Series wrong the Thursday night Game Five ended. The Mets had just won, 2-0, with Don Hahn and John Milner knocking in runs against Vida Blue, and Jerry Koosman and Tug McGraw combining on a three-hitter. The Mets were up, 3-2 in the best-of-seven set. Given that information, the minds behind the scoreboard controls decided to post a most hopeful message as if it were fact.

"MIRACLE NO. 2," the Stadiarama gleefully informed 54,817 frostbitten fans, awaited "3000 MILES AWAY".

Wrong on two counts, it turned out.

The Mets did fly back to California and they did need only one more win to clinch their second world championship, but it didn't come to pass. They lost Game Six on Saturday, 3-1, and Game Seven on Sunday, 5-2. The contests are remembered less for what happened than what didn't.

Yogi Berra didn't start George Stone in Game Six, which would have provided Tom Seaver with a precious extra day of rest in case Game Seven was needed — and skipping Stone meant overlooking a good bet to finish Oakland off (12-3 during the regular season, plus an outstanding playoff effort versus Cincinnati). Berra's not altogether muddled logic was Seaver was the best he had...the best anybody had. Still, his ace had a tired right arm after 314 innings pitched in the regular season, the NLCS and Game Three of the World Series. Nonetheless, the Franchise gave his manager seven more innings in Game Six, and they were probably decent enough to get by on against another team on another day.

But these were the Oakland A's and this was their third consecutive postseason and they had Reggie Jackson ready to cut loose. Jackson — who considered Seaver "so good, blind people come out to hear him pitch" — had missed the 1972 Fall Classic with a leg injury but was now making this October his own. He doubled home Joe Rudi in the first and Sal Bando (aided by Staub's continued inability to throw from right) in the third. Tom struck out six and didn't give up any other runs, but his fastball lacked its characteristic verve. Almost apologetically, Reggie judged the pitcher he bested twice as "not the real Tom Seaver today".

The only Seaver the Mets had gave way to Tug McGraw, who gave up another run in the eighth. Meanwhile, the Mets scratched out only one run all afternoon and lost to Catfish Hunter, the omnipresent Darold Knowles and Rollie Fingers, 3-1.

In Game Seven, with no Seaver, Berra again eschewed Stone and went with the more accomplished Matlack. But Jon, like Tom, had taken on a heavy workload just to get the Mets from the edge of extinction in August to the seventh game of the World Series this Sunday. In his second big league season and first postseason, the southpaw had already thrown 265 frames. Met pitching under the tutelage of coach Rube Walker had been nurtured to function on four days' rest. For a second straight day, Berra was interrupting his starters' established flow by demanding excellence on three days' rest.

While Stone sat in the bullpen, Matlack took the Mets to the third inning, nothing-nothing, until the Oakland Coliseum walls fell down around him. Ken

Holtzman once more remembered pitchers could hit and doubled with one out. Campy Campaneris, whose calling card was usually his legs (three stolen bases in the Series), belted a two-run homer. Rudi singled, Bando popped out and Reggie... well, Reggie homered. It was October, and that, Met pitchers were learning before anybody else did, was what Mr. Jackson, the impending Series MVP, did when available to play.

Down 4-0, Berra withdrew Matlack. Harry Parker got the Mets out of the third and threw a clean fourth. Ray Sadecki surrendered an additional run in the fifth to make it 5-0. By the time Stone was ushered in to pitch a scoreless seventh and eighth (striking out three), the Mets were down, 5-1. Four runs separated them from the A's and three outs separated them from winter.

The 1973 Mets being the 1973 Mets, they had one last way to make things interesting. With two out and two on against fireman Fingers, Ed Kranepool grounded to first. Gene Tenace couldn't handle the ball and was charged with an error, allowing the Mets' second run to score and cutting the Mets' deficit to three. Dick Williams — minutes from announcing his resignation from Charlie Finley's employ — removed Rollie and went to Knowles, allowing the veteran lefty to become the first pitcher to appear in all seven games of a World Series. The presence of a southpaw on the mound presented Berra with occasion to make one final decision.

Yogi needed a three-run homer in the worst way. The next batter was lefthanded Wayne Garrett, who slugged thirteen homers during the season against righthanded pitching, but only three against lefties. It might have made strategic sense to call back Garrett and insert a righthanded pinch-hitter with a power-laden track record against *all* kinds of pitching.

It also might have provided just the spiritual jolt a ballclub supercharged by an ethos of You Gotta Believe required at such a moment. Two on, two out, down by three and — a ferry ride from San Francisco, no less — New York sends to the plate, Willie Mays. The old man, who last swung in Game Three, grounding out as a pinch-hitter, was nonetheless a .300 hitter so far in this postseason (Garrett was down to .115). More to the point, he was Willie Mays. The credentials and the sentimentality aside, he found a way to get the big hit in the deciding game against the Reds. He found a way to put the Mets ahead of the A's in extra innings a week ago.

Plus the credentials and the sentimentality.

But Berra, who overlooked Stone as a starter, now ignored Mays as a sub. He stuck with Garrett, and Garrett popped to Campaneris, and Campaneris caught it, and the A's were 5-2 winners and world champions again.

So much for that miracle waiting 3,000 miles from Shea.

The scoreboard failing to post information that would have required prescience, however, wasn't its most glaring mistake. The second count on which Stadiarama erred was implying the 1973 Mets needed to travel to Oakland and win another ballgame to lay claim to a miracle.

These Mets were in a World Series, having willed themselves into division-titlists and pennant-winners in record time. Their surge of progress can't be overstated: last place on August 30, first place on September 21, champions of the East on October 1, champions of the league on October 10, leaders of the World Series on October 18. Whatever happened in Oakland — and no soul true to the orange and blue didn't want that one additional W — wasn't going to dim 1973's late-lighted lamp.

This team's personnel was about half-different from 1969's, which made all the difference in its competitive platform. The half of the 1973 Mets that had endured from four years earlier was comparatively grizzled. The veterans like Seaver, Koosman, McGraw, Harrelson, Grote, Jones, Garrett and Kranepool wouldn't have lasted this long without being pretty good since 1969, when there were no expectations attached to them as a unit. They were joined now by a knot of veterans who came to the Mets after '69: Staub, Millan, Stone, Sadecki and the twilight version of Mays. There were relatively few kids around — Matlack and Milner the most prominent of them. All told, it was a team that you wouldn't have thought incapable of contending when the season began.

But when the season was nearly over, you would have considered it next-to-impossible. They had been too battered by injury and almost buried by competition. Yet those with some miles on them revved their engines and the younger among them learned to pick up their pace. The bottom-line results far transcended the 82 wins that led to three more in a successful playoff and three others in a raucous Fall Classic. While keepsakes like Tom Seaver's richly deserved second Cy Young award and Rusty Staub's courageous .423 World Series batting average look great on the Met mantel and in the Met annals, what resonates most from 1973 is that while a pennant was being won, legends were being born.

• "It Ain't Over 'Til It's Over," which Yogi Berra more or less uttered to reporters one summer night as the Mets stayed close enough to their competitors to dream, instantly became a bromide applicable in all those situations in which one's fate only *appeared* sealed. Yogi's place in baseball history was plenty secure before he was lured to Queens to coach and eventually manage, but the Berra who is quoted to affable extremes in the 21st century is a product of his Met years — this one in particular.

• "You Gotta Believe" made a similarly lasting contribution to the American lexicon and has been adopted (sometimes with a "ya" instead of a "you") by countless teams down to their last out, pass, shot or what have you (or ya). Mets fans still reach for it whenever it makes sense — which is always, since it is rooted in a season when believing in the Mets didn't seem to make any. The explicit nod to positive thinking ensured Tug McGraw would remain an icon in the Met mindset well beyond his time throwing an insanely devastating screwball in their uniform.

• Willie Mays didn't need 1973 — or a ninth-inning Game Seven at-bat — to guarantee his legend, and his exit from active athleticism might have been cleaner had he just slipped away after his 1972 New York homecoming. But then we would have missed "Say Goodbye to America," a phrase perhaps second only to Lou Gehrig's "luckiest man on the face of the earth" as the most affecting ever delivered by a ballplayer on a ballfield. And even though his difficulties with the Oakland sun blotted out the rest of what he did in his final October, the Mets won a pennant and took a World Series to its limit with Willie Mays garnering two key hits in their colors. Mays's Met legacy comes off as complicated, given his advanced state when he arrived, the most-favored-nation status bestowed on him by a doting Joan Payson and the bouts of crankiness that wouldn't have made him any manager's ideal utilityman...but it can't be said enough that he was Willie Mays. Willie Mays of the 1973 National League champion New York Mets.

• Buddy Harrelson's profile rose from surehanded shortstop (one Gold Glove, two All-Star selections) to the Met who wouldn't be pushed around after absorbing a barreling from Pete Rose during the playoffs. While Pete was stuck in the role of Shea Stadium villain for much of the rest of his career, Buddy's decision to fight back in Game Three seemed to preordain his long-haul status as the quintessential Met: maybe a little undersized, maybe a little overmatched but never, ever to be pushed around or counted out. The next time the Mets would see a World Series, it somehow figured that the man waving their runners home would be a third base coach named Harrelson.

• Let us not forget the signature play of the stretch drive — the "wonder of wonders," as *Fiddler on the Roof* would have framed it — in which the ball the Pirates' Dave Augustine hit bounced off the top of the left field wall and into Cleon Jones's glove on September 20 at Shea Stadium. One inch, maybe less, in the wrong direction and Augustine has the two-out, thirteenth-inning home run that puts Pittsburgh ahead, 5-3. Or if the ball bounces back but not directly to Cleon, Richie Zisk scores from first and the Bucs are winning, 4-3. Or if the relay from Jones to Garrett goes awry...or if the second relay, from Garrett to rookie Ron Hodges, isn't on the mark...or if the catcher who emerged from Double-A Memphis in June, in just his second professional season, gives Zisk a route to the plate...or doesn't make the tag...

So much could have gone wrong for the 1973 Mets, and so much did for about five months, but then so much went right.

Like Hodges tagging Zisk for the third out...and getting the winning hit in the bottom of the thirteenth...and the Mets leapfrogging the Pirates into first place the next night...and extending their winning streak into the next week...and withstanding the rain, the odds and the Cubs the week after...and dismantling the Big Red Machine the week after that.

And, finally, these New York Mets prosecuted seven ceaselessly intriguing championship-round contests against an adversary history would judge an upper-tier dynasty and produced three victories — plus one last ninth-inning rally that brought the tying run to the plate with two out before falling ultimately short of matching 1969's indisputably more satisfying let alone more certifiably miraculous ending.

But just coming so close? Considering where they'd been?

That was a miracle, too.

A FEW WORDS ON SOURCES

Myriad books, articles, broadcasts and Web sites are directly cited and credited as providing historical source material across this first volume of *The Happiest Recap*. A comprehensive bibliography is planned to coincide with the completion of the final volume to fully reflect the array of works from which information was drawn to make this the richest New York Mets history possible.

Baseball-Reference and Retrosheet have been the most essential sources for *The Happiest Recap*, from its inception as a blog series to its iteration as a four-volume book project. Any historically minded baseball writer who wishes to delve into the slightest (never mind deepest) details of a given game would be lost without Baseball-Reference and Retrosheet. I was that much more "found" because of these sites.

Ultimate Mets Database adds a human element to raw data with its continued curating of Fan Memories of Met players, personalities and games throughout the years. UMDB is a great complement to the Met memory, serving as something of a Greek chorus when a writer is wondering to himself,

"Was that Tim Harkness game really as great as it sounds?"

UMDB's contributors confirm that it was.

Postgame quotes that appear in individual game entries in *The Happiest Recap*, unless otherwise noted, were recorded for posterity by the sportswriters who've covered Mets games for a half-century in the employ of New York dailies, out-of-town papers, dot-coms and wire services. The online archives of the *New York Times* and dozens of newspapers captured by Google News Archive proved particularly helpful in enriching what could be gleaned from box scores. From a weekly perspective, *The Sporting News* and *Sports Illustrated* have provided their share of information and insights.

One of the many valuable lessons Bob Murphy, Ralph Kiner and Lindsey Nelson taught me as part of my ongoing Met education was the importance of maintaining a "baseball library". Granted, they used the phrase to promote yearbook sales, but I took it fairly literally and have spent a lifetime acquiring, reading and mostly holding onto hundreds of baseball books, many of which I dug out and enjoyed again as *The Happiest Recap* took on a life of its own.

My thanks to all from 1962 forward who have seen fit to play a role in detailing the literally Amazin' story of the New York Mets.

ACKNOWLEDGEMENTS

Implicit in something called *The Happiest Recap* is the instrumental role the late Bob Murphy played in inspiring its existence. Like most Mets fans who picked up so much of the game from Murph, I am grateful that he was my companion for so many wonderful moments and even the mediocre ones. He made every game seem like a win.

It's fitting that when I became acquainted with fellow Mets fan Jeff Hysen in 2007, I knew him only by his online screen name "bmfcr". I asked what it stood for. Why, "Bob Murphy Fan Club," the name of his fantasy baseball team. Jeff has been *The Happiest Recap*'s biggest booster, its most patient sounding board and its author's most insightful focus group — and that's while he's busy being the Washington D.C. area's standout standup comedian.

In the earliest, conceptual stages of *The Happiest Recap*, it was another good friend, the Met-minded Mark Simon, who saw its potential as a book. Since I first came into contact with Mark in 2005, he has attained new levels of responsibility and fame as one of ESPN's leading statistical gurus, and I'm very proud of his advancement.

My co-blogger Jason Fry remains the best virtual roommate any Internet denizen has ever had, and there's nobody alongside whom I'd rather recap the next 50 years of Mets baseball.

A core of Faith and Fear in Flushing readers regularly showed up to comment on the blog version of *The Happiest Recap* when it ran during the 2011 baseball season. My thanks to all of them for their earnest interest and steadfast support of an admittedly esoteric project.

I also appreciate the ongoing encouragement of historically minded Mets fan friends like Mark Weinstein, Sharon Chapman, Matthew Silverman, Jon Springer, Charlie Hangley, Ed Leyro, Taryn Cooper, Joe Dubin, Kevin Connell, John Colella, Larry Arnold, Ray Stilwell, Matthew Artus, Dave Murray, Joe Figliola, Shannon Shark, Howard Megdal, Rob Emproto, Ryder Chasin and a fellow named Paul whose last name I've never managed to commit to memory but who presented me with a Mets pennant just like the one displayed in Lane Pryce's office on *Mad Men* — which was incredibly swell of him. You meet a lot of incredibly swell folks when you're a Mets fan, and I appreciate knowing all of them.

Dana Brand was one of the people who made Mets blogging, writing and rooting a joy. He passed away in May of 2011, and I haven't gone a day since without missing his friendship and talent.

Larry Jabbonsky is a friend for all seasons and I thank him for his unstinting support through every one of them.

Carlos Briceno leaps on and off the Mets' bandwagon with disturbing alacrity, but he's never budged from steering mine.

If you like the cover and design of this book, and there's no way you shouldn't, thank the extraordinary illustrator (and outstanding human being to boot) Jim Haines. I plan on doing just that for quite a while.

Deepest thanks for publishing and marketing consultation from the firm of Suzan Prince and Mark Trost, a.k.a. my sister and brother-in-law, two people who would do anything to help my baseball writing reach a wider audience as long as it doesn't entail them having to watch an actual baseball game. But that's OK, I watch plenty of them myself.

Charles Prince arranged to take me to the eye doctor on the morning of a school day when I was six years old, which just happened to leave my afternoon free to watch Game No. 85 in this volume. Thanks are due my dad for helping me see the Mets win the fifth and the final game of the 1969 World Series.

Every day with my wife, Stephanie Prince, provides me with the happiest recap possible and the promise of an even better one to follow.

UP NEXT...

THE HAPPIEST RECAP
Volume 2—Second Base: 1974-1986

Follow the saga of the New York Mets
from the aftermath of You Gotta Believe
through the quest to bring the Magic back to Shea Stadium
until a new generation of Rising Stars was playing
Baseball Like It Oughta Be.

Watch thehappiestrecap.com
and faithandfearinflushing.com for details!

16606060R00129

Made in the USA
Charleston, SC
31 December 2012